JONATHAN SWIFT

THE SELECTED POEMS

A. Norman Jeffares was born in Dublin and now lives in Fife Ness in Scotland. He has held several professorships and published many books including *A History of Anglo-Irish Literature* (1982), *W. B. Yeats: A New Biography* (1988), *Yeats: The Love Poems* (1990), *Jonathan Swift: The Selected Poems* (1992) and *Joycechoyce* (1992). Two volumes of his poetry, *Brought Up in Ireland* and *Brought Up to Leave*, were published in 1987.

Other titles in Kyle Cathie Poetry:

W. B. Yeats: The Love Poems edited by A. Norman Jeffares
Rudyard Kipling: The Complete Verse edited by M. M. Kaye
Joyce: The Poems in Verse and Prose edited by A. Norman Jeffares and Brendan Kennelly
The Love Poems of D. H. Lawrence edited by Roy Booth
The Love Poetry of Shakespeare edited by Roy Booth
Ireland's Women edited by Katie Donovan, A. Norman Jeffares and Brendan Kennelly
The Things That Matter: Women's Spiritual Poetry edited by Julia Neuberger

JONATHAN SWIFT

THE SELECTED
POEMS

Edited with an introduction and notes by
A. NORMAN JEFFARES

KYLE CATHIE LIMITED

Introduction copyright © A. N. Jeffares 1992

This edition published 1992 by
Kyle Cathie Limited
20 Vauxhall Bridge Road, London SW1V 2SA

Reprinted 1996

ISBN 1 85626 211 1

A CIP Catalogue record for this book is available from the British Library.

Typeset by DP Photosetting, Aylesbury, Bucks
Printed and bound in Great Britain by
Cox & Wyman Ltd, Reading, Berks

CONTENTS

CONTENTS

INTRODUCTION

Lemuel Gulliver knew the pygmies and the giants, the imaginative and
zany inventors and scientists, the rational horses as well as the brutish
Yahoos. His creator knew human life and related his poetry closely to
his own experience of it. Jonathan Swift wrote poems reflecting
extremes of tension and relaxation: savage irony, fierce indignation
fuelled flames that burnt through political pretence and public
hypocrisy; appreciation and affectionate amusement irradiate poems
written to and about friends whom he addressed with conversational
ease. Swift was a sensitive, observant man who recorded realistically
the physical details of life about him; he was equally sensitive in his
reactions to the idiosyncrasies of human beings, whether those he knew
or those he imagined. The range of human life he explored in his
poetry was wide, and within that exploration were many differences, of
subject, of treatment.

This selection of his poems is arranged chronologically, for Swift's
emphases changed with the circumstances of his life, though his
own character – often misunderstood – preserved essential elements
throughout a life that was marked by extreme intelligence, intervals
of intense intellectual industry, and an impressive integrity.

The life had its lacks, its sense of *temps perdu*; it seemed at times one
doomed to disappointment; and it was often interrupted by unpre-
dictable intervals of illness, the nausea, giddiness, and inner noises
produced by Ménière's disease. Jonathan Swift's father – also Jonathan
– a lawyer, the fifth son of a royalist parson who was driven out of his
parish of Goodrich in Herefordshire, had come, with three of his
brothers, to make a living in Ireland where there were family
connections. He died before his son was born in Dublin on 30
November 1667. Swift thought that his father's marriage, to Abigail

Errick, had been improvident: it occurred, he wrote, 'before he could make a sufficient establishment for his family: and his son (not then born) hath often been heard to say that he felt the consequences of that marriage not only through the whole course of his education but during the greatest part of his life'. His father's untimely death threw him upon his Uncle Godwin's charity. That uncle gave him the best education to be had in Ireland, at Kilkenny College, the fine school set up by the eighth Earl of Ormonde in the previous century. But before Jonathan Swift went to Kilkenny at the age of six there had been a curious episode in his childhood. When he was a year old his nurse 'stole him on shipboard' and took him from Dublin to Whitehaven in England where he stayed for three years with her. When he returned to Dublin his mother had left, about two years after her husband's death, for Leicester, bringing with her her elder child Jane (who had been baptized in 1666), and Swift was 'replaced under the care of his uncle Godwin' in Dublin. As a result, he may have developed in self-protection a determination not to be taken in by thoughts of the normal family life he had obviously missed. His memories of Kilkenny consisted mainly of a comment to Charles Ford about formerly enjoying his own happiness as a schoolboy (the delicious holidays, the Saturday afternoon, and the charming custards in a blind alley) and never considering 'the confinement ten hours a day, to nouns and verbs, the terror of the rod, the bloody noses, and broken shins.' There is, however, one incident that probably did occur during his time there and made a deep impression on him. He went fishing when he was a little boy and 'felt a great fish at the end of my line, which I drew up almost to the ground; but it dropped in, and the disappointment vexes me to this very day, and I believe it was the type of all my future disappointments.'

The disappointments continued when Swift entered Trinity College, Dublin, at the age of fourteen, where 'by the ill treatment of his nearest relations, he was so discouraged and sunk in his spirits, that he too much neglected his academic studies, for some parts of which he had no great relish by nature, and turned himself to reading history and poetry'. Godwin Swift had lost a lot of money in the failure of an ironworks at Swadlingbar and may not have funded his nephew generously when he was an undergraduate. If this was the case, it must have been galling to the pride of someone who had always wanted to be treated as a lord. The seven years Swift spent at Trinity, his BA awarded *speciali gratia* (not as disappointing a result as used to be thought), did not point him to the likelihood of making a successful academic career. In any case, he disliked the aridity and pedantry of the curriculum with its emphasis on 'logic, physics, metaphysics, natural philosophy, mathematics or anything of that sort', which he professed he could never understand. Yet he was firmly aware of his innate abilities: he wanted them to be recognized and while working for his MA degree he must have wondered how this recognition could be achieved. The frustration involved, the gulf between ambition and achievement probably prompted his cutting lectures, his town-haunting, his absences from evening roll-call, his anti-authoritarian attitudes.

Into the personal problem of how to pursue power that would enable him to develop his potential intruded the public perturbation of the Williamite war. James II came to the throne in 1685, and Richard Talbot, created Earl of Tyrconnel that year, began a policy in Ireland (which he virtually controlled as Lord Deputy from 1687) of Catholicization. This alarmed the Protestant settlers, many of whom fled to England. Like most of the staff and students of Trinity College, which had felt Tyrconnel's pressure when he influenced the appoint-ment of a Catholic Fellow, and which was to be occupied by his forces when the war between James II and the Prince of Orange moved to Ireland, Jonathan Swift left the country, probably in January 1689. He walked from Holyhead to Leicester, where he stayed for a few months with his mother before going to Surrey with a letter of introduction from her to Sir William Temple, whose father Sir John Temple had been 'a great friend' of the Swift family. Sir William took the young man into his household, 'took care of him' and had a profound influence upon him.

Temple had been an Irish MP, and then was Ambassador at The Hague. He was a most successful diplomat, negotiating the Triple Alliance and helping to arrange the marriage of William of Orange and Mary, the daughter of James II by Anne Hyde. He took little part in public life after 1680, refusing a Secretaryship of State, and instead devoted himself to essay-writing and gardening. Swift was fortunate to come into contact with a man of taste, of learning and refinement whose reflections upon literature had been shaped by experience of the world, of courts, of diplomacy; fortunate, too, to experience the culture of Temple's household where he acted as a secretary. There he met and gave lessons to Esther Johnson (Stella), the elder daughter of Mrs Johnson, the housekeeper. She was then a pretty child of eight, obviously very intelligent.

After Swift had spent about a year at Temple's home, Moor Park, Temple wrote to Sir Robert Southwell, who was going to Ireland as Secretary of State to William of Orange, now King William III. The letter described Swift as having Latin and Greek, and some French, as writing 'a good and current hand', and as being very honest and diligent. He suggested that Southwell might keep him in his service or recommend him for a Fellowship at Trinity. Nothing came of Swift's return to Ireland, however; by 1691 he was back as a member of Temple's household, a second stay which lasted until 1694. Some tension or misunderstanding then arose, and Swift left an 'extremely angry' Temple, who 'would not oblige himself any further than upon my good behaviour, nor would promise anything firmly to me at all'. But because Swift had 'a scruple of entering the church merely for support', once he had got the offer of becoming a clerk in the Rolls Office in Dublin (a post he would have owed to Temple) he now felt he could enter the Church from choice rather than financial necessity. He went to Ireland intending to be ordained (it was the most likely career to which his education at Trinity College, Dublin, would have led); he discovered, however, that his Dublin degree (to which he had added an Oxford MA in 1692) was not enough to qualify him for ordination. He was required to present to the Archbishop of Dublin, Narcissus Marsh (who had been Provost of Trinity College when Swift was a student there, and probably remembered well how Swift's behaviour had been censured), a certificate from his latest employer to show he was of good character. He wrote what Temple's sister, Lady Giffard, who didn't like him, called a 'penitential letter', and Temple magnanimously provided the necessary information. Swift was then appointed on 28 January 1695 to the living of Kilroot in County Antrim, on the shore of Belfast Lough.

A moralist rather than a theologian, a devout man whose sincerity was more in evidence than his spirituality, Swift was consistently a good churchman. He revered the established Church; it was historically justified, occupying a middle position between the extremes of what Ricardo Quintana has neatly called a Whig state–church and a Tory church–state. Christianity, Swift thought, tells its practitioners to accept certain mysteries: outside them, however, there was nothing to which reason could not immediately assent. *The Sentiments of a Church of England Man* (1708) and *An Argument against Abolishing Christianity* (1708) ultimately see the Church as promoting the life of reason, something emphasized in the *Thoughts on Religion*, in which Swift sees all men as fallible in their exercise of reason.

Being a Church of Ireland clergyman in a remote area proved a disappointing experience. When he arrived in Kilroot in March 1695 Swift found he had few parishioners, the area being preponderantly populated by Presbyterians of Scottish origin. Sir William Temple asked him to return to Moor Park: this time he was being 'offered the advantage to have the same acquaintance with greatness that I formerly enjoyed and with better prospect of interest'. Swift used these words in a long letter to Jane Waring, a cousin of two of his contemporaries at Trinity and a daughter of the Archdeacon of Dromore. He proposed to her; she apparently refused, or prevaricated, and so he accepted Temple's invitation.

Though Swift left Ulster for Moor Park a little over a year after his arrival – he was in England by May 1696 – he retained Kilroot until 1698, probably as an insurance in case things did not work out well in Surrey. He had escaped from marriage, even temporarily from making a career. This third stay gave Swift the opportunity of developing his powerful intellectual resources in the elegant ambience Temple created. Temple's taste, the opposite of pedantry, was influential. Swift's reading was impressively wide, in his own words 'indefatigable'; he could read for ten hours a day in the well-stocked library; he developed a lasting interest in style; and he had ample time to write poetry.

Between 1691 and 1693, he told his cousin Thomas Swift that he had 'writ, and burnt and writ again, upon almost all manner of subjects, more perhaps than any man in England'. At Trinity College he had written lampoons, but now he produced three Pindaric odes and two pieces in heroic couplets. The first of his poems that can be dated with certainty is the 'Ode to the King on his Irish Expedition and the Success of his Arms in General', written in 1691. He was now giving 'the flower of the whole day, two hours in the morning, to poetry'. Again he was to be disappointed; he had strong literary ambitions, but in this early exalted poetry, interesting as it can be, Swift did not find his own voice, did not achieve his own individuality. Despite the advice he gave his former schoolfellow in 'To Mr Congreve' – 'Beat not the dirty paths where vulgar feet have trod, / But give the vigorous fancy room' – he was himself echoing previously established fashion, such as the strained verse he found in Abraham Cowley, as well as, to a certain extent, some of the nuances of Edmund Waller. It is not surprising that John Dryden produced his famous put-down: 'Cousin Swift, you will never be a poet'. He was to be proved wrong, but during the final period at Moor Park Swift was first to find his independence of mind in prose, a more suitable outlet at that time for his brilliantly inventive, indeed unique, satiric powers. He moved from the seventeenth-century exuberant complexities of *The Battle of the Books* into the easier, more powerful style of *A Tale of a Tub* (published together in 1704). He was in the process of making himself able to express civilized taste, barbing it with a wicked wit, and achieving simplicity, conciseness, clarity of expression and an ability 'to drive some one particular point'. He was writing in order to be understood, and a later anecdote supplied by Faulkner, the Dublin bookseller, is decidedly relevant; when he brought the proofs of the *Works* and read them to the Dean, two menservants were also present, and if they did not comprehend, Swift 'would alter and amend, until they understood it perfectly well, and then would say, "This will do; for I write to the vulgar, more than to the learned." '

This was the final preparatory phase in Swift's life, a development of intellectual strength and certainty, an achievement of the capacity to drive home an argument, and an ability to think clearly when 'the properest words' offered themselves first, and his judgement directed him 'in what order to place them so that they could be best understood'. It came to an abrupt end when Temple died in January 1699, and Swift was left 'unprovided both of friend and living'. Temple had undertaken to get him a living in England and had persuaded the King to promise him a prebend of Canterbury or Westminster, but Swift's appeal to the

King through the Earl of Romney came to nothing. Disappointed in his hopes of gaining a living in England, he did obtain an invitation to go to Ireland as chaplain and secretary to the Earl of Berkeley, who had been appointed a Lord Justice there. Swift's disappointments, however, continued: he thought Arthur Bushe had contrived to push him out of the secretaryship and denied him the deanery of Derry to which he had considered himself entitled. Life in the Berkeley household in Dublin Castle did, however, hold some pleasure for him: something of the atmosphere can be caught in 'The Humble Petition of Frances Harris' (p. 23), which shows Swift at his ease and indulging his propensity for teasing, the raillery he so enjoyed. Another poem of this period, 'The Discovery', also demonstrates Swift's new-found mastery of the familiar style and his capacity to adapt it to satiric criticism of the behaviour – and misbehaviour – of others.

In 1700 Swift was presented to the living of Laracor in County Meath, about twenty miles from Dublin (along with those of Agher and Rathbeggan); he was then installed prebend of St Patrick's Cathedral in Dublin. His ambition, however, was not to be satisfied within the confines of a country parish, though he enjoyed being at Laracor. He rebuilt the vicarage, laid out a garden, planted a willow walk, put in apple, cherry and holly trees, made a stream resemble a canal and fished for trout, eels and pike. He travelled to England frequently; he was there, in London, from April to September 1701, from April to October 1702, from November 1703 to June 1704, and from November 1707 to June 1709. He was still searching for a satisfactory role in life. The anonymously published *A Discourse of the Contests and Dissentions Between the Nobles and the Commons in Athens and Rome* (1701), designed to defend the Whig Lords who had been impeached, caused a stir. It was Swift's first political work, and he let it be known that it was his. As a result, the Whig leaders, among them Lord Halifax, Lord Somers and Lord Sutherland, courted him when he was next in London. *A Tale of a Tub*, also published anonymously, appeared in 1704, its brilliance showing Swift's genius, his erudition and his capacity for satire. But ironically enough, though he did not acknowledge the authorship of it, the *Tale* was to militate later against his advance in the Church. Now, however, he was negotiating during 1707 on behalf of the Church of Ireland to obtain remission of the First Fruits (the first year's income of every benefice, which was no longer paid to the Crown by the English Church). This role had been entrusted to him by William King, the Archbishop of Dublin, probably because of his increasing activity in the affairs of the Church of Ireland and because he was on friendly terms with the Lord Lieutenant, the Earl of Pembroke. It looked as if Swift had succeeded: 'the Thing is done,' he wrote to the Archbishop. The Whigs' promises, however, came to nothing because the Earl of Godolphin, the head of the ministry, wanted the Irish Church to agree to the removal of the Test Act (which would allow dissenters to hold office). And Pembroke did not push matters forward; he was replaced by the Earl of Wharton, who treated Swift coldly. Not for nothing had Swift told Somers, in addition to the fact that he was inclined to be a Whig in politics, that he was a high churchman in religion. He was to attack the Whigs bitterly for their ill-treatment of the Church. He had not enjoyed being surrounded by dissenters in Kilroot (he seems to have been less apprehensive about the Catholics who surrounded Laracor) and, besides, had not the Swift family's funds been lost during the Civil War when the Commonwealth soldiers had invaded his grandfather's rectory? ('My grandfather', he wrote in 1739, 'was so persecuted and plundered two hundred and fifty times by the barbarity of Cromwell's hellish crew that the poor old gentleman was forced to sell the better half of his estate to support his family.') In his own opposition to the Repeal of the Test Act, Swift thought Godolphin's price impossible. He made no application to be appointed as a chaplain to Wharton, when he was about to go to Ireland as Lord Lieutenant (to pursue the removal of the Irish Test Act): he would not go 'against what becometh a man of conscience and truth, and an entire friend to the Established Church'.

During his dealings with those in political power in London Swift had become disillusioned: describing details of his negotiations, he wrote to Archbishop King in Dublin to remark that he had found, in the small conversation he had had with great men, one maxim that they constantly observed: 'that in any business before them, if you enquire how it proceeds, they only confide what is proper to answer without one single thought whether it be agreeable to fact or no'. His increasing distaste for the Whigs was to a certain extent offset by his new friendships, notably with Joseph Addison who got him to polish two poems, 'Vanbrugh's House' and 'Baucis and Philemon' (p. 26), in line with current neo-classical taste (the latter poem suffered from Addison's gentility and lost much of its original raciness in the process). The poetry reflects Swift's sense of humour well: he had employed it in 'An Elegy on the Supposed Death of Partridge the Almanac Maker' (p. 31), who suffered from Swift's prose and was foolish enough to respond to the hoax by pronouncing himself alive. These were light-hearted pieces, though Swift was also moving into political verse: 'Verses said to be written on the Union' (of Scotland and England in 1707) reflected Swift's dislike of the home of Presbyterianism; he compared the likely result of the Union to the fate of the double-bottomed boat invented by Sir William Petty, Surveyor-General of Ireland, which capsized on a trial voyage. Two descriptive poems, 'A Description of the Morning' (p. 35) and the subsequent 'A Description of a City Shower' (p. 35), with which Swift was particularly pleased – and with reason – demonstrated his sharp observation of scenes and incidents, his ability to avoid artificiality, and, in the case of the latter poem, to mock existing literary practice in the matter of triplets and alexandrines:

> *Sweepings from butchers' stalls, dung, guts, and blood,*
> *Drowned puppies, stinking sprats, all drenched in mud,*
> *Dead cats, and turnip-tops come tumbling down the flood.*

At last Swift found, through his association with the Tory ministry which came to power in 1710, a role that gave him scope not only to defend and further the interest of the Irish Established Church, but to mould public opinion, particularly in the furtherance of peace. His powerfully persuasive, punchy political propaganda was principled: this was the secret of its underlying strength. The energy, clarity and ironic wit of Swift's journalism, his pamphlets and his later histories of events were based upon a desire to aid those who seemed to him to be most likely to preserve Church and State. He came to London in September 1710 and met Robert Harley in October. Harley, the son of a parliamentarian, had entered the House of Commons as a Whig, and had become Secretary of State in 1704. He began to intrigue with the Tories, aided by his cousin Abigail Hill (Mrs Masham) and then resigned office in 1708 when his secretary was convicted of treasonable correspondence with France. Harley set himself to undermine the power of the Whigs, and when Godolphin was dismissed in 1710 he was made Chancellor of the Exchequer and head of the government. Harley realized Swift's brilliance and told him that 'he and his friends knew very well what useful things I had written against the principles of the late discarded faction'. There was 'an entirely new scene'; there was a need for 'those who were friends to the constitution of church and state'; and there was a need of 'some good pen, to keep up the spirit raised in the people, to assert the principles, and justify the proceedings of the new ministers'. Swift fitted the job description. He was now at the centre of power in London and he took up the editorship of the *Examiner* in November, then gave this up in June 1711 to work on *The Conduct of the Allies*, an impressively influential pamphlet. He followed it up with *The History of the Last Four Years of the Queen*, an account of the events which led to the peace formulated in the Treaty of Utrecht of 1713. (The Tory leaders, however, thought the *History* too dangerous to be published at the time and when he was hoping to have it published in 1738 his English friends dissuaded him, and it did not appear during his lifetime.) There were political poems as well, among them a fierce lampoon on Godolphin, 'The Virtues of Sid Hamlet the Magician's Rod'; the devastating attack upon the Duchess of Somerset, 'The Windsor Prophecy'; and a celebration of the fall of the Duke of Marlborough, 'The Fable of Midas'.

The four years from 1710 to 1714 were Swift's period of political power. He left Laracor, with a curate in charge, for London in September 1710. There his friendships with Addison and the playwright William Congreve continued; that with Richard Steele (another Anglo-Irishman, an army officer turned playwright, who started the *Tatler* in 1709) was to break off in three years' time. There were new friends, among them John Arbuthnot, Queen Anne's physician, an author and authority on medicine, and Matthew Prior, minor poet and diplomat, and, by 1713, Alexander Pope and John Gay, the poet and playwright, author of *The Beggar's Opera* and *Polly*. Swift dined with Harley, meeting Henry St John and Sir Simon Harcourt there, becoming privy to their plans and helping to shape government policy with them. He travelled with the ministers on their weekend visits to Windsor. He became a member of the Brothers' Club, a social gathering which dined together on Thursdays, discussing politics as well as literature and other topics which occupied the attention of 'such men of wit and interest' as St John, James Butler, the second Duke of Ormonde, George Gravil, Baron Lansdowne, and Swift's particular friend Arbuthnot. All was going splendidly; his merits were recognized; he was preserving his independence.

In 1712 Swift began to press for his own preferment; he was, after all, forty-five. Finally he was appointed Dean of St Patrick's Cathedral in Dublin: not at all what he had hoped for, this exile to Ireland, but something definite at last after the rumours of the deaneries of Wells, Ely and Lichfield and talk of a canonry at Windsor. After a quick trip to Dublin to be installed, on 13 June 1713, he was soon back in London to try to heal the quarrels between Harley, now Earl of Oxford, and St John, now Viscount Bolingbroke.

There were some moments of light relief, meetings of the Scriblerus Club, formed in 1713, to ridicule all 'the false tastes in learning', to which the Earl of Oxford could be invited by Swift, Pope, Arbuthnot, Thomas Parnell and Gay. There were the satirical *Memoirs of Martin Scriblerus* – Scriblerus, the son of an antiquary of Munster, was a burlesque creation through which the friends could mock contemporary pedantry – to be written jointly (they were to stimulate Swift into writing *Gulliver's Travels*, the first edition of which was published on 28 October 1726); they were eventually published by Pope in the second volume of his *Prose Works* in 1741). But Swift was deeply distressed by the events which were unfolding like some apparently inexorable tragedy, ending with the fall of the Tory ministry after the death of Queen Anne on 1 August 1714. Though Swift's feelings for Oxford and Bolingbroke were to survive, the two men had not fulfilled his hopes and his expectations of them. Poems such as 'The Faggot', 'Horace. Lib. 2, Sat. 6' (p. 67), 'The Author upon Himself' (p. 64) and 'In Sickness' (p. 66) reveal the extent of his despair and despondency. He now left England, perforce to live permanently in Ireland, for the vengeful Whigs who were now in power certainly would not aid his career in the Church, and indeed he was far safer in Ireland. Bolingbroke had fled to France in March 1715, some of Swift's friends, including Charles Ford, seemed to have sympathized overly with Jacobitism, and Swift's letters were being opened. Oxford as well as

Bolingbroke was impeached for high treason, and so was the Duke of Ormonde. It spurred Swift into writing *An Enquiry into the Behaviour of the Last Ministry*, a defence of his friends which, however, remained unpublished, probably because Bolingbroke compounded his error of fleeing to France by accepting an earldom from the Pretender and being appointed his Secretary of State. Swift had not imagined himself 'to be perpetually in the company of traitors'. So, sent, as he once put it bitterly to Pope, 'to die like a poisoned rat in a hole', he was finally back in Ireland. He arrived there on 24 August 1714 and made only two visits to England after that.

Once installed in the Deanery in Dublin, Swift had at first but a few friends in the city. After his departure into 'exile' he wrote to Pope on 28 June 1715 that he lived

> in the corner of a vast unfurnished house. My family consists of a
> steward, a groom, a helper in the stable, a footman and an old maid, who
> are all at board wages, and when I do not dine abroad, or make an
> entertainment, which last is very rare, I eat a mutton-pie, and drink half a
> pint of wine. My amusements are defending my small dominions against
> the Archbishop and endeavouring to reduce my rebellious choir.

It took time to recover from his depression – and, besides, Swift had been suffering from severe bouts of Ménière's disease. Recover he did, however, making new friends, among them Thomas Sheridan and Patrick Delany, twenty and twenty-two years younger than the Dean respectively, as well as Daniel Jackson and the Rochfort brothers, George and John ('Nim'). Sheridan, particularly, stimulated Swift into writing verse trifles, riddles and various pasquinades: both men enjoyed word games, and later writing *Latino-Anglicus*, an invented language in which English words were written in Latin formations. An example is 'A Love Song':

> *Apud in is almi des ire*
> *Mimis tres Ine ver re qui re*
> *Alo veri findit a gestis*
> *His mi seri ne ver at restis*

which can be 'translated' as

A pudding is all my desire,
My mistress I never require.
A lover, I find it a jest is,
His misery never at rest is.

Swift had taken to heart Prior's advice, written in a letter of May 1718, that 'if you are once got into *la bagatelle* you may despise the world'.

Something of Swift's invincible capacity for jocularity irradiated the *Journal to Stella*, the letters written to Esther Johnson from September 1710 to June 1713 to tell her and her companion Rebecca Dingley (some fifteen to twenty years Stella's senior) of his doings in London. Swift had been responsible for their going to Ireland after Temple's death; they took lodgings in Dublin in 1701, when Stella was twenty (and they occasionally visited friends in the country). Stella's money, Swift pointed out, would gain more interest there and go further. The *Journal* is well described by A. L. Rowse as 'astonishingly modern in the gritty completeness of its detail.' Not only do these superb letters describe vividly Swift's personal and political, his social and literary life in London, but they are full of fun, lively in their raillery, affectionate in their teasing. In them he speaks openly of his feelings, his health, his hopes, his disappointments, his achievements. They reveal his delight in the bagatelle, his enjoyment in punning and the dexterity with which he used language. Now that he was in Dublin he had the company of Stella and he recorded their friendship in the poems he wrote for her birthdays. There is affectionate gratitude in such poems as 'To Stella, Visiting Me in My Sickness' and 'To Stella, Who Collected and Transcribed His Poems' (p. 83), while in 'Stella at Woodpark' (p. 105) he tempers his jesting lest she think it too severe, excusing his raillery and turning it into a compliment. Later, when she was gravely ill and he was stuck in Holyhead waiting for a passage and then for a favourable wind, he wrote 'Holyhead. September 25, 1727' (p. 120), which conveys something of what violent friendship meant to him:

But now the danger of a friend
On whom my hopes and fears depend,
Absent from whom all climes are cursed,
With whom I'm happy in the worst,
With rage impatient makes me wait
A passage to the land I hate.

He regarded such friendship 'as much more lasting, and as much engaging as violent love'.

When he was in London Swift had seen much of the Vanhomrigh family: the widow of a wealthy Lord Mayor of Dublin of Dutch extraction, who had died in 1703, and her four children. The Vanhomrighs had come to London in 1707; and Swift, who had got to know them well in the next two years, resumed his friendship with them when he returned to London in the autumn of 1710. The *Journal to Stella* plays down the relationship, but he lived a few doors from the Vanhomrighs in St Alban's Street and when he moved to Chelsea in spring 1711 he visited them twice a day, changing into his best wig and gown (which he kept in their house) before going about his affairs. Swift taught the eldest daughter, Esther, as he had earlier taught Stella at Moor Park; he called her Mishessy and later Vanessa, and they became close friends. She seemed younger than her twenty-one years (she was actually twenty-three); she was vivacious, high-spirited, impressionable, impulsive and indiscreet. While Stella seems to have accepted the role of friend, Vanessa's friendship developed into love, a love she did not conceal. Swift had written to her from Ireland when he went to Dublin to be installed as Dean in June 1713, in reply to several of her increasingly demanding and declaratory letters, reminding her that he had told her when he left England he would try to forget everything there 'and would write as seldom as I could'. In the autumn of that year their relationship seems to have been cleared up and settled, to his satisfaction, as 'Cadenus and Vanessa' (p. 38), an ironic, playful poem ('a cavalier business', 'a trifle', he was to call it in 1726), implies; but before he finally left for Ireland in August 1714 he had been involved in helping her – her mother was by this time dead and her finances were temporarily in disarray – and she visited or tried to visit him in Letcombe Bassett where he had retired to be out of London during the chaotic period in August when the Tories split apart after Queen Anne's death. Vanessa then decided to go to Ireland; this was totally against Swift's strong advice. He warned her that if she were in Ireland when he was there he would see her very seldom: 'It is not a place for any freedom, but where everything is known in a week and magnified a hundred degrees', and, though he did not add this, it was where Stella lived. Despite his warnings, Vanessa crossed to Ireland

and stayed in Turnstile Alley in Dublin; she then settled into the family property, Celbridge Abbey, not far from Dublin, on the Liffey.

The situation was difficult indeed. Swift was obviously trying very hard to discourage Vanessa, to distance her; he wrote an alarmed letter as the result of some woman discussing Vanessa, reminding her that he 'ever feared the tattle of this nasty town'; he urged her to observe restraint; he reminded her, too, that he had said to her that he would see her seldom if she were in Ireland. But letters indicate that he did visit her, if rarely; one, written in French, expressed his warm regards for her, praising her character: hers, however, complain of his 'prodigious neglect' of her; she told him the love she had for him was not only seated in her soul, 'for there is not a single atom of my frame that is not blended with it.' What, she asked, had caused this 'prodigious change' in him? Some crisis, however, seems to have blown up after August 1722, seven years after she had arrived in Ireland; on 2 June the following year Vanessa died. Swift went to the south of Ireland and did not return until the autumn; Stella and Rebecca Dingley stayed with Charles Ford from April to early October. 'Stella's Distress on the 3rd fatal day of October 1723' and 'Stella at Woodpark' (p. 105) record their visit but we remain ignorant of the details of the break with Vanessa, of Stella's attitude to the situation, and can only surmise Swift's reactions. 'On Censure', a poem probably written in 1727, demonstrates an apparent indifference to the publication of 'Cadenus and Vanessa' in 1726, something probably directed by Vanessa before she died. But he wrote to Thomas Tickell – his belief that women could not keep secrets reinforced by hindsight – to say that 'Folly, malice, negligence and the incontinence in keeping secrets, for which we want a word, ought to caution men to keep the key of their cabinets.'

Whilst Swift obviously cared deeply for Vanessa and for Stella ('A Receipt to Restore Stella's Youth' shows his concern that she was eating 'but a mouthful a day' and hoping that the country air at Quilca, Thomas Sheridan's house in County Cavan, would do her good), he was not inhibited in his satiric portraits of women in general. In part these are inspired by an anti-romanticism, an ability to turn poetic conventions to ridicule; such poems as 'Phyllis; or the Progress of Love' (p. 76) and 'The Progress of Beauty' (p. 79) exhibit Swift's intellect busily finding subjects outside public life, though public events were to provide him with ample material for satire. 'Upon the South Sea Project' and 'The Run upon the Bankers' (p. 92) seem up to date in the late twentieth century with its pricked balloon of share prices in 1987 and the difficulties of the Bank of Commerce and Credit International (BCCI) in 1991.

Swift had determined to keep out of Irish politics when he returned to Ireland, but it proved impossible for him to do so. His *Proposal for the Universal Use of Irish Manufacture* brought the printer into court, charged with sedition; this provoked Swift into 'An Excellent New Song on a Seditious Pamphlet' (p. 91). He was disturbed by the poverty of the Irish weavers: there was, familiar word, a recession in 1721, and Westminster's restrictions on Irish trade had the effect of a high bank rate today. Swift wrote 'An Epilogue to a Play for the Benefit of the Weavers in Ireland' in 1721. He was not, however, to be drawn fully into Irish political life until 1724, when the first of his *Drapier's Letters* was published in March. The first poem against Wood, who had been granted a patent to mint a large amount of copper coins (far beyond what the Irish economy required), was 'A Serious Poem upon William Wood'. Others followed: 'An Epigram on Wood's Brass Money' and 'On Wood the Ironmonger'. Swift's *Drapier's Letters* were as effective as *The Conduct of the Allies* had been in influencing public opinion, and the government had to abandon the proposal, Wood surrendering his patent in 1725. Swift was a popular patriotic hero, as 'Drapier's Hill' (p. 138) and the notes on it in Faulkner's edition of 1735 indicate.

After two visits to England – these were largely concerned with the publication of *Gulliver's Travels* in 1726 and with the *Miscellanies* (containing many of his poems), published in 1726 in collaboration with Pope, with whom he stayed at Twickenham – and after Stella's death early in 1728 Swift was to remain in Ireland for the rest of his life. In Ireland he corrected his masterpiece, *Gulliver's Travels*, his portrait of man capable of reason but not a rational creature, his own view of humanity larger than the rational satiric one his invented character Lemuel Gulliver puts forward. In 1729 Swift produced his most devastating propaganda pamphlet, *A Modest Proposal*, the fiercest example of his *saeva indignatio*, the anger aroused by his contempla- tion of the stark poverty of Ireland, caused as much, he thought, by Irish

selfishness and apathy as by English politics, the treatment of Ireland
as a colony.

During this period Swift wrote some of his most impressive poems.
They include his clear view of the relations between Ireland and
England, put in the 'Verses Occasioned by the Sudden Drying Up of St
Patrick's Well near Trinity College, Dublin' (p. 135). His political
attitudes found expression in 'A Libel on the Reverend Dr Delany and
His Excellency John, Lord Carteret' (p. 141), written by an author

> *... in politics grown old,*
> *Whose thoughts are of a different mould,*
> *Who, from my soul, sincerely hate*
> *Both kings and ministers of state. ...*

The sharp comment in this poem in 'Walpole's more than royal will'
was developed in 'The Character of Sir Robert Walpole' (p. 157). But
not only English politicians were lashed in scorn: the Irish Parliament
got its come-uppance in the savage satire of 'A Character, Panegyric,
and Description of the Legion Club' (p. 193).

Swift despaired of Ireland, though, he wrote to Pope in 1729, 'I
confess freely that I have no discontent at living here.' His bouts of
illness, the loneliness of living in the Deanery, the recognition of
mortality as news of his English friends' deaths came across the Irish
Sea, his awareness of the approach of old age and its humiliating
infirmities, all could produce such despairingly negative poems as 'The
Place of the Damned' (p. 157). Its negativity, however, should be read
in conjunction with the jesting with which he invested 'On the Day of
Judgement' (p. 176). Swift's dislike of bodily decay, the repugnance it
aroused in him, inspired the details of 'The Lady's Dressing Room'
(p. 150), published in 1732, to become most popular with his
contemporary audience, 'A Beautiful Young Nymph Going to Bed'
(p. 155) and 'Strephon and Chloe', the excremental elements of which
have so excited some critics who failed to understand that Swift was
creating a carapace for his sensitivity in an age which would have
quickly overcome the same critics, were they transported back to Swift's
time, by its physical as well as political stinks and corruptions. It is well
to remember how Swift insisted upon the need for cleanliness. He was
disgusted by much of what he observed and purged himself of his

disgust by description of what offended him – in his imagination as well as in reality.

There was another way of dealing with the cruder side of life as well as giving it realistic treatment: this emerges in the flippancies of, say, 'A Pastoral Dialogue' (p. 138), another send-up of a genre, of artificial poetic conventions, for here the nymph and swain are rustic labourers weeding the courtyard of Market Hill, the seat of Sir Arthur Acheson, five miles from Armagh. The muse has duly been invoked:

> *Sing, heavenly Muse, in sweetly flowing strain,*
> *The soft endearments of the nymph and swain*

but the tender lovers speak firmly in the vernacular:

DERMOT
> *No more that briar thy tender leg shall rake:*
> *(I spare the thistle for Sir Arthur's sake.)*
> *Sharp are the stones, take thou this rushy mat;*
> *The hardest bum will bruise with sitting squat.*

SHEELAH
> *Thy breeches, torn behind, stand gaping wide;*
> *This petticoat shall save thy dear backside;*
> *Nor need I blush, although you feel it wet;*
> *Dermot, I vow, 'tis nothing else but sweat.*

Swift was a visitor at Market Hill on three occasions, in 1728, 1729 and 1730. Apart from 'writing family verses of mirth by way of libels on my Lady' on his first visit, his friendship with the Achesons led to several attractive poems such as 'On Cutting Down the Old Thorn at Market Hill', a satiric presentation of contemporary life in classic forms, the mock-heroic dominant. This was written in 1728, and while at Market Hill Swift completed 'The Journal of a Modern Lady', probably with Lady Acheson in mind. His friendship with her bred the didactic dimension which seems to have been almost inevitable in cementing his closer relationships with the women he liked as friends; he advised her on grammar and elocution, and gave her, in his usual way, nicknames: she was 'Skinny' and 'Snip'; her somewhat emaciated appearance is part and parcel of 'Death and Daphne' and 'Daphne' – poems, incidentally, which she enjoyed. You had to enjoy teasing if you were a friend of the Dean: but then teasing and punning have been acceptable in Irish life, perhaps because of the oral tradition that is part of the intellectual background.

This friendship led Swift to buy land on the Achesons' estate north of Market Hill with the idea of building a house there. 'Drapier's Hill' (p. 138) describes the plan – its abandonment is the subject of 'The Dean's Reasons for Not Building at Drapier's Hill'. His role in the household may have echoed his earlier ease in the Berkeley household, for 'The Revolution at Market Hill' brings in the staff, Dennis the butler and Peggy Dixon the housekeeper, in a way reminiscent of 'The Humble Petition of Frances Harris'. 'A Panegyric on the Dean in the Person of a Lady in the North' (obviously Lady Acheson) presents Swift as he would, presumably, have liked to see himself, and picks upon his ability to move with ease at all levels of society:

> *Now, as a jester, I accost you;*
> *Which never yet one friend has lost you.*
> *You judge so nicely to a hair,*
> *How far to go, and when to spare:*
> *By long experience grown so wise,*
> *Of every taste to know the size;*
> *There's none so ignorant or weak*
> *To take offence at what you speak.*
> *Whene'er you joke, 'tis all a case;*
> *Whether with Dermot, or his Grace;*
> *With Teague O'Murphy, or an earl;*
> *A duchess or a kitchen girl.*
> *With such dexterity you fit*
> *Their several talents to your wit,*
> *That Moll the chambermaid can smoke,*
> *And Gaghagan take every joke.*

Geoffrey Hill, a twentieth-century poet and academic, has ventured into the area of ignorance or weakness by labelling the poem coprophilous, failing to appreciate its comic appreciation of the Achesons' twin temples to Cloacina, goddess of sewers, a ladies' and a gentlemen's lavatory. Swift was, as usual, praising cleanliness, though in an ironic way.

Swift may possibly, it has been suggested, have somewhat worn out his welcome at Market Hill; he was, however, able to mock himself as a visitor in 'Lady Acheson Weary of the Dean', and we can also see that he could be decidedly exigent.

His own character, enigmatic in some respects, a mixture of self-deprecation and self-assessment – which, naturally enough, contained self-praise, for he knew what he had achieved and how far he had progressed – was sketched in two poems, 'The Life and Genuine Character of Dr Swift' and 'Verses on the Death of Dr Swift, D.S.P.D.' (p. 160). The latter is now probably his best-known poem, and deservedly so. Like 'On Poetry: a Rhapsody' (p. 176), it shows Swift's ability to keep his verse moving, to create the condensed phrase, to observe, to record and to comment, with incisive wit at the service of moral judgement and jest alike.

Swift had always realized his mortality. In old age he prepared for it by writing his will in 1740. He provided for Rebecca Dingley, for his cousin Mrs Whiteway, a kind and intelligent woman who cared for him in his last years. There were various bequests of objects to friends – portraits, miniatures, silver plates for decanters and wine bottles, snuff boxes, medals, writing materials, a bottle-screw, gold and silver boxes, a strongbox – but the bulk of his fortune went to the building of St Patrick's Hospital – generally known as Swift's Hospital – in Dublin, 'an hospital large enough for the reception of as many idiots and lunatics' as the income from the lands and 'worldly substance' could maintain. The 'Verses on the Death of Dr Swift, D.S.P.D.' allude to his gift with a characteristic jest:

> *He gave the little wealth he had,*
> *To build a house for fools and mad:*
> *And showed by one satiric touch,*
> *No nation wanted it so much....*

As he grew older, he recorded a mood of glumness in 'On his own Deafness' (p. 193) but finished the poem with a typically deft flick of fun, particularly in the first Dublin printed version:

> *Deaf, giddy, helpless, left alone,*
> *To all my friends a burthen grown,*
> *No more I hear my church's bell,*

Than if it rang out for my knell:
At thunder now no more I start,
Than at the rumbling of a cart:
Nay, what's incredible, alack!
I hardly hear a woman's clack.

It had been Stella's conversation that provided a haven for Swift in storms of rage; he had also escaped some of the doldrums of despair in her company. But bereft of her companionship in his later days, he occupied himself, as ever, with writing. *A Complete Collection of Genteel and Ingenious Conversation according to the Most Polite Mode and Method now Used at Court and in the Best Companies* was published in 1738. Cast in conversational mode, and apparently the work of Simon Wagstaff, yet another invented persona, its characters speak in cliches; it is a magnificently rich compendium of how his contemporaries conversed, using the currency of well-worn, indeed worn-out, phrases. Swift's last unfinished prose work, the *Directions to Servants*, published in 1745, illustrates his knowledge of how humans behave, and why – and it is extremely funny. Many of his poems remind us of the interest he took in the sounds and turns of speech used at all levels of society. The streets of Dublin, for instance, provided him not only with the eccentric Mad Mullinex (see pp. 122–31) but with the street cries of 'Verses Made for the Women Who Cry Apples, etc.' (p. 201).

Swift loved variety, individuality, independence. He respected his readers, and both in his poetry and his prose he strove, successfully, to make himself clear, to make his point, to achieve that simplicity 'without which no human performance can arrive to any great perfection.' The simplicity depended on his firm grip upon the crude reality of objects, as in, say, 'A Description of a City Shower' (p. 35), as well as on his sharp awareness of the comic differences between appearance and reality exemplified in 'The Lady's Dressing Room' (p. 150), 'A Beautiful Young Nymph Going to Bed' (p. 155) or 'Strephon and Chloe'. He wanted, even in his earliest poems, to get beneath surface appearances: though he regarded his verses as written upon trifles, they were never composed without a moral view; they can surprise his readers by making them see themselves more clearly and thus they can at times have a considerable shock-effect.

In his poetry, Swift shares with us his enjoyment of words in dexterity of punning or rhyming, his powerful sense of parody – he treated heroic and pastoral modes with sharp irony – and, especially, his delight in the accents of forthright speech. In his praising and denigrating alike, he captured the details of life with precision, the octosyllabic couplet giving his lines control and conveying the directness he valued so greatly. His satiric views have a vitality of invention in their interpretation of current events, public and private alike. He is appealingly, naturally direct in the poems he wrote to his friends; he can express his affection and regard straightforwardly or else in the teasing way he and his friends enjoyed, in raillery, in the spirit of the bagatelle. He defended himself with more solemn readers in view: '. . . malice never was his aim / He lashed the vice but not the Name.'

When senility (not the madness some critics, as opposed to medical experts, have fathered on him) eventually overtook Swift in his last three years, his physical energy remained. Though he seems to have had a stroke, he continued his lifelong pursuit of health through exercise, walking incessantly through the rooms of the Deanery and up and down the stairs. When he rocked himself in a chair he repeated, 'I am what I am: I am what I am.' He was buried in St Patrick's Cathedral, his grave near Stella's. His own epitaph seizes upon what he was, upon the essential element in him: he loved human liberty.

The Humble Petition of Frances Harris

To their Excellencies
The Lords Justices of Ireland.
The humble petition of Frances Harris,
Who must starve, and die a maid if it miscarries.

Humbly showeth

That I went to warm myself in Lady Betty's chamber, because I
    was cold;
And I had in a purse seven pounds, four shillings and six pence
    (besides farthings) in money and gold;
So, because I had been buying things for my Lady last night,
I was resolved to tell my money, to see if it was right.
Now you must know, because my trunk has a very bad lock,
Therefore all the money I have (which, God knows, is a very
    small stock)
I keep in my pocket, tied about my middle, next my smock.
So, when I went to put up my purse, as God would have it, my
    smock was unripped;
And instead of putting it into my pocket, down it slipped:
10   Then the bell rung, and I went down to put my Lady to bed;
And, God knows, I thought my money was as safe as my
    maidenhead.
So, when I came up again, I found my pocket feel very light,
But when I searched, and missed my purse, Lord! I thought I
    should have sunk outright:
Lord! Madam, says Mary, how d'ye do? Indeed, said I, never
    worse:
But pray, Mary, can you tell what I have done with my purse?
Lord help me, said Mary, I never stirred out of this place:
Nay, said I, I had it in Lady Betty's chamber, that's a plain case.
So Mary got me to bed, and covered me up warm;
However, she stole away my garters, that I might do myself no
    harm.

20   So I tumbled and tossed all night, as you may very well think;
      But hardly ever set my eyes together, or slept a wink.
      So I was a-dreamed, methought, that we went and searched the
          folks round;
      And in a corner of Mrs Duke's box, tied in a rag, the money
          was found.
      So next morning we told Whittle, and he fell a-swearing;
      Then my Dame Wadgar came, and she, you know, is thick of
          hearing:
      Dame, said I, as loud as I could bawl, do you know what a loss I
          have had?
      Nay, said she, my Lord Collway's folks are all very sad,
      For my Lord Dromedary comes a Tuesday without fail;
      Pugh! said I, but that's not the business that I ail.
30   Says Cary, says he, I have been a servant this five and twenty
          years, come spring,
      And in all the places I lived, I never heard of such a thing.
      Yes, says the steward, I remember when I was at my Lady
          Shrewsbury's,
      Such a thing as this happened, just about the time of
          gooseberries.
      So I went to the party suspected, and I found her full of grief;
      (Now you must know, of all things in the world, I hate a thief.)
      However, I was resolved to bring the discourse slily about;
      Mrs Dukes, said I, here's an ugly accident has happened out;
      'Tis not that I value the money three skips of a louse;
      But the thing I stand upon, is the credit of the house;
40   'Tis true, seven pounds, four shillings, and six pence, makes a
          great hole in my wages;
      Besides, as they say, service is no inheritance in these ages.
      Now, Mrs Dukes, you know, and everybody understands,
      That though 'tis hard to judge, yet money can't go without
          hands.
      The Devil take me, said she (blessing herself), if ever I saw't!
      So she roared like a Bedlam, as though I had called her all to
          naught;
      So you know, what could I say to her any more:

I e'en left her, and came away as wise as I was before.

Well: but then they would have had me gone to the cunning-
man:

No, said I, 'tis the same thing, the chaplain will be here anon.

50 So the chaplain came in. Now the servants say he is my
sweetheart,

Because he's always in my chamber, and I always take his part;

So, as the Devil would have it, before I was aware, out I
blundered,

Parson, said I, can you cast a nativity, when a body's plundered?

(Now you must know, he hates to be called 'Parson' like the
devil.)

Truly, says he, Mrs Nab, it might become you to be more civil:

If your money be gone, as a learned divine says, d'ye see,

You are no text for my handling, so take that from me:

I was never taken for a conjuror before, I'd have you to know.

Lord, said I, don't be angry, I am sure I never thought you so:

60 You know, I honour the cloth, I design to be a parson's wife;

I never took one in your coat for a conjuror in all my life.

With that, he twisted his girdle at me like a rope, as who
should say,

Now you may go hang yourself for me; and so went away.

Well; I thought I should have swooned: Lord, said I, what shall
I do?

I have lost my money; and I shall lose my true-love too.

So, my Lord called me; Harry, said my Lord, don't cry,

I'll give something towards thy loss; and says my Lady, so will I.

Oh! but, said I, what if after all, the chaplain won't come to?

For that, he said (an't please your Excellencies) I must petition
you.

70 The premises tenderly considered, I desire your Excellencies'
protection:

And that I may have a share in next Sunday's collection:

And over and above, that I may have your Excellencies' letter,

With an order for the chaplain aforesaid; or instead of him a
better.

And then your poor petitioner, both night and day,
Or the chaplain (for 'tis his trade) as in duty bound, shall ever
   pray.

Baucis and Philemon

IMITATED FROM THE EIGHTH BOOK OF OVID

In ancient times, as story tells,
The saints would often leave their cells
And stroll about, but hide their quality,
To try good people's hospitality.

   It happened on a winter night,
(As authors of the legend write)
Two brother-hermits, saints by trade,
Taking their tour in masquerade,
Disguised in tattered habits, went
10 To a small village down in Kent;
Where, in the stroller's canting strain,
They begged from door to door in vain;
Tried every tone might pity win,
But not a soul would let them in.

   Our wandering saints in woeful state,
Treated at this ungodly rate,
Having through all the village passed,
To a small cottage came at last;
Where dwelt a good old honest yeoman,
20 Called in the neighbourhood, Philemon.
Who kindly did the saints invite
In his poor hut to pass the night:
And then the hospitable sire
Bid Goody Baucis mend the fire;
While he from out the chimney took
A flitch of bacon off the hook;

And freely from the fattest side
Cut out large slices to be fried:
Then stepped aside to fetch 'em drink,
30 Filled a large jug up to the brink;
And saw it fairly twice go round;
Yet (what was wonderful) they found
'Twas still replenished to the top,
As if they ne'er had touched a drop.
The good old couple was amazed,
And often on each other gazed;
For both were frighted to the heart,
And just began to cry, 'What art!'
Then softly turned aside to view,
40 Whether the lights were burning blue.
The gentle pilgrims soon aware on't,
Told them their calling, and their errand:
'Good folks, you need not be afraid,
We are but saints,' the hermits said:
'No hurt shall come to you, or yours;
But, for that pack of churlish boors,
Not fit to live on Christian ground,
They and their houses shall be drowned:
Whilst you shall see your cottage rise,
50 And grow a church before your eyes.'

They scarce had spoke; when fair and soft
The roof began to mount aloft;
Aloft rose every beam and rafter;
The heavy wall climbed slowly after.

The chimney widened, and grew higher,
Became a steeple with a spire.

The kettle to the top was hoist,
And there stood fastened to a joist:
But with the up-side down, to show
60 Its inclination for below:

In vain; for some superior force,
Applied at bottom, stops its course;
Doomed ever in suspense to dwell,
'Tis now no kettle, but a bell.

A wooden jack, which had almost
Lost, by disuse, the art to roast,
A sudden alteration feels,
Increased by new intestine wheels:
And what exalts the wonder more,
70 The number made the motion slower,
The flier, which, though't had leaden feet,
Turned round so quick you scarce could see't;
Now slackened by some secret power,
Can hardly move an inch an hour.
The jack and chimney, near allied,
Had never left each other's side;
The chimney to a steeple grown,
The jack would not be left alone;
But up against the steeple reared,
80 Became a clock, and still adhered:
And still its love to household cares
By a shrill voice at noon declares,
Warning the cook-maid not to burn
That roast meat which it cannot turn.

The groaning chair was seen to crawl
Like an huge snail half up the wall;
There stuck aloft, in public view;
And with small change, a pulpit grew.

The porringers, that in a row
90 Hung high, and made a glittering show,
To a less noble substance changed,
Were now but leathern buckets, ranged.

The ballads pasted on the wall,
Of Joan of France, and English Moll,

Fair Rosamund, and Robin Hood,
The 'Little Children in the Wood';
Now seemed to look abundance better,
Improved in picture, size, and letter;
And high in order placed describe
100 The heraldry of every tribe.

A bedstead of the antique mode,
Compact of timber many a load;
Such as our grandsires wont to use,
Was metamorphosed into pews;
Which still their ancient nature keep,
By lodging folks disposed to sleep.

The cottage, by such feats as these,
Grown to a church by just degrees,
The hermits then desire their host
110 To ask for what he fancied most.
Philemon, having paused a while,
Returned 'em thanks in homely style;
Then said: 'My house is grown so fine,
Methinks I still would call it mine:
I'm old, and fain would live at ease,
Make me the parson, if you please.'

He spoke, and presently he feels
His grazier's coat fall down his heels;
He sees, yet hardly can believe,
120 About each arm a pudding-sleeve:
His waistcoat to a cassock grew,
And both assumed a sable hue;
But, being old, continued just
As thread-bare, and as full of dust.
His talk was now of tithes and dues:
Could smoke his pipe, and read the news;
Knew how to preach old sermons next,
Vamped in the preface and the text;
At christenings well could act his part,

130   And had the service all by heart:
       Wished women might have children fast,
       And thought whose sow had farrowed last:
       Against dissenters would repine,
       And stood up firm for Right Divine:
       Found his head filled with many a system,
       But classic authors – he ne'er missed 'em.

       Thus having furbished up a parson,
       Dame Baucis next they played their farce on:
       Instead of homespun coifs were seen
140   Good pinners edged with colbertine:
       Her petticoat transformed apace,
       Became black satin, flounced with lace.
       Plain Goody would no longer down;
       'Twas Madam, in her grogram gown.
       Philemon was in great surprise,
       And hardly could believe his eyes,
       Amazed to see her look so prim:
       And she admired as much at him.

       Thus, happy in their change of life,
150   Were several years the man and wife:
       When on a day, which proved their last,
       Discoursing o'er old stories past,
       They went by chance, amidst their talk,
       To the churchyard, to fetch a walk;
       When Baucis hastily cried out,
       'My dear, I see your forehead sprout!'
       'Sprout,' quoth the man, 'what's this you tell us?
       I hope you don't believe me jealous:
       But yet, methinks, I feel it true;
160   And really yours is budding too –
       Nay – now I cannot stir my foot:
       It feels as if 'twere taking root.'

       Description would but tire my muse:
       In short, they both were turned to yews.

Old Goodman Dobson, of the Green,
Remembers he the trees has seen;
He'll talk of them from noon to night,
And goes with folks to show the sight;
On Sundays, after evening prayer,
170 He gathers all the parish there;
Points out the place of either yew;
Here Baucis, there Philemon grew:
Till once, a parson of our town,
To mend his barn, cut Baucis down;
At which, 'tis hard to be believed,
How much the other tree was grieved;
Grew scrubby, died a-top, was stunted:
So, the next parson stubbed and burnt it.

An Elegy on the Supposed Death of Partridge, the Almanac Maker

Well, 'tis as Bickerstaff had guessed,
Though we all took it for a jest:
Partridge is dead, nay more, he died
E'er he could prove the good squire lied.
Strange, an astroioger should die,
Without one wonder in the sky!
Not one of all his crony stars
To pay their duty at his hearse?
No meteor, no eclipse appeared?
10 No comet with a flaming beard?
The sun has rose, and gone to bed,
Just as if Partridge were not dead:
Nor hid himself behind the moon,
To make a dreadful night at noon.
He at fit periods walks through Aries,
Howe'er our earthly motion varies;

And twice a year he'll cut the Equator,
As if there had been no such matter.

Some wits have wondered what analogy
20 There is 'twixt cobbling and astrology;
How Partridge made his optics rise,
From a shoe-sole to reach the skies.
A list the cobblers' temples ties,
To keep the hair out of their eyes;
From whence 'tis plain the diadem
That princes wear derives from them;
And therefore crowns are nowadays
Adorned with golden stars and rays;
Which plainly shows the near alliance
30 Betwixt cobbling and the planets' science.

Besides, that slow-paced sign Boötes,
As 'tis miscalled, we know not who 'tis:
But Partridge ended all disputes,
He knew his trade, and called it boots.

The hornèd moon, which heretofore
Upon their shoes the Romans wore,
Whose wideness kept their toes from corns,
And whence we claim our shoeing-horns,
Shows how the art of cobbling bears
40 A near resemblance to the spheres.

A scrap of parchment hung by geometry
(A great refinement in barometry)
Can like the stars foretell the weather;
And what is parchment else but leather?
Which an astrologer might use,
Either for almanacs or shoes.

Thus Partridge, by his wit and parts,
At once did practise both these arts:
And as the boding owl, or rather

50 The bat, because her wings are leather,
Steals from her private cell by night,
And flies about the candle-light;
So learned Partridge could as well
Creep in the dark from leathern cell,
And in his fancy fly as far,
To peep upon a twinkling star.

Besides, he could confound the spheres,
And set the planets by the ears:
To show his skill, he Mars could join
60 To Venus in aspect malign;
Then call in Mercury for aid,
And cure the wounds that Venus made.

Great scholars have in Lucian read,
When Philip King of Greece was dead,
His soul and spirit did divide,
And each part took a different side:
One rose a star; the other fell
Beneath, and mended shoes in hell.

Thus Partridge still shines in each art,
70 The cobbling and star-gazing part;
And is installed as good a star
As any of the Caesars are.

Triumphant star! Some pity show
On cobblers militant below,
Whom roguish boys in stormy nights
Torment, by pissing out their lights;
Or through a chink convey their smoke,
Enclosed artificers to choke.

Thou, high exalted in thy sphere,
80 Mayst follow still thy calling there.
To thee the Bull will lend his hide,

By Phoebus newly tanned and dried.
For thee they Argo's hulk will tax,
And scrape her pitchy sides for wax.
Then Ariadne kindly lends
Her braided hair to make thee ends.
The point of Sagittarius' dart
Turns to an awl, by heavenly art:
And Vulcan, wheedled by his wife,
90   Will forge for thee a paring-knife.
For want of room by Virgo's side,
She'll strain a point, and sit astride,
To take thee kindly in between,
And then the signs will be thirteen.

But do not shed thy influence down
Upon St James's end of the town;
Consider whether the moon and stars
Have their devoutest worshippers,
Astrologers and lunatics
100   Have in more fields than stations fix
Hither thy gentle aspect bend,
Nor look asquint on an old friend.

THE EPITAPH

Here, five feet deep, lies on his back
A cobbler, star-monger, and quack;
Who to the stars in pure good will
Does to his best look upward still.
Weep all you customers that use
His pills, his almanacs, or shoes:
And you that did your fortunes seek
110   Step to his grave but once a week:
This earth, which bears his body's print,
You'll find has so much virtue in't,
That I durst pawn my ears, 'twill tell
What'er concerns you full as well,

In physic, stolen goods, or love,
As he himself could, when above.

A Description of the Morning

Now hardly here and there a hackney-coach
Appearing, showed the ruddy morn's approach.
Now Betty from her master's bed has flown,
And softly stole to discompose her own.
The slipshod prentice from his master's door
Had pared the dirt, and sprinkled round the floor.
Now Moll had whirled her mop with dexterous airs,
Prepared to scrub the entry and the stairs.
The youth with broomy stumps began to trace
10   The kennel-edge, where wheels had worn the place.
The small-coal man was heard with cadence deep,
Till drowned in shriller notes of chimney-sweep.
Duns at his Lordship's gate began to meet;
And Brickdust Moll had screamed through half a street.
The turnkey now his flock returning sees,
Duly let out a-nights to steal for fees.
The watchful bailiffs take their silent stands;
And schoolboys lag with satchels in their hands.

A Description of a City Shower

Careful observers may foretell the hour
(By sure prognostics) when to dread a shower.
While rain depends, the pensive cat gives o'er
Her frolics, and pursues her tail no more.
Returning home at night you find the sink
Strike your offended sense with double stink.
If you be wise, then go not far to dine,
You spend in coach-hire more than save in wine.
A coming shower your shooting corns presage,

10   Old aches throb, your hollow tooth will rage.
     Sauntering in coffee-house is Dulman seen;
     He damns the climate, and complains of spleen.

      Meanwhile the South, rising with dabbled wings,
     A sable cloud athwart the welkin flings,
     That swilled more liquor than it could contain,
     And like a drunkard gives it up again.
     Brisk Susan whips her linen from the rope,
     While the first drizzling shower is born aslope:
     Such is that sprinkling which some careless quean
20   Flirts on you from her mop, but not so clean:
     You fly, invoke the gods; then turning, stop
     To rail; she singing, still whirls on her mop.
     Nor yet the dust had shunned the unequal strife,
     But, aided by the wind, fought still for life;
     And wafted with its foe by violent gust,
     'Twas doubtful which was rain, and which was dust.
     Ah! where must needy poet seek for aid,
     When dust and rain at once his coat invade?
     Sole coat, where dust cemented by the rain
30   Erects the nap, and leaves a cloudy stain.

      Now in contiguous drops the flood comes down,
     Threatening with deluge this devoted town.
     To shops in crowds the daggled females fly,
     Pretend to cheapen goods; but nothing buy.
     The Templar spruce, while every spout's abroach,
     Stays till 'tis fair, yet seems to call a coach.
     The tucked-up seamstress walks with hasty strides,
     While streams run down her oiled umbrella's sides.
     Here various kinds, by various fortunes led,
40   Commence acquaintance underneath a shed.
     Triumphant Tories, and desponding Whigs,
     Forget their feuds, and join to save their wigs.
     Boxed in a chair the beau impatient sits,
     While spouts run clattering o'er the roof by fits;

And ever and anon with frightful din
The leather sounds; he trembles from within.
So when Troy chair-men bore the wooden steed,
Pregnant with Greeks, impatient to be freed;
(Those bully Greeks, who, as the moderns do,
50 Instead of paying chair-men, run them through)
Laocoon struck the outside with his spear,
And each imprisoned hero quaked for fear.

    Now from all parts the swelling kennels flow,
And bear their trophies with them as they go:
Filths of all hues and odours, seem to tell
What streets they sailed from, by the sight and smell.
They, as each torrent drives with rapid force
From Smithfield, or St Pulchre's shape their course;
And in huge confluent join at Snow Hill ridge,
60 Fall from the conduit prone to Holborn Bridge.
Sweepings from butchers' stalls, dung, guts, and blood,
Drowned puppies, stinking sprats, all drenched in mud,
Dead cats, and turnip-tops come tumbling down the flood.

Corinna

This day (the year I dare not tell)
   Apollo played the midwife's part;
Into the world Corinna fell,
   And he endowed her with his art.

But Cupid with a satyr comes;
   Both softly to the cradle creep:
Both stroke her hands, and rub her gums,
   While the poor child lay fast asleep.

Then Cupid thus: 'This little maid
10   Of love shall always speak and write.'
'And I pronounce', the satyr said,
   'The world shall feel her scratch and bite.'

Her talent she displayed betimes;
   For, in a few revolving moons,
She seemed to laugh and squall in rhymes,
   And all her gestures were lampoons.

At six years old, the subtle jade
   Stole to the pantry-door, and found
The butler with my Lady's maid;
20   And you may swear the tale went round.

She made a song, how little Miss
   Was kissed and slobbered by a lad:
And how, when Master went to piss,
   Miss came, and peeped at all he had.

At twelve a poet, and coquette;
   Marries for love, half whore, half wife;
Cuckolds, elopes, and runs in debt;
   Turns authoress, and is Curll's for life.

Her commonplace book all gallant is,
30   Of scandal now a cornucopia;
She pours it out in an *Atlantis*,
   Or *Memoirs of the New Utopia*.

Cadenus and Vanessa

The shepherds and the nymphs were seen
Pleading before the Cyprian queen.
The counsel for the fair began,
Accusing that false creature, man:

The brief with weighty crimes was charged,
On which the pleader much enlarged:
That 'Cupid now has lost his art,
Or blunts the point of every dart;
His altar now no longer smokes,
10 His mother's aid no youth invokes:
This tempts freethinkers to refine,
And brings in doubt their power divine.
Now love is dwindled to intrigue,
And marriage grown a money-league.
Which crimes aforesaid' (with her leave)
'Were' (as he humbly did conceive)
'Against our sovereign lady's peace,
Against the statute in that case,
Against her dignity and crown.'
20 Then prayed an answer, and sat down.

The nymphs with scorn beheld their foes:
When the defendant's counsel rose;
And, what no lawyer ever lacked,
With impudence owned all the fact:
But, what the gentlest heart would vex,
Laid all the fault on t'other sex.
That 'Modern love is no such thing
As what those ancient poets sing;
A fire celestial, chaste, refined,
30 Conceived and kindled in the mind;
Which having found an equal flame,
Unites, and both become the same,
In different breasts together burn,
Together both to ashes turn.
But women now feel no such fire;
And only know the gross desire:
Their passions move in lower spheres,
Where'er caprice or folly steers:
A dog, a parrot, or an ape,
40 Or some worse brute in human shape,

Engross the fancies of the fair,
The few soft moments they can spare,
From visits to receive and pay;
From scandal, politics, and play;
From fans and flounces, and brocades;
From equipage and park-parades;
From all the thousand female toys;
From every trifle that employs
The out or inside of their heads,
50   Between their toilets and their beds.

      'In a dull stream, which moving slow
You hardly see the current flow;
If a small breeze obstructs the course,
It whirls about for want of force,
And in its narrow circle gathers
Nothing but chaff, and straws, and feathers:
The current of a female mind
Stops thus, and turns with every wind;
Thus whirling round, together draws
60   Fools, fops, and rakes, for chaff and straws.
Hence we conclude, no women's hearts
Are won by virtue, wit, and parts;
Nor are the men of sense to blame,
For breasts incapable of flame;
The fault must on the nymphs be placed,
Grown so corrupted in their taste.'

      The pleader, having spoke his best,
Had witness ready to attest,
Who fairly could on oath depose,
70   When questions on the fact arose,
That every article was true;
'Nor further those deponents knew':
Therefore he humbly would insist,
The bill might be with costs dismissed.

The cause appeared of so much weight,
That Venus, from her judgement-seat,
Desired them not to talk so loud,
Else she must interpose a cloud:
For if the heavenly folks should know
80 These pleadings in the courts below,
That mortals here disdain to love;
She ne'er could show her face above:
For gods, their betters, are too wise
To value that which men despise:
'And then,' said she, 'my son and I
Must stroll in air 'twixt land and sky;
Or else, shut out from heaven and earth,
Fly to the sea, my place of birth;
There live with daggled mermaids pent,
90 And keep on fish perpetual Lent.'

But since the case appeared so nice,
She thought it best to take advice.
The Muses, by their king's permission,
Though foes to love, attend the session;
And on the right hand took their places
In order; on the left, the Graces:
To whom she might her doubts propose
On all emergencies that rose.
The Muses oft were seen to frown;
100 The Graces half ashamed looked down;
And 'twas observed, there were but few ⎞
Of either sex, among the crew, ⎬
Whom she or her assessors knew. ⎠
The goddess soon began to see
Things were not ripe for a decree:
And said, she must consult her books,
The lovers' *Fleta*'s, Bractons, Cokes.
First to a dapper clerk she beckoned,
To turn to Ovid, Book the Second;
110 She then referred them to a place

In Virgil (*vide* Dido's case):
As for Tibullus's reports,
They never passed for law in courts;
For Cowley's briefs, and pleas of Waller,
Still their authority was smaller.

There was on both sides much to say:
She'd hear the cause another day;
And so she did, and then a third:
She heard it – there she kept her word;
120   But with rejoinders and replies,
Long bills, and answers, stuffed with lies;
Demur, imparlance, and essoign,
The parties ne'er could issue join:
For sixteen years the cause was spun,
And then stood where it first begun.

Now, gentle Clio, sing or say,
What Venus meant by this delay.
The goddess much perplexed in mind,
To see her empire thus declined,
130   When first this grand debate arose
Above her wisdom to compose,
Conceived a project in her head,
To work her ends; which, if it sped,
Would show the merits of the cause,
Far better than consulting laws.

In a glad hour Lucina's aid
Produced on earth a wondrous maid,
On whom the Queen of Love was bent
To try a new experiment:
140   She threw her law-books on the shelf,
And thus debated with herself.

'Since men allege they ne'er can find
Those beauties in a female mind,
Which raise a flame that will endure
For ever, uncorrupt and pure;
If 'tis with reason they complain,
This infant shall restore my reign.
I'll search where every virtue dwells,
From courts inclusive, down to cells,
150   What preachers talk, or sages write;
These I will gather and unite;
And represent them to mankind
Collected in that infant's mind.'

This said, she plucks in heaven's high bowers
A sprig of amaranthine flowers;
In nectar thrice infuses bays;
Three times refined in Titan's rays:
Then calls the Graces to her aid,
And sprinkles thrice the new-born maid:
160   From whence the tender skin assumes
A sweetness above all perfumes;
From whence a cleanliness remains,
Incapable of outward stains;
From whence that decency of mind,
So lovely in the female kind;
Where not one careless thought intrudes,
Less modest than the speech of prudes;
Where never blush was called in aid;
That spurious virtue in a maid;
170   A virtue but at second hand;
They blush because they understand.

The Graces next would act their part,
And showed but little of their art;
Their work was half already done,
The child with native beauty shone;
The outward form no help required:

Each breathing on her thrice, inspired
That gentle, soft, engaging air,
Which, in old times, adorned the fair;
180 And said, 'Vanessa be the name,
By which thou shalt be known to fame:
Vanessa, by the gods enrolled:
Her name on earth – shall not be told.'

But still the work was not complete,
When Venus thought on a deceit:
Drawn by her doves, away she flies,
And finds out Pallas in the skies:
'Dear Pallas, I have been this morn
To see a lovely infant born:
190 A boy in yonder isle below,
So like my own, without his bow:
By beauty could your heart be won,
You'd swear it is Apollo's son;
But it shall ne'er be said, a child
So hopeful, has by me been spoiled;
I have enough besides to spare,
And give him wholly to your care.'

Wisdom's above suspecting wiles:
The Queen of Learning gravely smiles;
200 Down from Olympus comes with joy,
Mistakes Vanessa for a boy;
Then sows within her tender mind
Seeds long unknown to womankind,
For manly bosoms chiefly fit,
The seeds of knowledge, judgement, wit.
Her soul was suddenly endued
With justice, truth and fortitude;
With honour, which no breath can stain,
Which malice must attack in vain;
210 With open heart and bounteous hand:
But Pallas here was at a stand;

She knew in our degenerate days
Bare virtue could not live on praise,
That meat must be with money bought;
She therefore, upon second thought,
Infused, yet as it were by stealth,
Some small regard for state and wealth:
Of which, as she grew up, there stayed
A tincture in the prudent maid:
220 She managed her estate with care,
Yet liked three footmen to her chair.
But lest he should neglect his studies
Like a young heir, the thrifty goddess
(For fear young master should be spoiled)
Would use him like a younger child;
And, after long computing, found
'Twould come to just five thousand pound.

The Queen of Love was pleased, and proud,
To see Vanessa thus endowed;
230 She doubted not but such a dame
Through every breast would dart a flame;
That every rich and lordly swain
With pride would drag about her chain;
That scholars would forsake their books
To study bright Vanessa's looks:
As she advanced, that womankind
Would by her model form their mind,
And all their conduct would be tried
By her, as an unerring guide.
240 Offending daughters oft would hear
Vanessa's praise rung in their ear:
Miss Betty, when she does a fault,
Lets fall a knife, or spills the salt,
Will thus be by her mother chid:
"'Tis what Vanessa never did.'
'Thus by the nymphs and swains adored,
My power shall be again restored,

And happy lovers bless my reign –'
So Venus hoped, but hoped in vain.

250   For when in time the martial maid
Found out the trick that Venus played,
She shakes her helm, she knits her brows,
And fired with indignation vows,
Tomorrow, ere the setting sun,
She'd all undo, that she had done.

But in the poets we may find,
A wholesome law, time out of mind,
Had been confirmed by fate's decree;
That gods, of whatsoe'er degree,
260   Resume not what themselves have given,
Or any brother-god in heaven:
Which keeps the peace among the gods,
Or they must always be at odds;
And Pallas, if she broke the laws,
Must yield her foe the stronger cause;
A shame to one so much adored
For wisdom at Jove's council-board.
Besides, she feared, the Queen of Love
Would meet with better friends above.

270   And though she must with grief reflect,
To see a mortal virgin decked
With graces hitherto unknown
To female breasts, except her own;
Yet she would act as best became
A goddess of unspotted fame:
She knew, by augury divine,
Venus would fail in her design:
She studied well the point, and found
Her foe's conclusions were not sound,
280   From premises erroneous brought,
And therefore the deductions naught;
And must have contrary effects
To what her treacherous foe expects.

In proper season Pallas meets
The Queen of Love, whom thus she greets
(For gods, we are by Homer told,
Can in celestial language scold),
'Perfidious goddess! but in vain
You formed this project in your brain,
290 A project for thy talents fit,
With much deceit and little wit:
Thou hast, as thou shalt quickly see,
Deceived thyself, instead of me;
For how can heavenly wisdom prove
An instrument to earthly love?
Knowst thou not yet that men commence
Thy votaries for want of sense?
Nor shall Vanessa be the theme
To manage thy abortive scheme:
300 She'll prove the greatest of thy foes:
And yet I scorn to interpose,
But using neither skill, nor force,
Leave all things to their natural course.'

The goddess thus pronounced her doom:
When, lo! Vanessa in her bloom
Advanced like Atalanta's star,
But rarely seen, and seen from far:
In a new world with caution stepped,
Watched all the company she kept,
310 Well knowing from the books she read
What dangerous paths young virgins tread:
Would seldom at the park appear,
Nor saw the playhouse twice a year;
Yet not incurious, was inclined
To know the converse of mankind.

First issued from perfumers' shops
A crowd of fashionable fops;
They asked her how she liked the play,

Then told the tattle of the day;
320 A duel fought last night at two,
About a Lady – you know who;
Mentioned a new Italian, come
Either from Muscovy or Rome;
Gave hints of who and who's together;
Then fell to talking of the weather:
'Last night was so extremely fine,
The ladies walked till after nine.'
Then in soft voice and speech absurd,
With nonsense every second word,
330 With fustian from exploded plays,
They celebrate her beauty's praise,
Run o'er their cant of stupid lies,
And tell the murders of her eyes.

With silent scorn Vanessa sat,
Scarce listening to their idle chat;
Further than sometimes by a frown,
When they grew pert, to pull them down.
At last she spitefully was bent
To try their wisdom's full extent;
340 And said, she valued nothing less
Than titles, figure, shape, and dress;
That merit should be chiefly placed
In judgement, knowledge, wit, and taste;
And these, she offered to dispute,
Alone distinguished man from brute:
That present times have no pretence
To virtue, in the noblest sense,
By Greeks and Romans understood,
To perish for our country's good.
350 She named the ancient heroes round,
Explained for what they were renowned;
Then spoke with censure, or applause,
Of foreign customs, rites, and laws.
Through nature, and through art she ranged,

And gracefully her subjects changed:
In vain: her hearers had no share
In all she spoke, except to stare.
Their judgement was upon the whole,
'That lady is the dullest soul' –
360 Then tipped their forehead in a jeer,
As who should say – 'she wants it here;
She may be handsome, young and rich,
But none will burn her for a witch.'

A party next of glittering dames,
From round the purlieus of St James,
Came early, out of pure good will,
To catch the girl in dishabille.
Their clamour 'lighting from their chairs,
Grew louder, all the way upstairs;
370 At entrance loudest, where they found
The room with volumes littered round.
Vanessa held Montaigne, and read,
Whilst Mrs Susan combed her head:
They called for tea and chocolate,
And fell into their usual chat,
Discoursing with important face,
On ribbons, fans, and gloves and lace;
Showed patterns just from India brought,
And gravely asked her what she thought;
380 Whether the red or green were best,
And what they cost? Vanessa guessed,
As came into her fancy first,
Named half the rates, and liked the worst.
To scandal next – 'What awkward thing
Was that, last Sunday in the Ring?'
– 'I'm sorry Mopsa breaks so fast;
I said her face would never last.'
'Corinna, with that youthful air,
Is thirty, and a bit to spare:
390 Her fondness for a certain earl

Began when I was but a girl.'
'Phyllis, who but a month ago
Was married to the Tunbridge beau,
I saw coquetting t'other night
In public with that odious knight.'

    They rallied next Vanessa's dress;
'That gown was made for old Queen Bess.'
'Dear madam, let me set your head:
Don't you intend to put on red?'
400 'A petticoat without a hoop!
Sure, you are not ashamed to stoop;
With handsome garters at your knees,
No matter what a fellow sees.'

    Filled with disdain, with rage inflamed,
Both of her self and sex ashamed,
The nymph stood silent out of spite,
Nor would vouchsafe to set them right.
Away the fair detractors went,
And gave, by turns, their censures vent.
410 'She's not so handsome in my eyes:
For wit, I wonder where it lies.'
'She's fair and clean, and that's the most;
But why proclaim her for a toast?'
'A babyface, no life, nor airs,
But what she learnt at country fairs;
Scarce knows what difference is between
Rich Flanders lace and colbertine.'
'I'll undertake my little Nancy
In flounces has a better fancy.'
420 'With all her wit, I would not ask
Her judgement, how to buy a mask.'
'We begged her but to patch her face,
She never hit one proper place;
Which every girl at five years old
Can do as soon as she is told.'

'I own, that out-of-fashion stuff
Becomes the creature well enough.'
'The girl might pass, if we could get her
To know the world a little better.'
430 (*To know the world*: a modern phrase,
For visits, ombre, balls and plays.)

Thus, to the world's perpetual shame,
The Queen of Beauty lost her aim.
Too late with grief she understood,
Pallas had done more harm than good;
For great examples are but vain,
Where ignorance begets disdain.
Both sexes, armed with guilt and spite,
Against Vanessa's power unite;
440 To copy her, few nymphs aspired;
Her virtues fewer swains admired:
So stars beyond a certain height
Give mortals neither heat nor light.

Yet some of either sex, endowed
With gifts superior to the crowd,
With virtue, knowledge, taste and wit,
She condescended to admit:
With pleasing arts she could reduce
Men's talents to their proper use;
450 And with address each genius held
To that wherein it most excelled;
Thus making others' wisdom known,
Could please them, and improve her own.
A modest youth said something new,
She placed it in the strongest view.
All humble worth she strove to raise;
Would not be praised, yet loved to praise.
The learned met with free approach,
Although they came not in a coach.
460 Some clergy too she would allow,

Nor quarrelled at their awkward bow.
But this was for Cadenus' sake;
A gownman of a different make;
Whom Pallas, once Vanessa's tutor,
Had fixed on for her coadjutor.

But Cupid, full of mischief, longs
To vindicate his mother's wrongs.
On Pallas all attempts are vain;
One way he knows to give her pain;
470   Vows, on Vanessa's heart to take
Due vengeance, for her patron's sake.
Those early seeds by Venus sown,
In spite of Pallas, now were grown;
And Cupid hoped they would improve
By time, and ripen into love.
The boy made use of all his craft,
In vain discharging many a shaft,
Pointed at colonels, lords, and beaux;
Cadenus warded off the blows:
480   For placing still some book betwixt,
The darts were in the cover fixed,
Or often blunted and recoiled,
On Plutarch's *Morals* struck, were spoiled.

The Queen of Wisdom could foresee,
But not prevent the Fates' decree;
And human caution tries in vain
To break that adamantine chain.
Vanessa, though by Pallas taught,
By Love invulnerable thought,
490   Searching in books for wisdom's aid,
Was, in the very search, betrayed.

Cupid, though all his darts were lost,
Yet still resolved to spare no cost;
He could not answer to his fame

The triumphs of that stubborn dame;
A nymph so hard to be subdued,
Who neither was coquette nor prude.
'I find,' said he, 'she wants a doctor,
Both to adore her and instruct her;
500   I'll give her what she most admires,
Among those venerable sires.
Cadenus is a subject fit,
Grown old in politics and wit;
Caressed by ministers of state,
Of half mankind the dread and hate.
Whate'er vexations Love attend,
She need no rivals apprehend.
Her sex, with universal voice,
Must laugh at her capricious choice.'

510   Cadenus many things had writ;
Vanessa much esteemed his wit,
And called for his poetic works;
Meantime the boy in secret lurks,
And, while the book was in her hand,
The urchin from his private stand
Took aim, and shot with all his strength
A dart of such prodigious length,
It pierced the feeble volume through,
And deep transfixed her bosom too.
520   Some lines, more moving than the rest,
Stuck to the point that pierced her breast;
And born directly to her heart,
With pains unknown increased the smart.

     Vanessa, not in years a score,
Dreams of a gown of forty-four;
Imaginary charms can find,
In eyes with reading almost blind:
Cadenus now no more appears
Declined in health, advanced in years:

530   She fancies music in his tongue,
Nor further looks, but thinks him young.
What mariner is not afraid,
To venture in a ship decayed?
What planter will attempt to yoke
A sapling with a fallen oak?
As years increase, she brighter shines,
Cadenus with each day declines,
And he must fall a prey to time,
While she continues in her prime.

540   Cadenus, common forms apart,
In every scene had kept his heart;
Had sighed and languished, vowed and writ,
For pastime, or to show his wit:
But books, and time, and state affairs,
Had spoiled his fashionable airs;
He now could praise, esteem, approve,
But understood not what was love:
His conduct might have made him styled
A father, and the nymph his child.

550   That innocent delight he took
To see the virgin mind her book,
Was but the master's secret joy
In school to hear the finest boy.
Her knowledge with her fancy grew;
She hourly pressed for something new:
Ideas came into her mind
So fast, his lessons lagged behind:
She reasoned, without plodding long;
Nor ever gave her judgement wrong.

560   But now a sudden change was wrought,
She minds no longer what he taught.
She wished her tutor were her lover;
Resolved she would her flame discover:
And when Cadenus would expound
Some notion subtle or profound,

The nymph would gently press his hand,
As if she seemed to understand;
Or dextrously dissembling chance,
Would sigh, and steal a secret glance.
570 Cadenus was amazed to find
Such marks of a distracted mind;
For though she seemed to listen more
To all he spoke, than e're before;
He found her thoughts would absent range,
Yet guessed not whence could spring the change.
And first he modestly conjectures
His pupil might be tired with lectures;
Which helped to mortify his pride,
Yet gave him not the heart to chide;
580 But in a mild dejected strain
At last he ventured to complain:
Said, she should be no longer teased;
Might have her freedom when she pleased:
Was now convinced he acted wrong,
To hide her from the world so long;
And in dull studies to engage
One of her tender sex and age.
That every nymph with envy owned,
How she might shine in the *grand monde*,
590 And every shepherd was undone
To see her cloistered like a nun.
This was a visionary scheme,
He waked, and found it but a dream;
A project far above his skill,
For nature must be nature still.
If he was bolder than became
A scholar to a courtly dame,
She might excuse a man of letters;
Thus tutors often treat their betters.
600 And since his talk offensive grew,
He came to take his last adieu.

Vanessa, filled with just disdain,
Would still her dignity maintain,
Instructed from her early years
To scorn the art of female tears.

Had he employed his time so long
To teach her what was right or wrong,
Yet could such notions entertain,
That all his lectures were in vain?
610   She owned the wandering of her thoughts,
But he must answer for her faults.
She well remembered, to her cost,
That all his lessons were not lost.
Two maxims she could still produce,
And sad experience taught their use:
That virtue, pleased by being shown,
Knows nothing which it dare not own;
Can make us without fear disclose
Our inmost secrets to our foes:
620   That common forms were not designed
Directors to a noble mind.
'Now,' said the nymph, 'to let you see
My actions with your rules agree,
That I can vulgar forms despise,
And have no secrets to disguise:
I knew by what you said and writ,
How dangerous things were men of wit;
You cautioned me against their charms,
But never gave me equal arms:
630   Your lessons found the weakest part,
Aimed at the head, but reached the heart.'

Cadenus felt within him rise
Shame, disappointment, guilt, surprise.
He knew not how to reconcile
Such language with her usual style:
And yet her words were so expressed

He could not hope she spoke in jest.
His thoughts had wholly been confined
To form and cultivate her mind.
He hardly knew, till he was told,
640 Whether the nymph were young or old:
Had met her in a public place,
Without distinguishing her face.
Much less could his declining age
Vanessa's earliest thoughts engage.
And if her youth indifference met,
His person must contempt beget.
Or, grant her passion be sincere,
How shall his innocence be clear?
650 Appearances were all so strong,
The world must think him in the wrong;
Would say, he made a treacherous use
Of wit, to flatter and seduce:
The town would swear he had betrayed,
By magic spells, the harmless maid;
And every beau would have his jokes,
That scholars were like other folks:
That when platonic flights are over,
The tutor turns a mortal lover.
660 So tender of the young and fair?
It showed a true paternal care:
'Five thousand guineas in her purse:
The doctor might have fancied worse . . .'

Hardly at length he silence broke,
And faltered every word he spoke;
Interpreting her complaisance,
Just as a man *sans consequence*.
She rallied well, he always knew;
Her manner now was something new;
670 And what she spoke was in an air,
As serious as a tragic player.
But whose who aim at ridicule

Should fix upon some certain rule,
Which fairly hints they are in jest,
Else he must enter his protest:
For, let a man be ne'er so wise,
He may be caught with sober lies;
A science, which he never taught,
And, to be free, was dearly bought:
680   For, take it in its proper light,
'Tis just what coxcombs call, 'a bite'.

   But, not to dwell on things minute;
Vanessa finished the dispute;
Brought weighty arguments to prove
That reason was her guide in love.
She thought he had himself described
His doctrines when she first imbibed;
What he had planted, now was grown;
His virtues she might call her own;
690   As he approves, as he dislikes,
Love or contempt, her fancy strikes.
Self-love, in nature rooted fast,
Attends us first, and leaves us last:
Why she likes him, admire not at her,
She loves herself, and that's the matter.
How was her tutor wont to praise
The geniuses of ancient days!
(Those authors he so oft had named
For learning, wit, and wisdom famed);
700   Was struck with love, esteem and awe,
For persons whom he never saw.
Suppose Cadenus flourished then,
He must adore such god-like men.
If one short volume could comprise
All that was witty, learned, and wise,
How would it be esteemed, and read,
Although the writer long were dead?
If such an author were alive,

How would all for his friendship strive;
710 And come in crowds to see his face:
And this she takes to be her case:
Cadenus answers every end,
The book, the author, and the friend.
The utmost her desires will reach,
Is but to learn what he can teach;
His converse is a system, fit
Alone to fill up all her wit;
While every passion of her mind
In him is centred and confined.

720   Love can with speech inspire a mute,
And taught Vanessa to dispute.
This topic, never touched before,
Displayed her eloquence the more:
Her knowledge, with such pains acquired,
By this new passion grew inspired:
Through this she made all objects pass,
Which gave a tincture o'er the mass:
As rivers, though they bend and twine,
Still to the sea their course incline:
730 Or, as philosophers, who find
Some favourite system to their mind,
In every point to make it fit,
Will force all nature to submit.

           Cadenus, who could ne'er suspect
His lessons would have such effect,
Or be so artfully applied,
Insensibly came on her side;
It was an unforeseen event,
Things took a turn he never meant.
740 Whoe'er excels in what we prize
Appears a hero to our eyes;
Each girl when pleased with what is taught,
Will have the teacher in her thought:

When Miss delights in her spinnet,
A fiddler may a fortune get;
A blockhead with melodious voice
In boarding schools can have his choice;
And oft the dancing-master's art
Climbs from the toe to touch the heart.
750   In learning let a nymph delight,
The pedant gets a mistress by't.
Cadenus, to his grief and shame,
Could scarce oppose Vanessa's flame;
But though her arguments were strong,
At least could hardly wish them wrong.
Howe'er it came, he could not tell,
But sure she never talked so well.
His pride began to interpose,
Preferred before a crowd of beaux:
760   So bright a nymph to come unsought,
Such wonder by his merit wrought:
'Tis merit must with her prevail,
He never knew her judgement fail;
She noted all she ever read,
And had a most discerning head.

       'Tis an old maxim in the schools,
That vanity's the food of fools;
Yet now and then your men of wit
Will condescend to take a bit.
770   So when Cadenus could not hide,
He chose to justify his pride;
Construing the passion she had shown,
Much to her praise, more to his own.
Nature in him had merit placed;
In her, a most judicious taste.
Love, hitherto a transient guest,
Ne'er held possession of his breast;
So, long attending at the gate,
Disdained to enter in so late.

780   Love, why do we one passion call?
When 'tis a compound of them all;
Where hot and cold, where sharp and sweet,
In all their equipages meet;
Where pleasures mixed with pains appear,
Sorrow with joy, and hope with fear:
Wherein his dignity and age
Forbid Cadenus to engage.
But friendship in its greatest height,
A constant, rational delight,
790   On virtue's basis fixed to last,
When love's allurements long are past;
Which gently warms, but cannot burn;
He gladly offers in return:
His want of passion will redeem,
With gratitude, respect, esteem:
With that devotion we bestow,
When goddesses appear below.

    While thus Cadenus entertains
Vanessa in exalted strains,
800   The nymph in sober words entreats
A truce with all sublime conceits.
For why such raptures, flights, and fancies,
To her, who durst not read romances;
In lofty style to make replies,
Which he had taught her to despise.
But when her tutor will affect
Devotion, duty, and respect,
He fairly abdicates his throne,
The government is now her own:
810   He has a forfeiture incurred:
She vows to take him at his word,
And hopes he will not think it strange
If both should now their stations change.
The nymph will have her turn, to be
The tutor; and the pupil, he:

Though she already can discern,
Her scholar is not apt to learn;
Or wants capacity to reach
The science she designs to teach:
820   Wherein his genius was below
The skill of every common beau;
Who, though he cannot spell, is wise
Enough to read a lady's eyes;
And will each accidental glance
Interpret for a kind advance.

But what success Vanessa met,
Is to the world a secret yet:
Whether the nymph, to please her swain,
Talks in a high romantic strain;
830   Or whether he at last descends
To act with less seraphic ends;
Or, to compound the business, whether
They temper love and books together;
Must never to mankind be told,
Nor shall the conscious Muse unfold.

Meantime the mournful Queen of Love
Led but a weary life above.
She ventures now to leave the skies,
Grown by Vanessa's conduct wise:
840   For though by one perverse event
Pallas had crossed her first intent;
Though her design was not obtained,
Yet had she much experience gained;
And, by the project vainly tried,
Could better now the cause decide.

She gave due notice, that both parties,
Coram Regina prox' die Martis,
Should at their peril, without fail,
'Come and appear, and save their bail.'

850 All met, and silence thrice proclaimed,
    One lawyer to each side was named.
    The judge discovered in her face
    Resentments for her late disgrace;
    And, full of anger, shame and grief,
    Directed them to mind their brief;
    Nor spend their time to show their reading;
    She'd have a summary proceeding.
    She gathered, under every head,
    The sum of what each lawyer said;
860 Gave her own reasons last; and then
    Decreed the cause against the men.

    But, in a weighty cause like this,
    To show she did not judge amiss,
    Which evil tongues might else report,
    She made a speech in open court;
    Wherein she grievously complains,
    'How she was cheated by the swains:
    On whose petition (humbly showing
    That women were not worth the wooing;
870 And that unless the sex would mend,
    The race of lovers soon must end)
    She was at Lord knows what expense
    To form a nymph of wit and sense;
    A model for her sex designed,
    Who never could one lover find.
    She saw her favour was misplaced;
    The fellows had a wretched taste;
    She needs must tell them to their face,
    They were a stupid, senseless race:
880 And were she to begin again,
    She'd study to reform the men;
    Or add some grains of folly more
    To women than they had before,
    To put them on an equal foot;
    And this, or nothing else, would do't.

This might their mutual fancy strike,
Since every being loves its like.

'But now, repenting what was done,
She left all business to her son:
890 She puts the world in his possession,
And let him use it at discretion.'

The crier was ordered to dismiss
The court, who made his last 'Oyez!'
The goddess would no longer wait;
But, rising from her chair of state,
Left all below at six and seven,
Harnessed her doves, and flew to heaven.

The Author upon Himself

By an old red-pate, murdering hag pursued,
A crazy prelate, and a royal prude.
By dull divines, who look with envious eyes,
On every genius that attempts to rise;
And pausing o'er a pipe, with doubtful nod,
Give hints, that poets ne'er believe in God.
So, clowns on scholars as on wizards look,
And take a folio for a conjuring book.

Swift had the sin of wit, no venial crime;
10   Nay, 'twas affirmed, he sometimes dealt in rhyme:
Humour, and mirth, had place in all he writ:
He reconciled divinity and wit.
He moved, and bowed, and talked with too much grace;
Nor showed the parson in his gait or face;
Despised luxurious wines, and costly meat;
Yet, still was at the tables of the great.
Frequented lords; saw those that saw the Queen;
At Child's or Truby's never once had been;

Where town and country vicars flock in tribes,
20 Secured by numbers from the laymen's gibes;
And deal in vices of the graver sort,
Tobacco, censure, coffee, pride, and port.

But, after sage monitions from his friends,
His talents to employ for nobler ends;
To better judgements willing to submit,
He turns to politics his dangerous wit.

And now, the public interest to support,
By Harley Swift invited comes to court.
In favour grows with ministers of state;
30 Admitted private, when superiors wait:
And, Harley, not ashamed his choice to own,
Takes him to Windsor in his coach, alone.
At Windsor Swift no sooner can appear,
But, St John comes and whispers in his ear;
The waiters stand in ranks; the yeomen cry,
'Make room', as if a duke were passing by.

Now Finch alarms the Lords; he hears for certain,
This dangerous priest is got behind the curtain:
Finch, famed for tedious elocution, proves
40 That Swift oils many a spring which Harley moves.
Walpole and Aislabie, to clear the doubt,
Inform the Commons, that the secret's out:
'A certain Doctor is observed of late,
To haunt a certain minister of state:
From whence, with half an eye we may discover,
The peace is made, and Perkin must come over.'
York is from Lambeth sent, to show the Queen
A dangerous treatise writ against the spleen;
Which by the style, the matter, and the drift,
50 'Tis thought could be the work of none but Swift.
Poor York! The harmless tool of others' hate;
He sues for pardon, and repents too late.

Now Madam Königsmark her vengeance vows
On Swift's reproaches for her murdered spouse:
From her red locks her mouth with venom fills;
And thence into the royal ear instils.
The Queen incensed, his services forgot,
Leaves him a victim to the vengeful Scot;
Now, through the realm a proclamation spread,
60   To fix a price on his devoted head.
While innocent, he scorns ignoble flight;
His watchful friends preserve him by a sleight.

By Harley's favour once again he shines;
Is now caressed by candidate divines;
Who change opinions with the changing scene:
Lord! how they were mistaken in the Dean!
Now, Delaware again familiar grows;
And in Swift's ear thrusts half his powdered nose.
The Scottish nation, whom he durst offend,
70   Again apply that Swift would be their friend.

By faction tired, with grief he waits a while,
His great contending friends to reconcile.
Performs what friendship, justice, truth require:
What could he more, but decently retire?

In Sickness

WRITTEN SOON AFTER THE AUTHOR'S COMING TO LIVE
IN IRELAND, UPON THE QUEEN'S DEATH, OCTOBER 1714

'Tis true – then why should I repine,
To see my life so fast decline?
But, why obscurely here alone?
Where I am neither loved nor known.
My state of health none care to learn;
My life is here no soul's concern.

And, those with whom I now converse,
Without a tear will tend my hearse.
Removed from kind Arbuthnot's aid,
10   Who knows his art but not his trade;
Preferring his regard for me
Before his credit or his fee.
Some formal visits, looks, and words,
What mere humanity affords,
I meet perhaps from three or four,
From whom I once expected more;
Which those who tend the sick for pay
Can act as decently as they.
But, no obliging, tender friend
20   To help at my approaching end,
My life is now a burden grown
To others, e'er it be my own.

    Ye formal weepers for the sick,
In your last offices be quick:
And spare my absent friends the grief
To hear, yet give me no relief;
Expired today, entombed tomorrow,
When known, will save a double sorrow.

Horace, Lib. 2, Sat. 6

PART OF IT IMITATED

I often wished that I had clear,
For life, six hundred pounds a year;
A handsome house to lodge a friend;
A river at my garden's end;
A terrace walk; and half a rood
Of land, set out to plant a wood.

Well: now I have all this and more,
I ask not to increase my store;
And should be perfectly content,
10   Could I but live on this side Trent;
Nor cross the Channel twice a year,
To spend six months with statesmen here.

      I must by all means come to town,
'Tis for the service of the crown.
'Lewis; the Dean will be of use,
Send for him up, take no excuse.'
The toil, the danger of the seas;
Great ministers ne'er think of these;
Or let it cost five hundred pound,
20   No matter where the money's found;
It is but so much more in debt,
And that they ne'er considered yet.

      'Good Mr Dean, go change your gown,
Let my Lord know you're come to town.'
I hurry me in haste away,
Not thinking it is levee day;
And find his honour in a pound,
Hemmed by a triple circle round,
Chequered with ribbons blue and green;
30   How should I thrust myself between?
Some wag observes me thus perplexed,
And smiling, whispers to the next,
'I thought the Dean had been too proud,
To jostle here among a crowd.'
Another in a surly fit,
Tells me I have more zeal than wit,
'So eager to express your love,
You ne'er consider whom you shove,
But rudely press before a duke.'
40   I own, I'm pleased with this rebuke;
And take it kindly meant to show
What I desire the world should know.

I get a whisper, and withdraw,
When twenty fools I never saw
Come with petitions fairly penned,
Desiring I would stand their friend.

This, humbly offers me his case:
That, begs my interest for a place.
A hundred other men's affairs
50   Like bees are humming in my ears.
'Tomorrow my appeal comes on,
Without your help the cause is gone –'
'The Duke expects my Lord and you,
About some great affair, at two –'
'Put my Lord Bolingbroke in mind,
To get my warrant quickly signed:
Consider, 'tis my first request.'
Be satisfied, I'll do my best –
Then presently he falls to tease:
60   'You may for certain, if you please;
I doubt not, if his Lordship knew –
And Mr Dean, one word from you –'

'Tis (let me see) three years and more
(October next, it will be four)
Since Harley bid me first attend,
And chose me for an humble friend:
Would take me in his coach to chat,
And question me of this and that;
As 'What's o-clock?' and 'How's the wind?
70   Whose chariot's that we left behind?'
Or gravely try to read the lines
Writ underneath the country signs:
Or, 'Have you nothing new today
From Pope, from Parnell or from Gay?'
Such tattle often entertains
My Lord and me as far as Staines:
As once a week we travel down

To Windsor, and again to town;
Where all that passes, *inter nos*,
80   Might be proclaimed at Charing Cross.

      Yet some I know with envy swell,
Because they see me used so well:
'How think you of our friend the Dean?
I wonder what some people mean;
My Lord and he are grown so great,
Always together, *tête à tête*:
What, they admire him for his jokes –
See but the fortune of some folks!'

      There flies about a strange report
90   Of some express arrived at court;
I'm stopped by all the fools I meet,
And catechized in every street.
'You, Mr Dean, frequent the great:
Inform us, will the Emperor treat?
Or do the prints and papers lie?'
Faith, Sir, you know as much as I.
'Ah Doctor, how you love to jest?
'Tis now no secret' – I protest
'Tis one to me. 'Then, tell us, pray
100   When are the troops to have their pay?'
And though I solemnly declare
I know no more than my Lord Mayor,
They stand amazed, and think me grown
The closest mortal ever known.

      Thus in a sea of folly tossed,
My choicest hours of life are lost;
Yet always wishing to retreat:
Oh, could I see my country seat!
There leaning near a gentle brook,
110   Sleep, or peruse some ancient book;
And there, in sweet oblivion, drown
Those cares that haunt a court and town.

The Author's Manner of Living

On rainy days alone I dine,
Upon a chick, and pint of wine.
On rainy days, I dine alone,
And pick my chicken to the bone:
But this my servants much enrages,
No scraps remain to save board-wages.
In weather fine I nothing spend,
But often sponge upon a friend:
Yet where he's not so rich as I;
10 I pay my club, and so God b' y' –

Mary the Cook-Maid's Letter to Dr Sheridan

Well; if ever I saw such another man since my mother bound
    my head,
You a gentleman! marry come up, I wonder where you were
    bred?
I am sure such words does not become a man of your cloth,
I would not give such language to a dog, faith and troth.
Yes; you called my master a knave: fie Mr Sheridan, 'tis a
    shame
For a parson, who should know better things, to come out with
    such a name.
Knave in your teeth, Mr Sheridan, 'tis both a shame and a sin,
And the Dean my master is an honester man than you and all
    your kin:
He has more goodness in his little finger, than you have in
    your whole body,
10 My master is a parsonable man, and not a spindle-shanked
    hoddy-doddy.
And now whereby I find you would fain make an excuse,
Because my master one day, in anger, called you goose.

Which, and I am sure I have been his servant four years since
    October,
And he never called me worse than 'sweetheart', drunk or
    sober:
Not that I know his Reverence was ever concerned to my
    knowledge,
Though you and your come-rogues keep him out so late in your
    wicked college.

You say you will eat grass on his grave; a Christian eat grass!
Whereby you now confess yourself to be a goose or an ass:
But that's as much as to say, that my master should die before
    ye;
20 Well, well, that's as God pleases, and I don't believe that's a
    true story,
And so say I told you so, and you may go tell my master; what
    care I?
And I don't care who knows it, 'tis all one to Mary.
Everybody knows that I love to tell truth, and shame the Devil;
I am but a poor servant, but I think gentlefolks should be civil.
Besides, you found fault with our victuals one day that you was
    here,
I remember it was upon a Tuesday, of all days in the year.
And Saunders the man says, you are always jesting and
    mocking,
'Mary', said he, (one day, as I was mending my master's
    stocking)
'My master is so fond of that minister that keeps the school;
30 I thought my master a wise man, but that man makes him a
    fool.'
'Saunders', said I, 'I would rather than a quart of ale,
He would come into our kitchen, and I would pin a dishclout to
    his tail.'
And now I must go, and get Saunders to direct this letter,
For I write but a sad scrawl, but sister Marget she writes better.
Well, but I must run and make the bed before my master comes
    from prayers,

And see now, it strikes ten, and I hear him coming upstairs:
Whereof I could say more to your verses, if I could write
   written hand,
And so I remain in a civil way, your servant to command,
MARY

Stella's Birthday, 1718

WRITTEN IN THE YEAR 1718 [/9]

Stella this day is thirty-four,
(We shan't dispute a year or more:)
However Stella, be not troubled,
Although thy size and years are doubled,
Since first I saw thee at sixteen,
The brightest virgin on the green.
So little is thy form declined;
Made up so largely in thy mind.

    Oh, would it please the gods to split
10 Thy beauty, size, and years, and wit;
No age could furnish out a pair
Of nymphs so graceful, wise and fair:
With half the lustre of your eyes,
With half your wit, your years, and size.
And then, before it grew too late,
How should I beg of gentle fate,
(That either nymph might have her swain,)
To split my worship too in twain.

A Quiet Life and a Good Name

TO A FRIEND, WHO MARRIED A SHREW

Nell scolded in so loud a din,
That Will durst hardly venture in:
He marked the conjugal dispute;
Nell roared incessant, Dick sat mute:
But, when he saw his friend appear,
Cried bravely, 'Patience, good my dear.'
At sight of Will she bawled no more,
But hurried out, and clapped the door.

'Why Dick! the Devil's in thy Nell,'
10   Quoth Will; 'thy house is worse than Hell:
Why, what a peal the jade has rung!
Damn her, why don't you slit her tongue?
For nothing else will make it cease.'
'Dear Will, I suffer this for peace;
I never quarrel with my wife:
I bear it for a quiet life.
Scripture you know exhorts us to it;
Bids us to *seek peace and ensue it.*'

Will went again to visit Dick;
20   And, entering in the very nick,
He saw virago Nell belabour,
With Dick's own staff, his peaceful neighbour.
Poor Will, who needs must interpose,
Received a brace or two of blows.

But now, to make my story short,
Will drew out Dick to take a quart.
'Why Dick, thy wife has devilish whims;
Od's-buds, why don't you break her limbs?
If she were mine, and had such tricks,
30   I'd teach her how to handle sticks:

Zounds, I would ship her to Jamaica,
And truck the carrion for tobacco;
I'd send her far enough away –'
'Dear Will; but what would people say?
Lord! I should get so ill a name,
The neighbours round would cry out *Shame*.'

    Dick suffered for his peace and credit;
But who believed him when he said it?
Can he who makes himself a slave,
40 Consult his peace, or credit save?
Dick found it by his ill success,
His quiet small, his credit less.
She served him at the usual rate;
She stunned, and then she broke his pate.
And, what he thought the hardest case,
The parish jeered him to his face;
Those men who wore the breeches least,
Called him a cuckold, fool and beast.
At home, he was pursued with noise;
50 Abroad, was pestered by the boys.
Within, his wife would break his bones,
Without, they pelted him with stones:
The prentices procured a riding,
To act his patience and her chiding.

    False patience, and mistaken pride!
There are ten thousand Dicks beside;
Slaves to their quiet and good name,
Are used like Dick, and bear the blame.

Phyllis

OR, THE PROGRESS OF LOVE

Desponding Phyllis was endued
With every talent of a prude:
She trembled when a man drew near;
Salute her, and she turned her ear;
If o'er against her you were placed
She durst not look above your waist:
She'd rather take you to her bed
Than let you see her dress her head;
In church you heard her, through the crowd,
10   Repeat the absolution loud;
In church, secure behind her fan,
She durst behold that monster, man:
There practised how to place her head,
And bit her lips to make them red;
Or, on the mat devoutly kneeling,
Would lift her eyes up to the ceiling,
And heave her bosom, unaware,
For neighbouring beaux to see it bare.

At length a lucky lover came,
20   And found admittance to the dame.
Suppose all parties now agreed,
The writings drawn, the lawyer fee'd,
The vicar and the ring bespoke:
Guess, how could such a match be broke?
See then what mortals place their bliss in!
Next morn betimes the bride was missing.
The mother screamed, the father chid;
Where can this idle wretch be hid?
No news of Phyl! The bridegroom came,
30   And thought his bride had skulked for shame;
Because her father used to say
The girl had such a bashful way.

Now John, the butler, must be sent
To learn the road that Phyllis went;
The groom was wished to saddle Crop;
For John must neither light nor stop,
But find her whereso'er she fled,
And bring her back, alive or dead.

See here again the devil to do;
40 For truly John was missing too.
The horse and pillion both were gone!
Phyllis, it seems, was fled with John.

Old Madam, who went up to find
What papers Phyl had left behind,
A letter on the toilet sees,
'To my much honoured father' – These:
('Tis always done, romances tell us,
When daughters run away with fellows)
Filled with the choicest commonplaces,
50 By others used in the like cases;
'That, long ago, a fortune-teller
Exactly said what now befell her;
And in a glass had made her see
A serving-man of low degree.
It was her fate, must be forgiven,
For *Marriages were made in heaven*:
His pardon begged, but to be plain,
She'd do't if 'twere to do again.
Thank God, 'twas neither shame nor sin;
60 For John was come of honest kin.
Love never thinks of rich and poor,
She'd beg with John from door to door.
Forgive her, if it be a crime,
She'll never do't another time.
She ne'er before in all her life
Once disobeyed him, maid nor wife.
One argument she summed up all in,

The thing was done and past recalling;
And therefore hoped she should recover
70   His favour, when his passion's over!
She valued not what others thought her,
And was – his most obedient daughter.'

    Fair maidens all, attend the Muse
Who now the wandering pair pursues.
Away they rode in homely sort,
Their journey long, their money short;
The loving couple well bemired;
The horse and both the riders tired:
Their victuals bad, their lodging worse;
80   Phyl cried, and John began to curse;
Phyl wished that she had strained a limb,
When first she ventured out with him:
John wished that he had broke a leg
When first for her he quitted Peg.

    But what adventures more befell 'em,
The Muse hath now no time to tell 'em.
How Johnny wheedled, threatened, fawned,
Till Phyllis all her trinkets pawned:
How oft she broke her marriage vows,
90   In kindness, to maintain her spouse,
Till swains unwholesome spoiled the trade;
For now the surgeon must be paid,
To whom those perquisites are gone,
In Christian justice due to John.

    When food and raiment now grew scarce,
Fate put a period to the farce,
And with exact poetic justice;
For John is landlord, Phyllis hostess:
They keep, at Staines, the Old Blue Boar,
100   Are cat and dog, and rogue and whore.

The Progress of Beauty

When first Diana leaves her bed,
Vapours and steams her looks disgrace,
A frowzy dirty-coloured red
Sits on her cloudy wrinkled face;

But, by degrees, when mounted high,
Her artificial face appears
Down from her window in the sky,
Her spots are gone, her visage clears.

'Twixt earthly females and the moon,
10 All parallels exactly run;
If Celia should appear too soon,
Alas, the nymph would be undone!

To see her from her pillow rise
All reeking in a cloudy steam,
Cracked lips, foul teeth, and gummy eyes;
Poor Strephon, how would he blaspheme!

The soot or powder which was wont
To make her hair look black as jet,
Falls from her tresses on her front
20 A mingled mass of dirt and sweat.

Three colours, black, and red, and white,
So graceful in their proper place,
Remove them to a different light.
They form a frightful hideous face.

For instance, when the lily skips
Into the precincts of the rose,
And takes possession of the lips,
Leaving the purple to the nose.

So, Celia went entire to bed,
30   All her complexions safe and sound;
But, when she rose, white, black, and red,
Though still in sight, had changed their ground.

The black, which would not be confined,
A more inferior station seeks,
Leaving the fiery red behind,
And mingles in her muddy cheeks.

The paint by perspiration cracks,
And falls in rivulets of sweat;
On either side you see the tracks,
40   While at her chin the confluents met.

A skilful housewife thus her thumb
With spittle, while she spins, anoints;
And thus the brown meanders come
In trickling streams betwixt her joints.

But Celia can with ease reduce,
By help of pencil, paint and brush,
Each colour to its place and use,
And teach her cheeks again to blush.

She knows her early self no more;
50   But filled with admiration stands,
As other painters oft adore
The workmanship of their own hands.

Thus, after four important hours
Celia's the wonder of her sex:
Say, which among the heavenly powers
Could cause such marvellous effects?

Venus, indulgent to her kind,
Gave women all their hearts could wish,
When first she taught them where to find
60 White lead and Lusitanian dish.

Love with white lead cements his wings;
White lead was sent us to repair
Two brightest, brittlest, earthly things,
A lady's face, and china-ware.

She ventures now to lift the sash,
The window is her proper sphere:
Ah, lovely nymph! be not too rash,
Nor let the beaux approach too near.

Take pattern by your sister star,
70 Delude at once, and bless our sight;
When you are seen, be seen from far;
And chiefly choose to shine by night.

In the Pall Mall when passing by,
Keep up the glasses of your chair;
Then each transported fop will cry,
'God damn me Jack, she's wondrous fair.'

But, art no longer can prevail
When the materials all are gone;
The best mechanic hand must fail,
80 When nothing's left to work upon.

Matter, as wise logicians say,
Cannot without a form subsist;
And form, say I, as well as they,
Must fail, if matter brings no grist.

And this is fa'r Diana's case;
For all astrolc ;ers maintain,
Each night a bit drops off her face,
While mortals say she's in her wane.

While Partridge wisely shows the cause
90   Efficient of the moon's decay,
That Cancer with his poisonous claws,
Attacks her in the Milky Way:

But Gadbury, in art profound,
From her pale cheeks pretends to show,
That swain Endymion is not sound,
Or else, that Mercury's her foe.

But, let the cause be what it will,
In half a month she looks so thin,
That Flamsteed can, with all his skill
100   See but her forehead and her chin.

Yet, as she wastes, she grows discreet,
Till midnight never shows her head:
So rotting Celia strolls the street,
When sober folks are all abed.

For sure if this be Luna's fate,
Poor Celia, but of mortal race,
In vain expects a longer date
To the materials of her face.

When Mercury her tresses mows
110   To think of black lead combs is vain;
No painting can restore a nose,
Nor will her teeth return again.

Two balls of glass may serve for eyes,
White lead can plaster up a cleft,
But these alas, are poor supplies
If neither cheeks, nor lips be left.

Ye powers, who over love preside!
Since mortal beauties drop so soon,
If you would have us well supplied,
120 Send us new nymphs with each new moon.

To Stella, Who Collected and Transcribed His Poems

As when a lofty pile is raised,
We never hear the workmen praised,
Who bring the lime, or place the stones;
But all admire Inigo Jones:
So if this pile of scattered rhymes
Should be approved in after-times;
If it both pleases and endures,
The merit and the praise are yours.

Thou, Stella, wert no longer young,
10 When first for thee my harp I strung:
Without one word of Cupid's darts,
Of killing eyes, or bleeding hearts:
With friendship and esteem possessed,
I ne'er admitted love a guest.

In all the habitudes of life,
The friend, the mistress, and the wife,
Variety we still pursue,
In pleasure seek for something new:
Or else, comparing with the rest,
20   Take comfort, that our own is best:
(The best we value by the worst,
As tradesmen show their trash at first:)
But his pursuits are at an end,
Whom Stella chooses for a friend.

A poet, starving in a garret,
Conning old topics like a parrot,
Invokes his mistress and his muse,
And stays at home for want of shoes:
Should but his muse descending drop
30   A slice of bread, and mutton-chop,
Or kindly when his credit's out,
Surprise him with a pint of stout,
Or patch his broken stocking soles,
Or send him in a peck of coals;
Exalted in his mighty mind
He flies, and leaves the stars behind;
Counts all his labours amply paid,
Adores her for her timely aid.

Or should a porter make enquiries
40   For Chloe, Sylvia, Phyllis, Iris;
Be told the lodging, lane, and sign,
The bowers that hold those nymphs divine;
Fair Chloe would perhaps be found
With footmen tippling underground;
The charming Sylvia beating flax,
Her shoulders marked with bloody tracks;
Bright Phyllis mending ragged smocks,
And radiant Iris in the pox.

These are the goddesses enrolled
50 In Curll's collections, new and old,
Whose scoundrel fathers would not know 'em,
If they should meet 'em in a poem.

True poets can depress and raise;
Are lords of infamy and praise:
They are not scurrilous in satire,
Nor will in panegyric flatter.
Unjustly poets we asperse;
Truth shines the brighter, clad in verse:
And all the fictions they pursue,
60 Do but insinuate what is true.

Now, should my praises owe their truth
To beauty, dress, paint, or youth,
What Stoics call *without our power*,
They could not be insured an hour:
'Twere grafting on an annual stock,
That must our expectation mock,
And making one luxuriant shoot,
Die the next year for want of root:
Before I could my verses bring,
70 Perhaps you're quite another thing.

So Maevius, when he drained his skull
To celebrate some suburb trull;
His similes in order set,
And every crambo he could get;
Had gone through all the commonplaces,
Worn out by wits who rhyme on faces;
Before he could his poem close,
The lovely nymph had lost her nose.

Your virtues safely I commend;
80 They on no accidents depend:
Let Malice look with all her eyes,
She dare not say the poet lies.

Stella, when you these lines transcribe,
Lest you should take them for a bribe;
Resolved to mortify your pride,
I'll here expose your weaker side.

Your spirits kindle to a flame,
Moved with the lightest touch of blame;
And when a friend in kindness tries
90 To show you where your error lies,
Conviction does but more incense;
Perverseness is your whole defence:
Truth, judgement, wit, give place to spite,
Regardless both of wrong and right.
Your virtues, all suspended, wait
Till time hath opened reason's gate:
And what is worse, your passion bends
Its force against your nearest friends;
Which manners, decency, and pride,
100 Have taught you from the world to hide.
In vain; for see, your friend hath brought
To public light your *only* fault;
And yet a fault we often find
Mixed in a noble generous mind;
And may compare to Etna's fire,
Which, though with trembling, all admire;
The heat that makes the summit glow,
Enriching all the vales below.
Those who in warmer climes complain,
110 From Phoebus' rays they suffer pain,
Must own, that pain is largely paid
By generous wines beneath a shade.

Yet when I find your passions rise,
And anger sparkling in your eyes,
I grieve those spirits should be spent,
For nobler ends by nature meant.
One passion, with a different turn,
Makes wit inflame, or anger burn;
So the sun's heat, by different powers,
120   Ripens the grape, the liquor sours.
Thus Ajax, when with rage possessed,
By Pallas breathed into his breast,
His valour would no more employ,
Which might alone have conquered Troy;
But, blinded by resentment, seeks
For vengeance on his friends the Greeks.

You think this turbulence of blood
From stágnating preserves the flood;
Which thus fermenting, by degrees
130   Exalts the spirits, sinks the lees.

Stella, for once you reason wrong;
For should this ferment last too long,
By time subsiding, you may find
Nothing but acid left behind.
From passion you may then be freed,
When peevishness and spleen succeed.

Say Stella, when you copy next,
Will you keep strictly to the text?
Dare you let these reproaches stand,
140   And to your failing set your hand?
Or if these lines your anger fire,
Shall they in baser flames expire?
Whene'er they burn, if burn they must,
They'll prove my accusation just.

An Elegy on the Much Lamented Death of Mr Demar, the Famous Rich Usurer, who Died the Sixth of July, 1720

Know all men by these presents, Death the tamer
By mortgage hath secured the corpse of Demar;
Nor can four hundred thousand sterling pound
Redeem him from his prison underground.
His heirs might well, of all his wealth possessed,
Bestow to bury him one iron chest.
Pluto, the god of wealth, will joy to know
His faithful steward, in the shades below.
He walked the streets, and wore a threadbare cloak;
10   He dined and supped at charge of other folk;
And by his looks, had he held out his palms,
He might be thought an object fit for alms.
So to the poor if he refused his pelf,
He used 'em full as kindly as himself.

Where'er he went he never saw his betters;
Lords, knights and squires were all his humble debtors;
And, under hand and seal, the Irish nation
Were forced to own to him their obligation.

He that could once have half a kingdom bought,
20   In half a minute is not worth a groat;
His coffers from the coffin could not save,
Nor all his *interest* keep him from the grave.
A golden monument would not be right,
Because we wish the earth upon him light.

Oh London Tavern! Thou hast lost a friend,
Though in thy walls he ne'er did farthing spend:
He touched the pence when others touched the pot;
The hand that signed the mortgage paid the shot.

Old as he was, no vulgar known disease
30 On him could ever boast a power to seize;
But as his gold he weighed, grim Death, in spite,
Cast in his dart, which made three moidores light;
And as he saw his darling money fail,
Blew his last breath to sink the lighter scale.

He, who so long was current, 'twould be strange
If he should now be cried down since his change.

The sexton shall green sods on thee bestow:
Alas the sexton is thy banker now!
A dismal banker must that banker be,
40 Who gives no bills, but of mortality.

THE EPITAPH

Beneath this verdant hillock lies
Demar the wealthy and the wise.
His heirs that he might safely rest,
Have put his carcass in a chest:
The very chest, in which, they say,
His other self, his money, lay.
And if his heirs continue kind,
To that dear self he left behind,
I dare believe, that four in five
50 Will think his better self alive.

Verses from Cadenus to Vanessa in Letters

[THE VERSES HE PROMISED]

Nymph, would you learn the only art
To keep a worthy lover's heart?
First, to adorn your person well,
In utmost cleanliness excel;
And though you must the fashions take,
Observe them but for fashion's sake.

The strongest reason will submit
To virtue, honour, sense, and wit.
To such a nymph the wise and good
10 Cannot be faithless if they would:
For vices all have different ends,
But virtue still to virtue tends.
And when your lover is not true,
'Tis virtue fails in him or you:
And either he deserves disdain,
Or you without a cause complain.
But here Vanessa cannot err,
Nor are these rules applied to her:
For who could such a nymph forsake
20 Except a blockhead or a rake,
Or how could she her heart bestow
Except where wit and virtue grow.

[AN EPIGRAM]

Dorinda dreams of dress abed,
    'Tis all her thought and art;
Her lace hath got within her head,
    Her stays stick to her heart.

[CAD IS WEARY OF TOWN]

A fig for partridges and quails –
Ye dainties, I know nothing of ye,
But on the highest mount in Wales
30 Would choose in peace to drink my coffee.

An Excellent New Song on a Seditious Pamphlet

TO THE TUNE OF PACKINGTON'S POUND

The Author having wrote a treatise, advising the people of Ireland
to wear their own manufactures, a prosecution was set on foot
against Waters the printer thereof, which was carried on with so
much violence, that one Whitshed, then Chief Justice, thought
proper, in a manner the most extraordinary, to keep the Grand-Jury
above twelve hours, and to send them eleven times out of court,
until he had wearied them into a special verdict.

I

Brocado's, and damasks, and tabbies, and gauzes,
   Are by Robert Ballentine lately brought over;
With forty things more: now hear what the law says,
   Whoe'er will not wear them, is not the King's lover.
      Though a printer and Dean
      Seditiously mean
Our true Irish hearts from old England to wean;
We'll buy English silks for our wives and our daughters,
In spite of his Deanship and journeyman Waters.

II

10 In England the dead in woollen are clad,
   The Dean and his printer then let us cry fie on;
To be clothed like a carcass would make a Teague mad,
   Since a living dog better is than a dead lion,
      Our wives they grow sullen
      At wearing of woollen,
   And all we poor shopkeepers must our horns pull in.
Then we'll buy English silks, &c.

III

Whoever our trading with England would hinder,
    To *inflame* both the nations do plainly conspire;
20 Because Irish linen will soon turn to tinder;
    And wool it is greasy, and quickly takes fire.
        Therefore I assure ye,
        Our noble Grand Jury,
    When they saw the Dean's book they were in a great fury:
They would buy English silks for their wives, &c.

IV

This wicked rogue Waters, who always is sinning,
    And before *Corum Nobus* so oft has been called,
Henceforward shall print neither pamphlets nor linen,
    And, if swearing can do't, shall be swingingly mauled:
30   And as for the Dean,
        You know whom I mean,
    If the printer will peach him, he'll scarce come off clean.
Then we'll buy English silks for our wives and our daughters,
In spite of his Deanship and journeyman Waters.

The Run upon the Bankers

The bold encroachers on the deep
    Gain by degrees huge tracts of land,
Till Neptune with one general sweep
    Turns all again to barren strand.

The multitude's capricious pranks
    Are said to represent the seas;
Breaking the bankers and the banks,
    Resume their own whene'er they please.

Money, the life-blood of the nation,
10   Corrupts and stágnates in the veins,
Unless a proper circulation
   Its motion and its heat maintains.

Because 'tis lordly not to pay,
   Quakers and aldermen, in state,
Like peers have levees every day
   Of duns attending at their gate.

We want our money on the nail;
   The banker's ruined if he pays;
They seem to act an ancient tale,
20   The birds are met to strip the jays.

Riches, the wisest monarch sings,
   Make pinions for themselves to fly:
They fly like bats, on parchment wings,
   And geese their silver plumes supply.

No money left for squandering heirs!
   Bills turn the lenders into debtors:
The wish of Nero now is theirs,
   That they had never known their letters.

Conceive the works of midnight hags,
30   Tormenting fools behind their backs;
Thus bankers o'er their bills and bags
   Sit squeezing images of wax.

Conceive the whole enchantment broke,
   The witches left in open air,
With power no more than other folk,
   Exposed with all their magic ware.

So powerful are a banker's bills
    Where creditors demand their due,
They break up counter, doors, and tills,
40   And leave the empty chests in view.

Thus when an earthquake lets in light
    Upon the god of gold and hell,
Unable to endure the sight,
    He hides within his darkest cell.

As when a conjuror takes a lease
    From Satan for a term of years,
The tenant's in a dismal case
    Whene'er the bloody bond appears.

A baited banker thus desponds,
50   From his own hand foresees his fall;
They have his soul who have his bonds;
    'Tis like the writing on the wall.

How will that caitiff wretch be scared
    When first he finds himself awake
At the last trumpet, unprepared,
    And all his grand account to make?

For in that universal call
    Few bankers will to heaven be mounters:
They'll cry, 'ye shops upon us fall,
60   Conceal and cover us, ye counters.'

When other hands the scales shall hold,
    And they in men and angels' sight
Produced with all their bills and gold,
    Weighed in the balance, and found light.

The Description of an Irish Feast

TRANSLATED ALMOST LITERALLY OUT OF THE ORIGINAL IRISH

O'Rourk's noble fare
    Will ne'er be forgot,
By those who were there,
    Or those who were not.
His revels to keep,
    We sup and we dine,
On seven score sheep,
    Fat bullocks and swine.
Usquebagh to our feast
10   In pails was brought up,
An hundred at least,
    And a madder our cup.
O there is the sport,
    We rise with the light,
In disorderly sort,
    From snoring all night.
O how was I tricked,
    My pipe it was broke,
My pocket was picked,
20   I lost my new cloak.
I'm rifled, quoth Nell,
    Of mantle and kercher,
Why then fare them well,
    The de'il take the searcher.
Come, harper, strike up,
    But first by your favour,
Boy, give us a cup;
    Ay, this has some savour:
O'Rourk's jolly boys
30   Ne'er dreamt of the matter,
Till roused by the noise,
    And musical clatter,
They bounce from their nest,

No longer will tarry,
They rise ready dressed,
     Without one *Ave Mary*.
They dance in a round,
     Cutting capers and ramping,
A mercy the ground
40   Did not burst with their stamping,
The floor is all wet
     With leaps and with jumps,
While the water and sweat,
     Splish, splash in their pumps.
Bless you late and early,
     Laughlin O' Enagin,
By my hand, you dance rarely,
     Margery Grinagin.
Bring straw for our bed,
50   Shake it down to the feet,
Then over us spread,
     The winnowing sheet.
To show, I don't flinch,
     Fill the bowl up again,
Then give us a pinch
     Of your sneezing, a *Yean*.
Good Lord, what a sight,
     After all their good cheer,
For people to fight
60   In the midst of their beer:
They rise from their feast,
     And hot are their brains,
A cubit at least
     The length of their *skenes*.
What stabs and what cuts,
     What clattering of sticks,
What strokes on the guts,
     What bastings and kicks!
With cudgels of oak,
70   Well hardened in flame,

An hundred heads broke,
    An hundred struck lame.
You churl, I'll maintain
    My father built Lusk,
The castle of Slane,
    And Carrickdrumrusk:
The Earl of Kildare,
    And Moynalta, his brother,
As great as they are,
80   I was nursed by their mother.
Ask that of old Madam,
    She'll tell you who's who,
As far up as Adam,
    She knows it is true,
Come down with that beam,
    If cudgels are scarce,
A blow on the wame,
    Or a kick on the arse.

Stella's Birthday, 1720

WRITTEN IN THE YEAR 1720–21

All travellers at first incline
Where'er they see the fairest sign;
And if they find the chamber neat,
And like the liquor, and the meat,
Will call again, and recommend
The Angel Inn to every friend:
What though the painting grows decayed,
The house will never lose its trade:
Nay, though the treacherous tapster Thomas
10 Hangs a new angel two doors from us,
As fine as dauber's hands can make it,
In hopes that strangers may mistake it;
We think it both a shame and sin
To quit the true old Angel Inn.

Now, this is Stella's case in fact,
An angel's face, a little cracked;
(Could poets, or could painters fix
How angels look at thirty-six:)
This drew us in at first, to find
20   In such a form an angel's mind:
And every virtue now supplies
The fainting rays of Stella's eyes.
See, at her levee, crowding swains,
Whom Stella freely entertains
With breeding, humour, wit, and sense;
And puts them to so small expense:
Their mind so plentifully fills,
And makes such reasonable bills;
So little gets for what she gives,
30   We really wonder how she lives!
And had her stock been less, no doubt,
She must have long ago run out.

Then who can think we'll quit the place
When Doll hangs out a newer face;
Nailed to her window full in sight
All Christian people to invite:
Or stop and light at Chloe's head
With scraps and leavings to be fed.

Then Chloe, still go on to prate
Of thirty-six and thirty-eight;
Pursue your trade of scandal-picking,
40   Your hints that Stella is no chicken;
Your innuendos, when you tell us
That Stella loves to talk with fellows:
But let me warn you to believe
A truth, for which your soul should grieve:
That, should you live to see the day
When Stella's locks must all be grey;
When age must print a furrowed trace

On every feature of her face;
Though you, and all your senseless tribe,
50 Could art, or time, or nature bribe,
To make you look like beauty's queen,
And hold forever at fifteen;
No bloom of youth can ever blind
The cracks and wrinkles of your mind:
All men of sense will pass your door,
And crowd to Stella's at fourscore.

A Satirical Elegy on the Death of a Late Famous General

His Grace! Impossible! What, dead!
Of old age too, and in his bed!
And could that Mighty Warrior fall?
And so inglorious, after all!
Well, since he's gone, no matter how,
The last loud trump must wake him now:
And, trust me, as the noise grows stronger,
He'd wish to sleep a little longer.
And could he be indeed so old
10 As by the newspapers we're told?
Threescore, I think, is pretty high;
'Twas time in conscience he should die.
This world he cumbered long enough;
He burnt his candle to the snuff;
And that's the reason, some folks think,
He left behind *so great a stink*.
Behold his funeral appears,
Nor widow's sighs, nor orphan's tears,
Wont at such times each heart to pierce,
20 Attend the progress of his hearse.
But what of that, his friends may say,
He had those honours in his day.

True to his profit and his pride,
He made them weep before he died.

Come hither, all ye empty things,
Ye bubbles raised by breath of kings;
Who float upon the tide of state,
Come hither, and behold your fate.
Let pride be taught by this rebuke,
30   How very mean a thing's a Duke;
From all his ill-got honours flung,
Turned to that dirt from whence he sprung.

The Progress of Marriage

Aetatis suae fifty-two,
A rich divine began to woo
A handsome young imperious girl
Nearly related to an Earl.
Her parents and her friends consent,
The couple to the temple went:
They first invite the Cyprian queen,
'Twas answered, she would not be seen:
The Graces next, and all the Muses
10   Were bid in form, but sent excuses:
Juno attended at the porch
With farthing candle for a torch,
While Mistress Iris held her train,
The faded bow distilling rain.
Then Hebe came and took her place
But showed no more than half her face.

Whate'er these dire forebodings meant,
In mirth the wedding-day was spent;
The wedding-day, you take me right,
20 I promise nothing for the night:
The bridegroom dressed, to make a figure,
Assumes an artificial vigour;
A flourished nightcap on, to grace
His ruddy, wrinkled, smirking face,
Like the faint red upon a pippin
Half withered by a winter's keeping.

And, thus set out this happy pair,
The swain is rich, the nymph is fair;
But, what I gladly would forget,
30 The swain is old, the nymph coquette.
Both from the goal together start;
Scarce run a step before they part;
No common ligament that binds
The various textures of their minds,
Their thoughts, and actions, hopes, and fears,
Less corresponding than their years.
Her spouse desires his coffee soon,
She rises to her tea at noon.
While he goes out to cheapen books,
40 She at the glass consults her looks
While Betty's buzzing at her ear,
Lord, what a dress these parsons wear!
So odd a choice, how could she make?
Wished him a colonel for her sake.
Then on her fingers' ends she counts
Exact to what his age amounts,
The Dean, she heard her uncle say,
Is sixty, if he be a day;
His ruddy cheeks are no disguise;
50 You see the crow's-feet round his eyes.

At one she rambles to the shops,
To cheapen tea, and talk with fops.
Or calls a council of her maids,
And tradesmen, to compare brocades.
Her weighty morning business o'er,
Sits down to dinner just at four;
Minds nothing that is done or said,
Her evening work so fills her head;
The Dean, who used to dine at one,
60   Is mawkish, and his stomach gone;
In threadbare gown, would scarce a louse hold,
Looks like the chaplain of the household,
Beholds her from the chaplain's place
In French brocades and Flanders lace;
He wonders what employs her brain;
But never asks, or asks in vain;
His mind is full of other cares,
And, in the sneaking parson's airs,
Computes, that half a parish dues
70   Will hardly find his wife in shoes.

Canst thou imagine, dull divine,
'Twill gain her love to make her fine?
Hath she no other wants beside?
You raise desire as well as pride,
Enticing coxcombs to adore,
And teach her to despise thee more.

If in her coach she'll condescend
To place him at the hinder end
Her hoop is hoist above his nose,
80   His odious gown would soil her clothes,
And drops him at the church, to pray,
While she drives on to see the play.
He, like an orderly divine,
Comes home a quarter after nine,
And meets her hasting to the ball:

Her chairmen push him from the wall.
He enters in, and walks upstairs,
And calls the family to prayers;
Then goes alone to take his rest
90 In bed, where he can spare her best.
At five the footmen make a din,
Her ladyship is just come in,
The masquerade began at two,
She stole away with much ado,
And shall be chid this afternoon
For leaving company so soon;
She'll say, and she may truly say't,
She can't abide to stay out late.

But now, though scarce a twelve month married,
100 His lady has twelve times miscarried,
The cause, alas, is quickly guessed,
The town has whispered round the jest:
Think on some remedy in time,
You find his Reverence past his prime,
Already dwindled to a lath;
No other way but try the Bath.

For Venus, rising from the ocean,
Infused a strong prolific potion,
That mixed with Achelous' spring,
110 The 'hornèd flood', as poets sing:
Who with an English beauty smitten
Ran underground from Greece to Britain,
The genial virtue with him brought,
And gave the Nymph a plenteous draught;
Then fled, and left his horn behind
For husbands past their youth to find;
The Nymph, who still with passion burned,
Was to a boiling fountain turned,
Where childless wives crowd every morn
120 To drink in Achelous' horn.

And here the father often gains
That title by another's pains.

    Hither, though much against his grain,
The Dean has carried Lady Jane.
He for a while would not consent,
But vowed his money all was spent:
His money spent! a clownish reason!
And must my Lady slip her season?
The doctor, with a double fee,
130 Was bribed to make the Dean agree.

    Here, all diversions of the place
Are proper in my Lady's case,
With which she patiently complies,
Merely because her friends advise;
His money and her time employs
In music, raffling-rooms, and toys,
Or in the Cross Bath, seeks an heir
Since others oft have found one there;
Where, if the Dean by chance appears,
140 It shames his cassock and his years.
He keeps his distance in the gallery
Till banished by some coxcomb's raillery;
For, it would his character expose
To bathe among the belles and beaux.

    So have I seen, within a pen,
Young ducklings fostered by a hen;
But when let out, they run and muddle
As instinct leads them, in a puddle;
The sober hen, not born to swim,
150 With mournful note clucks round the brim.

The Dean with all his best endeavour
Gets not an heir, but gets a fever;
A victim to the last essays
Of vigour in declining days.
He dies, and leaves his mourning mate
(What could he less?) his whole estate.

The widow goes through all the forms;
New lovers now will come in swarms.
Oh, may I see her soon dispensing
160 Her favours to some broken ensign!
Him let her marry for his face,
And only coat of tarnished lace;
To turn her naked out of doors,
And spend her jointure on his whores:
But for a parting present leave her
A rooted pox to last forever.

Stella at Woodpark

A HOUSE OF CHARLES FORD ESQ. EIGHT MILES FROM DUBLIN

Cuicunque nocere volebat
Vestimenta dabat pretiosa.

Don Carlos in a merry spite
Did Stella to his house invite:
He entertained her half a year
With generous wines and costly cheer.
Don Carlos made her chief director,
That she might o'er the servants hector.
In half a week the dame grew nice,
Got all things at the highest price.
Now at the table-head she sits,
10 Presented with the nicest bits:
She looked on partridges with scorn,

Except they tasted of the corn:
A haunch of venison made her sweat,
Unless it had the right *fumette*.
Don Carlos earnestly would beg,
'Dear madam, try this pigeon's leg';
Was happy when he could prevail
To make her only touch a quail.
Through candle-light she viewed the wine,
20   To see that every glass was fine.
At last grown prouder than the Devil,
With feeding high, and treatment civil,
Don Carlos now began to find
His malice work as he designed:
The winter sky began to frown,
Poor Stella must pack off to town.
From purling streams and fountains bubbling,
To Liffey's stinking tide in Dublin:
From wholesome exercise and air
30   To sossing in an easy chair;
From stomach sharp and hearty feeding,
To piddle like a lady breeding:
From ruling there the household singly,
To be directed here by Dingley:
From every day a lordly banquet,
To half a joint, and God be thank it:
From every meal Pontac in plenty,
To half a pint one day in twenty.
From Ford attending at her call,
40   To visits of Archdeacon Wall.
From Ford, who thinks of nothing mean,
To the poor doings of the Dean.
From growing richer with good cheer,
To running out by starving here.

But now arrives the dismal day:
She must return to Ormond Quay:
The coachman stopped, she looked, and swore
The rascal had mistook the door:
At coming in you saw her stoop;
50   The entry brushed against her hoop:
Each moment rising in her airs,
She cursed the narrow winding stairs:
Began a thousand faults to spy;
The ceiling hardly six foot high;
The smutty wainscot full of cracks;
And half the chairs with broken backs:
Her quarter's out at Lady Day,
She vows she will no longer stay,
In lodgings, like a poor *grisette*,
60   While there are houses to be let.

Howe'er, to keep her spirits up,
She sent for company to sup;
When all the while, you might remark,
She strove in vain to ape Woodpark.
Two bottles called for, (half her store;
The cupboard could contain but four;)
A supper worthy of her self,
Five nothings in five plates of Delf.

Thus, for a week the farce went on;
70   When all her country-savings gone,
She fell into her former scene.
Small beer, a herring, and the Dean.

Thus far in jest. Though now I fear
You think my jesting too severe:
But poets when a hint is new
Regard not whether false or true:
Yet raillery gives no offence,
Where truth has not the least pretence;

Nor can be more securely placed
80   Than on a nymph of Stella's taste.
I must confess, your wine and victual
I was too hard upon *a little*;
Your table neat, your linen fine;
And, though in miniature, you shine.
Yet, when you sigh to leave Woodpark,
The scene, the welcome, and the spark,
To languish in this odious town,
And pull your haughty stomach down;
We think you quite mistake the case;
90   The virtue lies not in the place:
For though my raillery were true,
A cottage is Woodpark with you.

Pethox the Great

From Venus born, thy beauty shows;
But who thy father, no man knows;
Nor can the skilful herald trace
The founder of thy ancient race.
Whether thy temper, full of fire,
Discovers Vulcan for thy sire;
The god who made Scamander boil,
And round his margin singed the soil;
(From whence, philosophers agree,
10   An equal power descends to thee.)
Whether from dreadful Mars you claim
The high descent from whence you came,
And, as a proof, show numerous scars
By fierce encounters made in wars;
(Those honourable wounds you bore
From head to foot, and *all before*;)
And still the bloody field frequent,
Familiar in each leader's tent.
Or whether, as the learn'd contend,

20   You from your neighbouring Gaul descend;
Or from Parthenope the proud,
Where numberless thy votaries crowd:
Whether thy great forefathers came
From realms that bear Vesputio's name:
For so conjectors would obtrude,
And from thy painted skin conclude.
Whether, as Epicurus shows,
The world from jostling seeds arose;
Which mingling with prolific strife
30   In chaos, kindled into life;
So your production was the same,
And from the contending atoms came.

    Thy fair indulgent mother crowned
Thy head with sparkling rubies round;
Beneath thy decent steps, the road
Is all with precious jewels strewed.
The bird of Pallas knows his post,
Thee to attend where'er thou goest.

    Byzantians boast, that on the clod
40   Where once their sultan's horse hath trod,
Grows neither grass, nor shrub, nor tree;
The same thy subjects boast of thee.

    The greatest lord, when you appear,
Will deign your livery to wear,
In all thy various colours seen,
Of red, and yellow, blue, and green.

    With half a word, when you require,
The man of business must retire.

The haughty minister of state
50 With trembling must thy leisure wait;
    And while his fate is in thy hands
    The business of the nation stands.

    Thou darest the greatest prince attack,
    Canst hourly set him on the rack,
    And, as an instance of thy power,
    Enclose him in a wooden tower,
    With pungent pains on every side:
    So Regulus in torments died.

    From thee our youth all virtues learn,
60 Dangers with prudence to discern;
    And well thy scholars are endued
    With temperance and with fortitude;
    With patience, which all ills supports;
    And secrecy, the art of courts.

    The glittering beau could hardly tell,
    Without your aid, to read or spell;
    But, having long conversed with you,
    Knows how to scrawl a billet-doux.

    With what delight, methinks, I trace
70 Thy blood in every noble race!
    In whom thy features, shape, and mien
    Are to the life distinctly seen.

    The Britons, once a savage kind,
    By you were brightened and refined:
    Descendants of the barbarous Huns,
    With limbs robust, and voice that stuns;
    But you have moulded them afresh,
    Removed the tough superfluous flesh,
    Taught them to modulate their tongues,
80 And speak without the help of lungs.

Proteus on you bestowed the boon
To change your visage like the moon;
You sometimes half a face produce,
Keep t'other half for private use.

How famed thy conduct in the fight,
With Hermes, son of Pleias bright:
Outnumbered, half encompassed round,
You strove for every inch of ground;
Then, by a soldierly retreat,
90 Retired to your imperial seat.
The victor, when your steps he traced,
Found all the realms before him waste;
You, o'er the high triumphal arch
Pontific, made your glorious march;
The wondrous arch behind you fell,
And left a chasm profound as hell:
You, in your Capitol secured,
A siege as long as Troy endured.

Stella's Birthday, 1725

As, when a beauteous nymph decays,
We say, she's past her dancing days;
So, poets lose their feet by time,
And can no longer dance in rhyme.
Your annual bard had rather chose
To celebrate your birth in prose;
Yet, merry folks, who want by chance
A pair to make a country dance,
Call the old housekeeper, and get her
10 To fill a place, for want of better;
While Sheridan is off the hooks,
And friend Delany at his books,
That Stella may avoid disgrace,
Once more the Dean supplies their place.

Beauty and wit, too sad a truth,
Have always been confined to youth;
The god of wit, and beauty's queen,
He twenty-one, and she fifteen:
No poet ever sweetly sung,
20   Unless he were, like Phoebus, young;
Nor ever nymph inspired to rhyme,
Unless, like Venus, in her prime.
At fifty-six, if this be true,
Am I a poet fit for you?
Or at the age of forty-three,
Are you a subject fit for me?
Adieu bright wit, and radiant eyes;
You must be grave, and I be wise.
Our fate in vain we would oppose,
30   But I'll be still your friend in prose:
Esteem and friendship to express,
Will not require poetic dress;
And if the muse deny her aid
To have them *sung*, they may be *said*.

But, Stella say, what evil tongue
Reports you are no longer young?
That Time sits with his scythe to mow
Where erst sat Cupid with his bow;
That half your locks are turned to grey;
40   I'll ne'er believe a word they say.
'Tis true, but let it not be known,
My eyes are somewhat dimmish grown;
For nature, always in the right,
To your decays adapts my sight,
And wrinkles undistinguished pass,
For I'm ashamed to use a glass;
And till I see them with these eyes,
Whoever says you have them, lies.

No length of time can make you quit
50 Honour and virtue, sense and wit;
Thus you may still be young to me,
While I can better *hear* than *see*;
Oh, ne'er may fortune show her spite,
To make me *deaf*, and mend my *sight*.

Verses Left in a Window of Dublin Castle

My very good Lord, 'tis a very hard task,
For a man to wait here, who has nothing to ask.

To Quilca

A COUNTRY HOUSE IN NO VERY GOOD REPAIR, WHERE THE
SUPPOSED AUTHOR, AND SOME OF HIS FRIENDS, SPENT A
SUMMER IN THE YEAR 1725

Let me my properties explain,
A rotten cabin, dropping rain;
Chimneys with scorn rejecting smoke;
Stools, tables, chairs, and bedsteads broke:
Here elements have lost their uses,
Air ripens not, nor earth produces:
In vain we make poor Sheelah toil,
Fire will not roast, nor water boil.
Through all the valleys, hills, and plains,
10 The goddess Want in triumph reigns;
And her chief officers of state,
Sloth, Dirt, and Theft around her wait.

Stella's Birthday, 1727

This day, whate'er the fates decree,
Shall still be kept with joy by me:
This day then, let us not be told,
That you are sick, and I grown old,
Nor think on our approaching ills,
And talk of spectacles and pills.
Tomorrow will be time enough
To hear such mortifying stuff.
Yet, since from reason may be brought
10   A better and more pleasing thought,
Which can, in spite of all decays,
Support a few remaining days:
From not the gravest of divines,
Accept for once some serious lines.

Although we now can form no more
Long schemes of life, as heretofore;
Yet you, while time is running fast,
Can look with joy on what is past.

Were future happiness and pain
20   A mere contrivance of the brain,
As atheists argue, to entice,
And fit their proselytes for vice;
(The only comfort they propose,
To have companions in their woes.)
Grant this the case, yet sure 'tis hard,
That virtue, styled its own reward,
And by all sages understood
To be the chief of human good,
Should acting, die, nor leave behind
30   Some lasting pleasure in the mind;
Which by remembrance will assuage
Grief, sickness, poverty, and age;

And strongly shoot a radiant dart,
To shine through life's declining part.

   Say, Stella, feel you no content,
Reflecting on a life well spent?
Your skilful hand employed to save
Despairing wretches from the grave;
And then supporting with your store,
40 Those whom you dragged from death before:
(So Providence on mortals waits,
Preserving what it first creates)
Your generous boldness to defend
An innocent and absent friend:
That courage which can make you just,
To merit humbled in the dust:
The detestation you express
For vice in all its glittering dress:
That patience under torturing pain,
50 Where stubborn Stoics would complain.

   Shall these like empty shadows pass,
Or forms reflected from a glass?
Or mere chimaeras in the mind,
That fly and leave no marks behind?
Does not the body thrive and grow
By food of twenty years ago?
And, had it not been still supplied,
It must a thousand times have died.
Then, who with reason can maintain,
60 That no effects of food remain?
And, is not virtue in mankind
The nutriment that feeds the mind?
Upheld by each good action past,
And still continued by the last:
Then, who with reason can pretend,
That all effects of virtue end?

   Believe me Stella, when you show
   That true contempt for things below,
   Nor prize your life for other ends
70 Than merely to oblige your friends;
   Your former actions claim their part,
   And join to fortify your heart.
   For virtue in her daily race,
   Like Janus, bears a double face;
   Looks back with joy where she has gone,
   And therefore goes with courage on.
   She at your sickly couch will wait,
   And guide you to a better state.

   O then, whatever heaven intends,
80 Take pity on your pitying friends;
   Nor let your ills affect your mind,
   To fancy they can be unkind.
   Me, surely me, you ought to spare,
   Who gladly would your sufferings share;
   Or give my scrap of life to you,
   And think it far beneath your due;
   You, to whose care so oft I owe,
   That I'm alive to tell you so.

Clever Tom Clinch Going to be Hanged

As clever Tom Clinch, while the rabble was bawling,
Rode stately through Holborn, to die in his calling;
He stopped at the George for a bottle of sack,
And promised to pay for it when he came back.
His waistcoat and stockings, and breeches were white,
His cap had a new cherry ribbon to tie't.
The maids to the doors and the balconies ran,
And said, lackaday! he's a proper young man.
But, as from the windows the ladies he spied,
10 Like a beau in the box, he bowed low on each side;

And when his last speech the loud hawkers did cry,
He swore from his cart, it was all a damned lie.
The hangman for pardon fell down on his knee;
Tom gave him a kick in the guts for his fee.
Then said, 'I must speak to the people a little,
But I'll see you all damned before I will whittle.
My honest friend Wild, may he long hold his place,
He lengthened my life with a whole year of grace.
Take courage, dear comrades, and be not afraid,
20   Nor slip this occasion to follow your trade.
My conscience is clear, and my spirits are calm,
And thus I go off without prayer-book or psalm.'
Then follow the practice of clever Tom Clinch,
Who hung like a hero, and never would flinch.

Advice to the Grub Street Verse-Writers

Ye poets ragged and forlorn,
   Down from your garrets haste,
Ye rhymers, dead as soon as born,
   Nor yet consigned to paste;

I know a trick to make you thrive;
   O, 'tis a quaint device:
Your still-born poems shall revive,
   And scorn to wrap up spice.

Get all your verses printed fair,
10   Then let them well be dried;
And Curll must have a special care
   To leave the margin wide.

Lend these to paper-sparing Pope;
   And, when he sits to write,
No letter with an envelope
   Could give him more delight.

When Pope has filled the margins round,
    Why, then recall your loan;
Sell them to Curll for fifty pound,
20   And swear they are your own.

The Furniture of a Woman's Mind

A set of phrases learned by rote;
A passion for a scarlet coat;
When at a play to laugh, or cry,
Yet cannot tell the reason why:
Never to hold her tongue a minute;
While all she prates has nothing in it,
Whole hours can with a coxcomb sit,
And take his nonsense all for wit:
Her learning mounts to read a song,
10   But half the words pronouncing wrong;
Has every repartee in store
She spoke ten thousand times before.
Can ready compliments supply
On all occasions, cut and dry.
Such hatred to a parson's gown,
The sight will put her in a swown.
For conversation well endued;
She calls it witty to be rude;
And, placing raillery in railing,
20   Will tell aloud your greatest failing;
Nor makes a scruple to expose
Your bandy leg, or crooked nose.
Can, at her morning tea, run o'er
The scandal of the day before.
Improving hourly in her skill,
To cheat and wrangle at quadrille.

     In choosing lace a critic nice,
     Knows to a groat the lowest price;
     Can in her female clubs dispute
30 What lining best the silk will suit;
     What colours each complexion match:
     And where with art to place a patch.

     If chance a mouse creeps in her sight,
     Can finely counterfeit a fright;
     So, sweetly screams if it comes near her,
     She ravishes all hearts to hear her.
     Can dexterously her husband tease,
     By taking fits whene'er she please:
     By frequent practice learns the trick
40 At proper seasons to be sick;
     Thinks nothing gives one airs so pretty;
     At once creating love and pity.
     If Molly happens to be careless,
     And but neglects to warm her hair-lace,
     She gets a cold as sure as death;
     And vows she scarce can fetch her breath.
     Admires how modest women can
     Be so *robustious* like a man.

     In party, furious to her power;
50 A bitter Whig, or Tory sour;
     Her arguments directly tend
     Against the side she would defend:
     Will prove herself a Tory plain,
     From principles the Whigs maintain;
     And, to defend the Whiggish cause,
     Her topics from the Tories draws.

O yes! If any man can find
More virtues in a woman's mind,
Let them be sent to Mrs Harding;
60   She'll pay the charges to a farthing:
Take notice, she has my commission
To add them in the next edition;
They may outsell a better thing;
So halloo boys! God save the King.

Holyhead. September 25, 1727

Lo here I sit at Holyhead
With muddy ale and mouldy bread:
All Christian victuals stink of fish,
I'm where my enemies would wish.
Convict of lies is every sign,
The inn has not one drop of wine.
I'm fastened both by wind and tide,
I see the ship at anchor ride.
The captain swears the sea's too rough,
10   He has not passengers enough.
And thus the Dean is forced to stay
Till others come to help the pay.
In Dublin they'd be glad to see
A packet though it brings in me.
They cannot say the winds are cross:
Your politicians at a loss
For want of matter swears and frets,
Are forced to read the old gazettes.
I never was in haste before
20   To reach that slavish hateful shore.
Before, I always found the wind
To me was most malicious kind,
But now the danger of a friend
On whom my hopes and fears depend,
Absent from whom all climes are cursed,

With whom I'm happy in the worst,
With rage impatient makes me wait
A passage to the land I hate.
Else, rather on this bleaky shore
30   Where loudest winds incessant roar,
Where neither herb nor tree will thrive,
Where nature hardly seems alive,
I'd go in freedom to my grave,
Than rule yon isle, and be a slave.

An Elegy on Dicky and Dolly

Under this stone lie Dicky and Dolly;
Doll dying first, Dick grew melancholy,
For Dick without Doll thought living a folly.

Dick lost in Doll a wife tender and dear,
But Dick lost by Doll, twelve hundred a year,
A loss that Dick thought, no mortal could bear.

Dick sighed for his Doll and his mournful arms crossed,
Thought much of his Doll, and the jointure he lost;
The first vexed him much, but the other vexed most.

10   Thus loaded with grief, Dick sighed and he cried;
To live without both full three days he tried:
But liked neither loss, and so quietly died.

One bed while alive held both Doll and Dick,
One coach oft carried them when they were quick,
One grave now contains them both *haec et hic*.

Dick left a pattern few will copy after:
Then, reader, pray shed some tears of salt water,
For so sad a tale is no subject of laughter.

Meath smiles for the jointure, though gotten so late;
20   The son laughs that got the hard-gotten estate;
And Cuff grins for getting the Alicant plate.

Here quiet they lie, in hopes to rise one day,
Both solemnly put, in this hole on a Sunday,
And here rest, *sic transit gloria mundi.*

Mad Mullinix and Timothy

M.   I own 'tis not my bread and butter,
But prithee Tim, why all this clutter?
Why ever in these raging fits,
Damning to hell the Jacobites?
When, if you search the kingdom round,
There's hardly twenty to be found:
No, not among the priests and friars.

T.   'Twixt you and me God damn the liars.

M.   The Tories are gone every man over
10   To our illustrious house of Hanover.
From all their conduct this is plain,
And then –   T.   God damn the liars again.
Did not an earl but lately vote
To bring in (I could cut his throat)
Our whole account of public debts?

M.   Lord, how this frothy coxcomb frets! [*aside*]

T.   Did not an able statesman bishop
This dangerous horrid motion dish up?
As Popish craft? Did he not rail on't?
20   Show fire and faggot in the tail on't?
Proving the earl a grand offender,
And in a plot for the Pretender?
Whose fleet, in all our friends' opinion,
Was then embarking at Avignon.

    M.   These brangling jars of Whig and Tory
Are stale, and worn as Troy-Town story.
The wrong, 'tis certain, you were both in,
And now you found you fought for nothing.
Your faction, when their game was new,
30   Might want such noisy fools as you;
But you, when all the show is past,
Resolve to stand it out the last;
Like Martin Marall, gaping on,
Not minding when the song is done.
When all the bees are gone to settle,
You clatter still your brazen kettle.
The leaders whom you listed under,
Have dropped their arms, and seized the plunder.
And when the war is past you come
40   To rattle in their ears your drum:
And, as that hateful hideous Grecian
Thersites (he was your relation)
Was more abhorred, and scorned by those
With whom he served, than by his foes,
So thou art grown the detestation
Of all thy party through the nation.
Thy peevish, and perpetual teasing,
With plots, and Jacobites and treason;
Thy busy never-meaning face;
50   Thy screwed-up front; thy state grimace;
Thy formal nods; important sneers;
Thy whisperings foisted in all ears;
(Which are, whatever you may think,
But nonsense wrapped up in a stink)
Have made thy presence, in a true sense,
To thy own side so damned a nuisance,
That when they have you in their eye,
As if the Devil drove, they fly.

    T.   My good friend Mullinix forbear.
60 I vow to God you're too severe.
    If it could ever yet be known
    I took advice except my own,
    It should be yours. But damn my blood,
    I must pursue the public good.
    The faction, (is it not notorious?)
    Keck at the memory of *Glorious.*
    'Tis true, nor need I to be told,
    My quondam friends are grown so cold,
    That scarce a creature can be found,
70 To prance with me his statue round.
    The public safety, I foresee,
    Henceforth depends alone on me:
    And while this vital breath I blow,
    Or from above, or from below,
    I'll sputter, swagger, curse and rail,
    The Tories' terror, scourge and flail.

    M.   Tim, you mistake the matter quite,
    The Tories! you are their delight;
    And should you act a different part,
80 Be grave and wise, 'twould break their heart.
    Why, Tim, you have a taste I know,
    And often see a puppet-show.
    Observe, the audience is in pain,
    While Punch is hid behind the scene;
    But when they hear his rusty voice,
    With what impatience they rejoice!
    And then they value not two straws
    How Solomon decides the cause,
    Which the true mother, which Pretender,
90 Nor listen to the witch of Endor;
    Should Faustus, with the Devil behind him,
    Enter the stage, they never mind him;
    If Punch, to spur their fancy, shows
    In at the door his monstrous nose,

Then sudden draws it back again,
O what a pleasure mixed with pain!
You every moment think an age,
Till he appears upon the stage:
And first his bum you see him clap
100 Upon the Queen of Sheba's lap.
The Duke of Lorraine drew his sword,
Punch roaring ran, and running roared,
Reviled all people in his jargon,
And sold the King of Spain a bargain.
St George himself he plays the wag on,
And mounts astride upon the dragon.
He gets a thousand thumps and kicks
Yet cannot leave his roguish tricks;
In every action thrusts his nose,
110 The reason why no mortal knows.
In doleful scenes, that break our heart,
Punch comes, like you, and lets a fart.
There's not a puppet made of wood,
But what would hang him if they could.
While teasing all, by all he's teased,
How well are the spectators pleased!
Who in the motion have no share;
But purely come to hear, and stare;
Have no concern for Sabra's sake,
120 Which gets the better, saint or snake.
Provided Punch (for there's the jest)
Be soundly mauled, and plagues the rest.

    Thus Tim, philosophers suppose,
The world consists of puppet-shows;
Where petulant, conceited fellows
Perform the part of Pulcinellos;
So at this booth, which we call Dublin,
Tim, thou'rt the Punch to stir up trouble in;
You wriggle, fidge, and make a rout,
130 Put all your brother puppets out,

Run on in one perpetual round,
To tease, perplex, disturb, confound,
Intrude with monkey grin, and clatter,
To interrupt all serious matter,
Are grown the nuisance of your clan,
Who hate and scorn you, to a man;
But then the lookers-on, the Tories,
You still divert with merry stories;
They would consent, that all the crew
140   Were hanged, before they'd part with you.

But tell me, Tim, upon the spot,
By all this coil what has thou got?
If Tories must have all the sport,
I feel you'll be disgraced at court.

T.   Got? Damn my blood, I frank my letters,
Walk by my place, before my betters,
And, simple as I now stand here,
Expect in time to be a peer.
Got? Damn me, why I got my will!
150   Ne'er hold my peace, and ne'er stand still.
I fart with twenty ladies by;
They call me beast, and what care I?
I bravely call the Tories Jacks,
And sons of whores – behind their backs.
But could you bring me once to think,
That when I strut, and stare, and stink,
Revile and slander, fume and storm,
Betray, make oath, impeach, inform,
With such a constant, loyal zeal,
160   To serve myself and common weal,
And fret the Tories' souls to death,
I did but lose my precious breath,
And when I damn my soul to plague 'em,
Am, as you tell me, but their May-game,
Consume my vitals! they shall know,

I am not to be treated so,
I'd rather hang myself by half,
Than give those rascals cause to laugh.

But how, my friend, can I endure,
170   Once so renowned, to live obscure?
No little boys and girls to cry
'There's nimble Tim a-passing by.'
No more my dear delightful way tread,
Of keeping up a party hatred.
Will none the Tory dogs pursue,
When through the streets I cry 'halloo'?
Must all my damme's, bloods and wounds
Pass only now for empty sounds?
Shall Tory rascals be elected,
180   Although I swear them disaffected?
And when I roar 'a plot, a plot',
Will our own party mind me not?
So qualified to swear and lie,
Will they not trust me for a spy?
Dear Mullinix, your good advice
I beg, you see the case is nice:
O, were I equal in renown,
Like thee, to please this thankless town!
Or blessed with such engaging parts,
190   To win the truant schoolboys' hearts!
Thy virtues meet their just reward,
Attended by the sable guard,
Charmed by thy voice the prentice drops
The snowball destined at thy chops;
Thy graceful steps, and colonel's air,
Allure the cinder-picking fair.

   M.   No more – in mark of true affection
I take thee under my protection.
Thy parts are good, 'tis not denied,
200   I wish they had been well applied.

But now observe my counsel, *viz.*
Adapt your habit to your phiz.
You must no longer thus equip ye,
As Horace says, '*Optat ephippia.*'
(There's Latin too that you may see
How much improved by Dr Lee).
I have a coat at home, that you may try,
'Tis just like this, which hangs by geometry.
My hat has much the nicer air,
210   Your block will fit it to a hair.
That wig, I would not for the world
Have it so formal, and so curled,
'Twill be so oily, and so sleek,
When I have lain in it a week!
You'll find it well prepared to take
The figure of toupee and snake.
Thus dressed alike from top to toe,
That which is which 'tis hard to know;
When first in public we appear,
220   I'll lead the van, keep you the rear;
Be careful, as you walk behind,
Use all the talents of your mind;
Be studious well to imitate
My portly motion, mien, and gate.
Mark my address, and learn my style,
When to look scornful, when to smile,
Nor sputter out your oaths so fast,
But keep your swearing to the last.
Then at your leisure we'll be witty,
230   And in the streets divert the city:
The ladies from the windows gaping,
The children all our motions aping.
Your conversation to refine,
I'll take you to some friends of mine;
Choice spirits, who employ their parts,
To mend the world by useful arts.
Some cleansing hollow tubes, to spy

Direct the Zenith of the sky;
Some have the city in their care,
240   From noxious steams to purge the air;
Some teach us in these dangerous days,
How to walk upright in our ways;
Some whose reforming hands engage,
To lash the lewdness of the age;
Some for the public service go,
Perpetual envoys to and fro;
Whose able heads support the weight
Of twenty ministers of state.
We scorn, for want of talk, to jabber
250   Of parties o'er our bonnyclabber:
Nor are we studious to enquire,
Who votes for manners, who for hire:
Our care is to improve the mind,
With what concerns all humankind,
The various scenes of mortal life,
Who beats her husband, who his wife;
Or how the bully at a stroke
Knocked down the boy, the lanthorn broke;
One tells the rise of cheese, and oatmeal;
260   Another when he got a hot meal;
One gives advice in proverbs old,
Instructs us how to tame a scold;
Or how by almanacs 'tis clear,
That herrings will be cheap this year.

     T.   Dear Mullinix, I now lament
My precious time, so long misspent,
By nature meant for nobler ends,
O, introduce me to your friends!
For whom, by birth, I was designed,
270   Till politics debased my mind.
I give myself entire to you,
God damn the Whigs and Tories too.

Tom Mullinex and Dick

Tom and Dick had equal fame,
　　And both had equal knowledge;
Tom could write and spell his name,
　　But Dick had seen a college.

Dick a coxcomb, Tom was mad,
　　And both alike diverting,
Tom was held the merrier lad,
　　But Dick the best at farting.

Dick would cock his nose in scorn,
10　　But Tom was kind and loving;
Tom a footboy bred and born,
　　But Dick was from an oven.

Dick could neatly dance a jig,
　　But Tom was best at borees;
Tom would pray for every Whig,
　　And Dick curse all the Tories.

Dick would make a woeful noise,
　　And scold at an election;
Tom huzza'd the blackguard boys,
20　　And held them in subjection.

Tom could move with lordly grace,
　　Dick nimbly skip the gutter;
Tom could talk with solemn face,
　　But Dick could better sputter.

Dick was come to high renown
　　Since he commenced physician;
Tom was held by all the town
　　The deeper politician.

Tom had the genteeler swing,
30   His hat could nicely put on;
Dick knew better how to swing
        His cane upon a button.

Dick for repartee was fit,
        And Tom for deep discerning;
Dick was thought the brighter wit,
        But Tom had better learning.

Dick with zealous no's and aye's,
        Could roar as loud as Stentor;
In the House 'tis all he says;
40   But Tom is eloquenter.

Dick, a Maggot

As when rooting in a bin,
All powdered o'er from tail to chin,
A lively maggot sallies out,
You know him by his hazel snout:
So, when the grandson of his grandsire,
Forth issues wriggling Dick Drawcansir,
With powdered rump, and back and side,
You cannot blanch his tawny hide;
For 'tis beyond the power of meal,
10   The gypsy visage to conceal:
For, as he shakes his wainscot chops,
Down every mealy atom drops
And leaves the Tartar phiz, in show
Like a fresh turd just dropped on snow.

An Answer to the Ballyspellin Ballad

Dare you dispute,
You saucy brute,
And think there's no rebelling
Your scurvy lays,
And senseless praise
You give to Ballyspellin?

Howe'er you bounce,
I here pronounce
Your medicine is repelling;
10   Your water's mud,
And sours the blood
When drank at Ballyspellin.

Those pocky drabs,
To cure their scabs,
You thither are compelling,
Will back be sent
Worse than they went
From nasty Ballyspellin.

Llewellyn! why,
20   As well may I
Name honest Doctor Pelling;
So hard sometimes
You tug for rhymes,
To bring in Ballyspellin.

No subject fit
To try your wit
When you went colonelling;
But dull intrigues
'Twixt jades and teagues
30   That met at Ballyspellin.

Our lasses fair,
Say what you dare,
Who sowens make with shelling,
At Market Hill
More beaux can kill
Than yours at Ballyspellin.

Would I was whipped
When Sheelah stripped,
To wash herself our well in;
40 A bum so white
Ne'er came in sight
At paltry Ballyspellin.

Your mawkins there
Smocks hempen wear;
Of Holland, not an ell in;
No, not a rag,
Whate'er you brag,
Is found at Ballyspellin.

But Tom will prate
50 At any rate,
All other nymphs expelling:
Because he gets
A few grisettes
At lousy Ballyspellin.

There's bonny Jane
In yonder lane,
Just o'er against the Bell Inn;
Where can you meet
A lass so sweet
60 Round all your Ballyspellin?

We have a girl
Deserves an earl,
She came from Enniskillen;
So fair, so young,
No such among
The belles of Ballyspellin.

How would you stare
To see her there,
The foggy mists dispelling,
70   That cloud the brows
Of every blowze
Who lives at Ballyspellin.

Now, as I live,
I would not give
A stiver or a skilling
To touse and kiss
The fairest miss
That leaks at Ballyspellin.

Whoe'er will raise
80   Such lies as these
Deserves a good cudgelling;
Who falsely boasts
Of belles and toasts
At dirty Ballyspellin.

My rhymes are gone
To all but one,
Which is, our trees are felling;
As proper quite
As those you write
90   To force in Ballyspellin.

Verses Occasioned by the Sudden Drying Up of St Patrick's Well near Trinity College, Dublin

By holy zeal inspired, and led by fame,
To thee, once favourite isle, with joy I came;
What time the Goth, the Vandal, and the Hun,
Had my own native Italy o'errun.
Ierne, to the world's remotest parts,
Renowned for valour, policy and arts.

    Hither from Colchus, with the fleecy ore,
Jason arrived two thousand years before.
Thee, happy island, Pallas called her own,
10 When haughty Britain was a land unknown.
From thee, with pride, the Caledonians trace
The glorious founder of their kingly race:
Thy martial sons, whom now they dare despise,
Did once their land subdue and civilize:
Their dress, their language, and the Scottish name,
Confess the soil from whence the victors came.
Well may they boast that ancient blood, which runs
Within their veins, who are thy younger sons,
A conquest and a colony from thee,
20 The mother-kingdom left her children free;
From thee no mark of slavery they felt,
Not so with thee thy base invaders dealt;
Invited here to vengeful Morough's aid,
Those whom they could not conquer, they betrayed.
Britain, by thee we fell, ungrateful isle!
Not by thy valour, but superior guile:
Britain, with shame confess, this land of mine
First taught thee human knowledge and divine;
My prelates and my students, sent from hence,
30 Made your sons converts both to God and sense:

Not like the pastors of thy ravenous breed,
Who come to fleece the flocks, and not to feed.

Wretched Ierne! with what grief I see
The fatal changes time hath made in thee.
The Christian rites I introduced in vain:
Lo! Infidelity returned again.
Freedom and Virtue in thy sons I found,
Who now in Vice and Slavery are drowned.

By faith and prayer, this crozier in my hand,
40   I drove the venomed serpent from thy land;
The shepherd in his bower might sleep or sing,
Nor dread the adder's tooth, nor scorpion's sting.

With omens oft I strove to warn thy swains,
Omens, the types of thy impending chains.
I sent the magpie from the British soil,
With restless beak thy blooming fruit to spoil,
To din thine ears with unharmonious clack,
And haunt thy holy walls in white and black.
What else are those thou seest in bishop's gear
50   Who crop the nurseries of learning here?
Aspiring, greedy, full of senseless prate,
Devour the church, and chatter to the state.

As you grew more degenerate and base,
I sent you millions of the croaking race;
Emblems of insects vile, who spread their spawn
Through all thy land, in armour, fur and lawn:
A nauseous brood, that fills your senate walls,
And in the chambers of your Viceroy crawls.

See where the new-devouring vermin runs,
60   Sent in my anger from the land of Huns;
With harpy claws it undermines the ground,
And sudden spreads a numerous offspring round;
The amphibious tyrant, with his ravenous band,
Drains all thy lakes of fish, of fruits thy land.

Where is the sacred well, that bore my name?
Fled to the fountain back, from whence it came!
Fair Freedom's emblem once, which smoothly flows,
And blessings equally on all bestows.
Here, from the neighbouring nursery of arts,
70   The students drinking, raised their wit and parts;
Here, for an age and more, improved their vein,
Their Phoebus I, my spring their Hippocrene.
Discouraged youths, now all their hopes must fail,
Condemned to country cottages and ale;
To foreign prelates make a slavish court,
And by their sweat procure a mean support;
Or, for the classics read the attorney's guide;
Collect excise, or wait upon the tide.

O! had I been apostle to the Swiss,
80   Or hardy Scot, or any land but this;
Combined in arms, they had their foes defied,
And kept their liberty, or bravely died.
Thou still with tyrants in succession cursed,
The last invaders trampling on the first:
Nor fondly hope for some reverse of fate,
Virtue herself would now return too late.
Not half thy course of misery is run,
Thy greatest evils yet are scarce begun.
Soon shall thy sons, the time is just at hand,
90   Be all made captives in their native land;
When, for the use of no Hibernian born,
Shall rise one blade of grass, one ear of corn;
When shells and leather shall for money pass,
Nor thy oppressing lords afford thee brass.
But all turn leasers to that mongrel breed,
Who from thee sprung, yet on thy vitals feed;
Who to yon ravenous isle thy treasures bear,
And waste in luxury thy harvests there;
For pride and ignorance a proverb grown,
100   The jest of wits, and to the court unknown.

I scorn thy spurious and degenerate line,
And from this hour my patronage resign.

Drapier's Hill

We give the world to understand,
Our thriving Dean has purchased land;
A purchase which will bring him clear,
Above his rent four pounds a year;
Provided, to improve the ground,
He will but add two hundred pound,
And from his endless hoarded store,
To build a house five hundred more.
Sir Arthur too shall have his will,
10   And call the mansion Drapier's Hill;
That when the nation long enslaved,
Forgets by whom it once was saved;
When none the Drapier's praise shall sing;
His signs aloft no longer swing;
His medals and his prints forgotten,
And all his handkerchiefs are rotten;
His famous *Letters* made waste paper;
This hill may keep the name of Drapier:
In spite of envy flourish still,
20   And Drapier's vie with Cooper's Hill.

A Pastoral Dialogue

A nymph and swain, Sheelah and Dermot hight,
Who wont to weed the court of Gosford knight,
While each with stubbed knife removed the roots
That raised between the stones their daily shoots;
As at their work they sat in counterview,
With mutual beauty smit, their passion grew.
Sing, heavenly Muse, in sweetly flowing strain,
The soft endearments of the nymph and swain.

DERMOT

My love to Sheelah is more firmly fixed
10   Than strongest weeds that grow these stones betwixt:
My spud these nettles from the stones can part;
No knife so keen to weed thee from my heart.

SHEELAH

My love for gentle Dermot faster grows
Than yon tall dock that rises to thy nose.
Cut down the dock, 'twill sprout again; but O!
Love rooted out, again will never grow.

DERMOT

No more that briar thy tender leg shall rake:
(I spare the thistle for Sir Arthur's sake.)
Sharp are the stones, take thou this rushy mat;
20   The hardest bum will bruise with sitting squat.

SHEELAH

Thy breeches, torn behind, stand gaping wide;
This petticoat shall save thy dear backside;
Nor need I blush, although you feel it wet;
Dermot, I vow, 'tis nothing else but sweat.

DERMOT

At an old stubborn root I chanced to tug,
When the Dean threw me this tobacco plug:
A longer ha'porth never did I see;
This, dearest Sheelah, thou shalt share with me.

SHEELAH

In at the pantry door this morn I slipped,
30   And from the shelf a charming crust I whipped:
Dennis was out, and I got hither safe;
And thou, my dear, shalt have the bigger half.

DERMOT

When you saw Tady at long-bullets play,
You sat and loused him all a sunshine day.
How could you, Sheelah, listen to his tales,
Or crack such lice as his betwixt your nails?

SHEELAH

When you with Oonagh stood behind a ditch,
I peeped, and saw you kiss the dirty bitch.
Dermot, how could you touch those nasty sluts!
40   I almost wish this spud were in your guts.

DERMOT

If Oonagh once I kissed, forbear to chide;
Her aunt's my gossip by my father's side:
But, if I ever touch her lips again,
May I be doomed for life to weed in rain.

SHEELAH

Dermot, I swear, though Tady's locks could hold
Ten thousand lice, and every louse was gold,
Him on my lap you never more should see;
Or may I lose my weeding-knife – and thee.

DERMOT

O, could I earn for thee, my lovely lass,
50   A pair of brogues to bear thee dry to mass!
But see where Norah with the sowens comes –
Then let us rise, and rest our weary bums.

On Burning a Dull Poem

An ass's hoof alone can hold
That poisonous juice which kills by cold.
Methought, when I this poem read,
No vessel but an ass's head,

Such frigid fustian could contain;
I mean the head without the brain.
The cold conceits, the chilling thoughts,
Went down like stupefying draughts:
I found my head began to swim,
10   A numbness crept through every limb:
In haste, with imprecations dire,
I threw the volume in the fire:
When, who could think, though cold as ice,
It burnt to ashes in a trice.

How could I more enhance its fame?
Though born in snow, it died in flame.

A Libel on the Reverend Dr Delany and His Excellency John, Lord Carteret

TO DR DELANY, OCCASIONED BY HIS EPISTLE TO HIS
EXCELLENCY JOHN, LORD CARTERET

Deluded mortals, whom the great
Choose for companions *tête à tête*,
Who at their dinners, *en famille*,
Get leave to sit whene'er you will;
Then, boasting tell us where you dined,
And, how his Lordship was so kind;
How many pleasant things he spoke,
And, how you laughed at every joke:
Swear, he's a most facetious man:
10   That you and he are cup and can.
You travel with a heavy load,
And quite mistake preferment's road.

Suppose my Lord and you alone;
Hint the least interest of your own;
His visage drops, he knits his brow,

He cannot talk of business now:
Or, mention but a vacant post,
He'll turn it off with, 'Name your toast.'
Nor could the nicest artist paint
20   A countenance with more constraint.

For, as their appetites to quench,
Lords keep a pimp to bring a wench;
So, men of wit are but a kind
Of pandars to a vicious mind;
Who proper objects must provide
To gratify their lust of pride,
When wearied with intrigues of state,
They find an idle hour to prate.
Then, should you dare to ask a place,
30   You forfeit all your patron's grace,
And disappoint the sole design,
For which he summoned you to dine.

Thus, Congreve spent, in writing plays,
And one poor office, half his days;
While Montagu, who claimed the station
To be Maecenas of the nation,
For poets open table kept,
But ne'er considered where they slept:
Himself as rich as fifty Jews,
40   Was easy, though they wanted shoes;
And, crazy Congreve scarce could spare
A shilling to discharge his chair;
Till prudence taught him to appeal
From Paean's fire to party zeal;
Not owing to his happy vein
The fortunes of his latter scene;
Took proper principles to thrive;
And so might every dunce alive.

Thus, Steele who owned what others writ,
50   And flourished by imputed wit,
From perils of a hundred gaols,
Withdrew to starve, and die in Wales.

Thus Gay, the hare with many friends,
Twice seven long years the court attends,
Who, under tales conveying truth,
To virtue formed a princely youth:
Who paid his courtship with the crowd,
As far as modest pride allowed;
Rejects a servile usher's place,
60   And leaves St James's in disgrace.

Thus Addison, by lords caressed,
Was left in foreign lands distressed;
Forgot at home, became for hire,
A travelling tutor to a squire.
But, wisely left the Muses' hill;
To business shaped the poet's quill,
Let all his barren laurels fade;
Took up himself the courtier's trade:
And, grown a minister of state,
70   Saw poets at his levee wait.

Hail! happy Pope, whose generous mind,
Detesting all the statesman kind!
Contemning courts, at courts unseen,
Refused the visits of a queen;
A soul with every virtue fraught
By sages, priests, or poets taught:
Whose filial piety excels
Whatever Grecian story tells:
A genius for all stations fit,
80   Whose meanest talent is his wit:
His heart too great, though fortune little,
To lick a rascal statesman's spittle;

Appealing to the nation's taste,
Above the reach of want is placed:
By Homer dead was taught to thrive,
Which Homer never could alive:
And, sits aloft on Pindus' head,
Despising slaves that cringe for bread.

    True politicians only pay
90 For solid work, but not for play;
Nor ever choose to work with tools
Forged up in colleges and schools.
Consider how much more is due
To all their journeymen, than you.
At table you can Horace quote;
They at a pinch can bribe a vote:
You show your skill in Grecian story,
But, they can manage Whig and Tory:
You, as a critic, are so curious
100 To find a verse in Virgil spurious;
But, they can smoke the deep designs,
When Bolingbroke with Pulteney dines.

    Besides; your patron may upbraid ye,
That you have got a place already:
An office for your talents fit,
To flatter, carve and show your wit;
To snuff the lights and stir the fire,
And get a dinner for your hire.
What claim have you to place, or pension?
110 He overpays in condescension.

    But, reverend Doctor, you, we know,
Could never condescend so low:
The Viceroy, whom you now attend,
Would, if he durst, be more your friend;
Nor will *in you* those gifts despise,
By which himself was taught to rise:

When he has virtue to retire,
He'll grieve he did not raise you higher,
And place you in a better station,
120   Although it might have pleased the nation.

    This may be true – submitting still
To Walpole's more than royal will.
And what condition can be worse?
He comes to drain a beggar's purse:
He comes to tie our chains on faster,
And show us, England is our master:
Caressing knaves and dunces wooing,
To make them work their own undoing.
What has he else to bait his traps,
130   Or bring his vermin in, but scraps?
The offals of a church distressed,
A hungry vicarage at best;
Or, some remote inferior post,
With forty pounds a year at most.

    But, here again you interpose;
Your favourite Lord is none of those,
Who owe their virtues to their stations,
And characters to dedications:
For keep him in, or turn him out,
140   His learning none will call in doubt:
His learning, though a poet said it,
Before a play, would lose no credit:
Nor Pope would dare deny him wit,
Although to praise it Philips writ.
I own, he hates an action base,
His virtues battling with his place;
Nor wants a nice discerning spirit,
Betwixt a true and spurious merit:
Can sometimes drop a voter's claim,
150   And give up party to his fame.
I do the most that friendship can;
I hate the Viceroy, love the man.

But, you, who till your fortune's made
Must be a sweetener by your trade,
Should swear he never meant us ill;
We suffer sore against his will;
That, if we could but see his heart,
He would have chose a milder part:
We rather should lament his case,
160 Who must obey, or lose his place.

Since this reflection slipped your pen,
Insert it when you write again:
And, to illustrate it, produce
This simile for his excuse.

'So, to destroy a guilty land,
An angel sent by Heaven's command,
While he obeys Almighty will,
Perhaps, may feel compassion still;
And wish the task had been assigned
170 To spirits of less gentle kind.'

But I, in politics grown old,
Whose thoughts are of a different mould,
Who, from my soul, sincerely hate
Both kings and ministers of state:
Who look on courts with stricter eyes,
To see the seeds of vice arise,
Can lend you an allusion fitter,
Though flattering knaves may call it bitter:
Which, if you durst but give it place,
180 Would show you many a statesman's face.
Fresh from the tripod of Apollo,
I had it in the words that follow.
(Take notice, to avoid offence
I here except His Excellence.)

    So, to effect his monarch's ends,
From Hell a Viceroy devil ascends,
His budget with corruptions crammed,
The contributions of the damned;
Which with unsparing hand, he strews
190   Through courts and senates as he goes;
And then at Belzebub's Black Hall,
Complains his budget was too small.

    Your simile may better shine
In verse; but there is truth in mine.
For, no imaginable things
Can differ more than God and kings.
And statesmen, by ten thousand odds
Are angels, just as kings are gods.

An Excellent New Ballad

OR, THE TRUE ENGLISH DEAN TO BE HANGED FOR A RAPE

I

Our brethren of England, who love us so dear,
   And in all they do for us so kindly do mean,
A blessing upon them, have sent us this year,
   For the good of our church, a true English Dean.
A holier priest ne'er was wrapped up in crape,
The worst you can say, he committed a rape.

II

In his journey to Dublin, he lighted at Chester,
   And there he grew fond of another man's wife,
Burst into her chamber, and would have caressed her,
10   But she valued her honour much more than her life.
She bustled and struggled, and made her escape,
To a room full of guests for fear of a rape.

III

The Dean he pursued to recover his game,
    And now to attack her again he prepares,
But the company stood in defence of the dame,
    They cudgelled and cuffed him, and kicked him downstairs.
His Deanship was now in a damnable scrape,
And this was no time for committing a rape.

IV

To Dublin he comes, to the bagnio he goes,
20   And orders the landlord to bring him a whore;
No scruple came on him his gown to expose,
    'Twas what all his life he had practised before.
He had made himself drunk with the juice of the grape,
And got a good clap, but committed no rape.

V

The Dean, and his landlord, a jolly comrade,
    Resolved for a fortnight to swim in delight;
For why, they had both been brought up to the trade
    Of drinking all day, and of whoring all night.
His landlord was ready his Deanship to ape
30   In every debauch, but committing a rape.

VI

This Protestant zealot, this English divine,
    In church and in state was of principles sound,
Was truer than Steele to the Hanover line,
    And grieved that a Tory should live above ground.
Shall a subject so loyal be hanged by the nape,
For no other crime but committing a rape?

VII

By old popish canons, as wise men have penned 'em,
    Each priest had a concubine, *jure ecclesiae*;
Who'd be Dean of Ferns without a *commendam*?
40   And precedents we can produce, if it please ye:
Then, why should the Dean, when whores are so cheap,
Be put to the peril, and toil of a rape?

VIII

If fortune should please but to take such a crotchet,
    (To thee I apply great Smedley's successor)
To give thee lawn-sleeves, a mitre and rochet,
    Whom wouldst thou resemble? I leave thee a guesser;
But I only behold thee in Atherton's shape,
For sodomy hanged, as thou for a rape.

IX

Ah! dost thou not envy the brave Colonel Chartres,
50   Condemned for thy crime, at three score and ten?
To hang him all England would lend him their garters;
    Yet he lives, and is ready to ravish again,
Then throttle thyself with an ell of strong tape,
For thou hast not a groat to atone for a rape.

X

The Dean he was vexed that his whores were so willing:
    He longed for a girl that would struggle and squall;
He ravished her fairly, and saved a good shilling;
    But, here was to pay the Devil and all.
His trouble and sorrows now come in a heap,
60   And hanged he must be for committing a rape.

XI

If maidens are ravished, it is their own choice;
    Why are they so wilful to struggle with men?
If they would but lie quiet, and stifle their voice,
    No Devil or Dean could ravish 'em then,
Nor would there be need of a strong hempen cape,
Tied round the Dean's neck, for committing a rape.

XII

Our church and our state dear England maintains,
    For which all true Protestant hearts should be glad;
She sends us our bishops and judges and deans,
70   And better would give us, if better she had;
But, Lord how the rabble will stare and will gape,
When the good English Dean is hanged up for a rape.

The Lady's Dressing Room

Five hours, (and who can do it less in?)
By haughty Celia spent in dressing;
The goddess from her chamber issues,
Arrayed in lace, brocade and tissues:
Strephon, who found the room was void,
And Betty otherwise employed,
Stole in, and took a strict survey
Of all the litter as it lay:
Whereof, to make the matter clear,
10   An *inventory* follows here.

And first, a dirty smock appeared,
Beneath the arm-pits well besmeared;
Strephon, the rogue, displayed it wide,
And turned it round on every side:
In such a case few words are best,
And Strephon bids us guess the rest;
But swears how damnably the men lie,
In calling Celia sweet and cleanly.

Now listen while he next produces,
20 The various combs for various uses,
Filled up with dirt so closely fixed,
No brush could force a way betwixt;
A paste of composition rare,
Sweat, dandruff, powder, lead and hair,
A forehead cloth with oil upon't
To smooth the wrinkles on her front;
Here, alum flower to stop the steams,
Exhaled from sour unsavoury streams;
There, night-gloves made of Tripsy's hide,
30 Bequeathed by Tripsy when she died;
With puppy water, beauty's help,
Distilled from Tripsy's darling whelp.
Here gallipots and vials placed,
Some filled with washes, some with paste;
Some with pomatum, paints and slops,
And ointments good for scabby chops.
Hard by, a filthy basin stands,
Fouled with the scouring of her hands;
The basin takes whatever comes,
40 The scrapings from her teeth and gums,
A nasty compound of all hues,
For here she spits, and here she spews.

But oh! it turned poor Strephon's bowels
When he beheld and smelt the towels;
Begummed, bemattered, and beslimed;
With dirt, and sweat, and ear-wax grimed.
No object Strephon's eye escapes;
Here, petticoats in frowzy heaps;
Nor be the handkerchiefs forgot,
50 All varnished o'er with snuff and snot.
The stockings why should I expose,
Stained with the moisture of her toes;
Or greasy coifs and pinners reeking,
Which Celia slept at least a week in?

A pair of tweezers next he found,
To pluck her brows in arches round,
Or hairs that sink the forehead low,
Or on her chin like bristles grow.

The virtues we must not let pass
60   Of Celia's magnifying glass;
When frighted Strephon cast his eye on't,
It showed the visage of a giant:
A glass that can to sight disclose
The smallest worm in Celia's nose,
And faithfully direct her nail
To squeeze it out from head to tail;
For, catch it nicely by the head,
It must come out, alive or dead.

Why, Strephon, will you tell the rest?
70   And must you needs describe the chest?
That careless wench! No creature warn her
To move it out from yonder corner,
But leave it standing full in sight,
For you to exercise your spite!
In vain the workman showed his wit,
With rings and hinges counterfeit
To make it seem in this disguise,
A cabinet to vulgar eyes;
Which Strephon ventured to look in,
80   Resolved to go through *thick and thin*,
He lifts the lid: there need no more,
He smelt it all the time before.

As, from within Pandora's box,
When Epimethus oped the locks,
A sudden universal crew
Of human evils upward flew;
He still was comforted to find
That hope at last remained behind.

So, Strephon, lifting up the lid,
90 To view what in the chest was hid,
    The vapours flew from out the vent;
    But Strephon, cautious, never meant
    The bottom of the pan to grope,
    And foul his hands in search of hope.

    O! ne'er may such a vile machine
    Be once in Celia's chamber seen!
    O! may she better learn to keep
    'Those secrets of the hoary deep.'

    As mutton cutlets, prime of meat,
100 Which though with art you salt and beat,
    As laws of cookery require,
    And roast them at the clearest fire;
    If from adown the hopeful chops
    The fat upon a cinder drops,
    To stinking smoke it turns the flame,
    Poisoning the flesh from whence it came;
    And up exhales a greasy stench,
    For which you curse the careless wench:
    So things which must not be expressed,
110 When *plumped* into the reeking chest,
    Send up an excremental smell
    To taint the parts from which they fell:
    The petticoats and gown perfume,
    And waft a stink round every room.

    Thus finishing his grand survey,
    The swain disgusted slunk away,
    Repeating in his amorous fits,
    'Oh! Celia, Celia, Celia shits!'

But Vengeance, goddess never sleeping,
120 Soon punished Strephon for his peeping.
His foul imagination links
Each dame he sees with all her stinks:
And, if unsavoury odours fly,
Conceives a lady standing by:
All women his description fits,
And both ideas jump like wits,
By vicious fancy coupled fast,
And still appearing in contrast.

I pity wretched Strephon, blind
130 To all the charms of womankind;
Should I the Queen of Love refuse,
Because she rose from stinking ooze?
To him that looks behind the scene,
Statira's but some pocky quean.

When Celia in her glory shows,
If Strephon would but stop his nose,
Who now so impiously blasphemes
Her ointments, daubs, and paints and creams;
Her washes, slops, and every clout,
140 With which he makes so foul a rout;
He soon would learn to think like me,
And bless his ravished eyes to see
Such order from confusion sprung,
Such gaudy *tulips* raised from *dung*.

A Beautiful Young Nymph Going to Bed

WRITTEN FOR THE HONOUR OF THE FAIR SEX, IN 1731

Corinna, pride of Drury Lane,
For whom no shepherd sighs in vain;
Never did Covent Garden boast
So bright a battered, strolling toast;
No drunken rake to pick her up,
No cellar where on tick to sup;
Returning at the midnight hour;
Four storeys climbing to her bower;
Then, seated on a three-legged chair,
10   Takes off her artificial hair:
Now, picking out a crystal eye,
She wipes it clean, and lays it by.
Her eyebrows from a mouse's hide,
Stuck on with art on either side,
Pulls off with care, and first displays 'em,
Then in a play-book smoothly lays 'em.
Now dexterously her plumpers draws,
That serve to fill her hollow jaws.
Untwists a wire; and from her gums
20   A set of teeth completely comes.
Pulls out the rags contrived to prop
Her flabby dugs, and down they drop.
Proceeding on, the lovely goddess
Unlaces next her steel-ribbed bodice;
Which, by the operator's skill,
Press down the lumps, the hollows fill.
Up goes her hand, and off she slips
The bolsters that supply her hips.
With gentlest touch, she next explores
30   Her shankers, issues, running sores;
Effects of many a sad disaster.
And then to each applies a plaster.
But must, before she goes to bed,

Rub off the daubs of white and red;
And smooth the furrows in her front,
With greasy paper stuck upon't.
She takes a bolus e'er she sleeps;
And then between two blankets creeps.
With pains of love tormented lies;
40   Or, if she chance to close her eyes,
Of Bridewell and the compter dreams,
And feels the lash, and faintly screams.
Or, by a faithless bully drawn,
At some hedge-tavern lies in pawn.
Or, to Jamaica seems transported,
Alone, and by no planter courted.
Or, near Fleet Ditch's oozy brinks,
Surrounded with a hundred stinks,
Belated, seems on watch to lie,
50   And snap some cully passing by.
Or, struck with fear, her fancy runs
On watchmen, constables and duns,
From whom she meets with frequent rubs;
But, never from religious clubs;
Whose favour she is sure to find,
Because she pays them all in kind.

Corinna wakes. A dreadful sight!
Behold the ruins of the night!
A wicked rat her plaster stole,
60   Half ate, and dragged it to his hole.
The crystal eye, alas, was missed;
And Puss had on her plumpers pissed.
A pigeon picked her issue-peas,
And Shock her tresses filled with fleas.

The nymph, though in this mangled plight,
Must every morn her limbs unite.
But how shall I describe her arts
To recollect the scattered parts?

Or show the anguish, toil, and pain,
70 Of gathering up herself again?
The bashful Muse will never bear
In such a scene to interfere.
Corinna in the morning dizened,
Who sees, will spew; who smells, be poisoned.

The Character of Sir Robert Walpole

With favour and fortune fastidiously blessed,
He's loud in his laugh and he's coarse in his jest;
Of favour and fortune unmerited vain,
A sharper in trifles, a dupe in the main;
Achieving of nothing, still promising wonders,
By dint of experience improving in blunders;
Oppressing true merit, exalting the base,
And selling his country to purchase his peace.
A jobber of stocks by retailing false news;
10 A prater at court in the style of the stews;
Of virtue and worth by profession a giber;
Of juries and senates the bully and briber.
Though I name not the wretch you know who I mean –
'Tis the cur-dog of Britain and spaniel of Spain.

The Place of the Damned

All folks who pretend to religion and grace,
Allow there's a Hell, but dispute of the place;
But if Hell may by logical rules be defined,
The place of the damned – I will tell you my mind.

Wherever the damned do chiefly abound,
Most certainly there is Hell to be found;
Damned poets, damned critics, damned blockheads, damned
knaves,

Damned senators bribed, damned prostitute slaves;
Damned lawyers and judges, damned lords and damned squires,
10   Damned spies and informers, damned friends and damned
        liars;
Damned villains, corrupted in every station;
Damned time-serving priests all over the nation.
And into the bargain I'll readily give you
Damned ignorant prelates, and councillors privy.
Then let us no longer by parsons be flammed,
For we know by these marks, the place of the damned:
And Hell to be sure is at Paris or Rome,
How happy for us, that it is not at home!

Helter Skelter

OR, THE HUE AND CRY AFTER THE ATTORNEYS,
GOING TO RIDE THE CIRCUIT

Now the active young attorneys
Briskly travel on their journeys,
Looking big as any giants,
On the horses of their clients;
Like so many little Mars's,
With their tilters at their arses,
Brazen hilted, lately burnished,
And with harness-buckles furnished;
And with whips and spurs so neat,
10   And with jockey-coats complete;
And with boots so very greasy,
And with saddles eke so easy,
And with bridles fine and gay,
Bridles borrowed for a day,
Bridles destined far to roam,
Ah! never to come home;
And with hats so very big, sir,
And with powdered caps and wigs, sir;
And with ruffles to be shown,

20   Cambric ruffles not their own;
     And with holland shirts so white,
     Shirts becoming to the sight,
     Shirts bewrought with different letters,
     As belonging to their betters:
     With their pretty tinselled boxes,
     Gotten from their dainty doxies,
     And with rings so very trim,
     Lately taken out of lim –
     And with very little pence,
30   And as very little sense:
     With some law but little justice,
     Having stolen from my hostess,
     From the barber and the cutler,
     Like the soldier from the sutler;
     From the vintner and the tailor,
     Like the felon from the gaoler,
     Into this and t'other county,
     Living on the public bounty;
     Thorough town and thorough village,
40   All to plunder, all to pillage;
     Thorough mountains, thorough valleys;
     Thorough stinking lanes and alleys;
     Some to cuckold farmers' spouses,
     And make merry in their houses;
     Some to tumble country wenches
     On their rushy beds and benches;
     And, if they begin a fray,
     Draw their swords and run away:
     All to murder equity,
50   And to take a double fee;
     Till the people all are quiet,
     And forget to broil and riot,
     Low in pocket, cowed in courage,
     Safely glad to sup their porridge,
     And vacation's over – then
     Hey for Dublin town again!

Verses on the Death of Dr Swift, D.S.P.D.

OCCASIONED BY READING A MAXIM IN ROCHEFOUCAULD

*Dans l'adversité de nos meilleurs amis nous trouvons quelque
chose, qui ne nous deplaist pas.*

In the adversity of our best friends, we find something that
    doth not displease us.

As Rochefoucauld his maxims drew
From Nature, I believe 'em true:
They argue no corrupted mind
In him; the fault is in mankind.

This maxim more than all the rest
Is thought too base for human breast;
'In all distresses of our friends
We first consult our private ends,
While Nature kindly bent to ease us,
10 Points out some circumstance to please us.'

If this perhaps your patience move,
Let reason and experience prove.

We all behold with envious eyes,
Our equal raised above our size;
Who would not at a crowded show,
Stand high himself, keep others low?
I love my friend as well as you,
But would not have him stop my view;
Then let me have the higher post;
20 I ask but for an inch at most.

If in a battle you should find,
One, whom you love of all mankind,
Had some heroic action done,
A champion killed, or trophy won;
Rather than thus be overtopped,
Would you not wish his laurels cropped?

Dear honest Ned is in the gout,
Lies racked with pain, and you without:
How patiently you hear him groan!
30 How glad the case is not your own!

What poet would not grieve to see,
His brethren write as well as he?
But rather than they should excel,
He'd wish his rivals all in Hell.

Her end when Emulation misses,
She turns to envy, stings and hisses:
The strongest friendship yields to pride,
Unless the odds be on our side.

Vain humankind! Fantastic race!
40 Thy various follies, who can trace?
Self-love, ambition, envy, pride,
Their empire in our hearts divide:
Give others riches, power, and station,
'Tis all on me a usurpation.
I have no title to aspire;
Yet, when you sink, I seem the higher.
In Pope, I cannot read a line,
But with a sigh, I wish it mine:
When he can in one couplet fix
50 More sense than I can do in six:
It gives me such a jealous fit,
I cry, 'Pox take him, and his wit.'

Why must I be outdone by Gay,
In my own humorous biting way?

Arbuthnot is no more my friend,
Who dares to irony pretend;
Which I was born to introduce,
Refined it first, and showed its use.

St John, as well as Pulteney knows,
60   That I had some repute for prose;
And till they drove me out of date
Could maul a minister of state:
If they have mortified my pride,
And made me throw my pen aside;
If with such talents Heaven hath blest 'em,
Have I not reason to detest 'em?

To all my foes, dear Fortune, send
Thy gifts, but never to my friend:
I tamely can endure the first,
70   But, this with envy makes me burst.

Thus much may serve by way of proem,
Proceed we therefore to our poem.

The time is not remote, when I
Must by the course of nature die:
When I foresee my special friends,
Will try to find their private ends:
Though it is hardly understood,
Which way my death can do them good;
Yet thus, methinks, I hear 'em speak;
80   'See, how the Dean begins to break:
Poor gentleman, he droops apace,
You plainly find it in his face:
That old vertigo in his head,
Will never leave him, till he's dead:

Besides, his memory decays,
He recollects not what he says;
He cannot call his friends to mind;
Forgets the place where last he dined:
Plies you with stories o'er and o'er,
90   He told them fifty times before.
How does he fancy we can sit,
To hear his out-of-fashioned wit?
But he takes up with younger folks,
Who for his wine will bear his jokes:
Faith, he must make his stories shorter,
Or change his comrades once a quarter:
In half the time, he talks them round;
There must another set be found.

    'For poetry, he's past his prime,
100   He takes an hour to find a rhyme:
His fire is out, his wit decayed,
His fancy sunk, his Muse a jade.
I'd have him throw away his pen;
But there's no talking to some men.'

    And, then their tenderness appears,
By adding largely to my years:
'He's older than he would be reckoned,
And well remembers Charles the Second.

    'He hardly drinks a pint of wine;
110   And that, I doubt, is no good sign.
His stomach too begins to fail:
Last year we thought him strong and hale;
But now, he's quite another thing;
I wish he may hold out till spring.'

    Then hug themselves, and reason thus;
'It is not yet so bad with us.'

In such a case they talk in tropes,
And, by their fears express their hopes:
Some great misfortune to portend,
120   No enemy can match a friend;
With all the kindness they profess,
The merit of a lucky guess,
(When daily 'Howd'y's' come of course,
And servants answer: 'Worse and worse')
Would please 'em better than to tell,
That, God be praised, the Dean is well.
Then he who prophesied the best
Approves his foresight to the rest:
'You know, I always feared the worst,
130   And often told you so at first':
He'd rather choose that I should die,
Than his prediction prove a lie.
No one foretells I shall recover;
But, all agree, to give me over.

Yet should some neighbour feel a pain,
Just in the parts, where I complain;
How many a message would he send?
What hearty prayers that I should mend?
Enquire what regimen I kept?
140   What gave me ease, and how I slept?
And more lament, when I was dead,
Than all the snivellers round my bed.

My good companions, never fear,
For though you may mistake a year;
Though your prognostics run too fast,
They must be verified at last.

'Behold the fatal day arrive!
How is the Dean? He's just alive.
Now the departing prayer is read:
150   He hardly breathes. The Dean is dead.

Before the passing-bell begun,
The news through half the town has run.
O, may we all for death prepare!
What has he left? And who's his heir?
I know no more than what the news is,
'Tis all bequeathed to public uses.
To public use! A perfect whim!
What had the public done for him?
Mere envy, avarice, and pride!
160   He gave it all. – But first he died.
And had the Dean, in all the nation,
No worthy friend, no poor relation?
So ready to do strangers good,
Forgetting his own flesh and blood?'

    Now Grub Street wits are all employed;
With elegies, the town is cloyed:
Some paragraph in every paper,
To curse the Dean, or bless the Drapier.

    The doctors, tender of their fame,
170   Wisely on me lay all the blame:
'We must confess his case was nice;
But he would never take advice:
Had he been ruled, for ought appears,
He might have lived these twenty years:
For when we opened him we found
That all his vital parts were sound.'

    From Dublin soon to London spread,
'Tis told at court, the Dean is dead.

    Kind Lady Suffolk in the spleen,
180   Runs laughing up to tell the Queen.
The Queen, so gracious, mild, and good,
Cries, 'Is he gone? 'Tis time he should.
He's dead you say, why let him rot;

I'm glad the medals were forgot.
I promised them, I own; but when?
I only was the princess then;
But now as consort of the King,
You know 'tis quite a different thing.'

    Now Chartres, at Sir Robert's levee,
190 Tells, with a sneer, the tidings heavy:
'Why, is he dead without his shoes?'
(Cries Bob) 'I'm sorry for the news;
Oh, were the wretch but living still,
And in his place my good friend Will;
Or had a mitre on his head
Provided Bolingbroke were dead.'

    Now Curll his shop from rubbish drains;
Three genuine tomes of Swift's remains.
And then to make them pass the glibber,
200 Revised by Tibbalds, Moore, and Cibber.
He'll treat me as he does my betters.
Publish my will, my life, my letters.
Revive the libels born to die;
Which Pope must bear, as well as I.

    Here shift the scene, to represent
How those I love, my death lament.
Poor Pope will grieve a month; and Gay
A week; and Arbuthnot a day.

    St John himself will scarce forbear,
210 To bite his pen, and drop a tear.
The rest will give a shrug and cry,
'I'm sorry; but we all must die.'
Indifference clad in wisdom's guise,
All fortitude of mind supplies:
For how can stony bowels melt,
In those who never pity felt;
When *we* are lashed, *they* kiss the rod;
Resigning to the will of God.

The fools, my juniors by a year,
220 Are tortured with suspense and fear.
Who wisely thought my age a screen,
When death approached, to stand between:
The screen removed, their hearts are trembling,
They mourn for me without dissembling.

My female friends, whose tender hearts
Have better learnt to act their parts,
Receive the news in doleful dumps,
'The Dean is dead, (*and what is trumps?*)
Then Lord have mercy on his soul.
230 (*Ladies, I'll venture for the vole.*)
Six deans they say must bear the pall.
(*I wish I knew which king to call.*)'
'Madam, your husband will attend
The funeral of so good a friend.'
'No madam, 'tis a shocking sight,
And he's engaged tomorrow night!
My Lady Club would take it ill,
If he should fail her at quadrille.
He loved the Dean, (*I lead a heart.*)
240 But dearest friends, they say, must part.
His time was come, he ran his race;
We hope he's in a better place.'

Why do we grieve that friends should die?
No loss more easy to supply.
One year is past; a different scene;
No further mention of the Dean;
Who now, alas, no more is missed,
Than if he never did exist.
Where's now this favourite of Apollo?
250 Departed; and his works must follow:
Must undergo the common fate;
His kind of wit is out of date.
Some country squire to Lintot goes,

Inquires for Swift in verse and prose:
Says Lintot, 'I have heard the name:
He died a year ago.' The same.
He searcheth all his shop in vain;
'Sir, you may find them in Duck Lane:
I sent them with a load of books,
260   Last Monday to the pastry-cook's.
To fancy they could live a year!
I find you're but a stranger here.
The Dean was famous in his time;
And had a kind of knack at rhyme:
His way of writing now is past;
The town hath got a better taste:
I keep no antiquated stuff;
But, spick and span I have enough.
Pray, do but give me leave to show 'em;
270   Here's Colley Cibber's birthday poem.
This ode you never yet have seen,
By Stephen Duck, upon the Queen.
Then, here's a letter finely penned,
Against the *Craftsman* and his friend;
It clearly shows that all reflection
On ministers, is disaffection.
Next, here's Sir Robert's vindication,
And Mr Henley's last oration:
The hawkers have not got 'em yet,
280   Your honour please to buy a set?

    'Here's Woolston's tracts, the twelfth edition;
'Tis read by every politician:
The country members, when in town,
To all their boroughs send them down:
You never met a thing so smart;
The courtiers have them all by heart:
Those maids of honour (who can read)
Are taught to use them for their creed.
The reverend author's good intention

290 Hath been rewarded with a pension:
  He doth an honour to his gown,
  By bravely running priestcraft down:
  He shows, as sure as God's in Gloucester,
  That Jesus was a grand impostor:
  That all his miracles were cheats,
  Performed as jugglers do their feats:
  The church had never such a writer:
  A shame he hath not got a mitre!'

  Suppose me dead; and then suppose
300 A club assembled at the Rose;
  Where from discourse of this and that,
  I grow the subject of their chat:
  And, while they toss my name about,
  With favour some, and some without;
  One quite indifferent in the cause,
  My character impartial draws:

  'The Dean, if we believe report,
  Was never ill received at court:
  As for his works in verse and prose,
310 I own myself no judge of those:
  Nor can I tell what critics thought 'em;
  But, this I know, all people bought 'em;
  As with a moral view designed
  To cure the vices of mankind:
  His vein, ironically grave,
  Exposed the fool, and lashed the knave:
  To steal a hint was never known,
  But what he writ was all his own.

  'He never thought an honour done him,
320 Because a duke was proud to own him:
  Would rather slip aside, and choose
  To talk with wits in dirty shoes:
  Despised the fools with stars and garters,

So often seen caressing Chartres:
He never courted men in station,
Nor persons had in admiration;
Of no man's greatness was afraid,
Because he sought for no man's aid.
Though trusted long in great affairs,
330   He gave himself no haughty airs:
Without regarding private ends,
Spent all his credit for his friends:
And only chose the wise and good;
No flatterers; no allies in blood;
But succoured virtue in distress,
And seldom failed of good success;
As numbers in their hearts must own,
Who, but for him, had been unknown.

'With princes kept a due decorum,
340   But never stood in awe before 'em:
And to her Majesty, God bless her,
Would speak as free as to her dresser,
She thought it his peculiar whim,
Nor took it ill as come from him.
He followed David's lesson just,
"In princes never put thy trust."
And, would you make him truly sour;
Provoke him with a slave in power:
The Irish senate, if you named,
350   With what impatience he declaimed!
Fair LIBERTY was all his cry;
For her he stood prepared to die;
For her he boldly stood alone;
For her he oft exposed his own.
Two kingdoms, just as factions led,
Had set a price upon his head;
But, not a traitor could be found,
To sell him for six hundred pound.

'Had he but spared his tongue and pen,
360 He might have rose like other men:
But, power was never in his thought;
And, wealth he valued not a groat:
Ingratitude he often found,
And pitied those who meant the wound:
But, kept the tenor of his mind,
To merit well of humankind:
Nor made a sacrifice of those
Who still were true, to please his foes.
He laboured many a fruitless hour
370 To reconcile his friends in power;
Saw mischief by a faction brewing,
While they pursued each other's ruin.
But, finding vain was all his care,
He left the court in mere despair.

'And, oh! how short are human schemes!
Here ended all our golden dreams.
What St John's skill in state affairs,
What Ormonde's valour, Oxford's cares,
To save their sinking country lent,
380 Was all destroyed by one event.
Too soon that precious life was ended,
On which alone our weal depended.
When up a dangerous faction starts,
With wrath and vengeance in their hearts:
By solemn league and covenant bound,
To ruin, slaughter, and confound;
To turn religion to a fable,
And make the government a Babel:
Pervert the law, disgrace the gown,
390 Corrupt the senate, rob the crown;
To sacrifice old England's glory,
And make her infamous in story.
When such a tempest shook the land,
How could unguarded virtue stand?

'With horror, grief, despair the Dean
Beheld the dire destructive scene:
His friends in exile, or the Tower,
Himself within the frown of power;
Pursued by base envenomed pens,
400   Far to the land of slaves and fens;
A servile race in folly nursed,
Who truckle most, when treated worst.

'By innocence and resolution,
He bore continual persecution;
While numbers to preferment rose;
Whose merits were, to be his foes.
When, *ev'n his own familiar friends*
Intent upon their private ends,
Like renegadoes now he feels,
410   *Against him lifting up their heels.*

'The Dean did by his pen defeat
An infamous destructive cheat;
Taught fools their interest to know;
And gave them arms to ward the blow.
Envy hath owned it was his doing,
To save that helpless land from ruin,
While they who at the steerage stood,
And reaped the profit, sought his blood.

'To save them from their evil fate,
420   In him was held a crime of state.
A wicked monster on the bench,
Whose fury blood could never quench;
As vile and profligate a villain,
As modern Scroggs, or old Tresilian;
Who long all justice had discarded,
Nor feared he God, nor man regarded;
Vowed on the Dean his rage to vent,
And make him of his zeal repent;

But Heaven his innocence defends,
430 The grateful people stand his friends:
Not strains of law, nor judges' frown,
Nor topics brought to please the crown,
Nor witness hired, nor jury picked,
Prevail to bring him in convict.

'In exile with a steady heart,
He spent his life's declining part;
Where folly, pride, and faction sway,
Remote from St John, Pope, and Gay.

'His friendship there to few confined,
440 Were always of the middling kind:
No fools of rank, a mongrel breed,
Who fain would pass for lords indeed:
Where titles give no right or power,
And peerage is a withered flower,
He would have held it a disgrace,
If such a wretch had known his face.
On rural squires, that kingdom's bane,
He vented oft his wrath in vain:
Biennial squires, to market brought;
450 Who sell their souls and votes for naught;
The nation stripped, go joyful back,
To rob the church, their tenants rack,
Go snacks with thieves and rapparees,
And keep the peace, to pick up fees:
In every job to have a share,
A gaol or barrack to repair;
And turn the tax for public roads
Commodious to their own abodes.

'Perhaps I may allow the Dean
460 Had too much satire in his vein;
And seemed determined not to starve it,
Because no age could more deserve it.

Yet, malice never was his aim;
He lashed the vice but spared the name.
No individual could resent,
Where thousands equally were meant.
His satire points at no defect,
But what all mortals may correct;
For he abhorred that senseless tribe,
470   Who call it humour when they jibe:
He spared a hump or crooked nose,
Whose owners set not up for beaux.
True genuine dullness moved his pity,
Unless it offered to be witty.
Those, who their ignorance confessed,
He ne'er offended with a jest;
But laughed to hear an idiot quote,
A verse from Horace, learnt by rote.

'He knew an hundred pleasant stories,
480   With all the turns of Whigs and Tories:
Was cheerful to his dying day,
And friends would let him have his way.

'He gave the little wealth he had,
To build a house for fools and mad:
And showed by one satiric touch,
No nation wanted it so much:
That kingdom he hath left his debtor,
I wish it soon may have a better.'

Verses on I Know Not What

My latest tribute here I send,
With this let your collection end.
Thus I consign you down to fame,
A character to praise and blame;
And, if the whole may pass for true,
Contented rest; you have your due.
Give future times the satisfaction
To leave one handle for detraction.

[A Paper Book is Sent by Boyle]

A paper book is sent by Boyle,
Too neatly gilt for me to soil.
Delany sends a silver standish,
When I no more a pen can brandish.
Let both around my tomb be placed,
As trophies of a Muse deceased:
And let the friendly lines they writ
In praise of long departed wit,
Be graved on either side in columns,
10   More to my praise than all my volumes;
To burst with envy, spite, and rage,
The vandals of the present age.

On the Day of Judgement

With a whirl of thought oppressed,
I sink from reverie to rest.
An horrid vision seized my head,
I saw the graves give up their dead.
Jove, armed with terrors, burst the skies,
And thunder roars, and lightning flies!
Amazed, confused, its fate unknown,
The world stands trembling at his throne.
While each pale sinner hangs his head,
10   Jove, nodding, shook the heavens, and said,
'Offending race of humankind,
By nature, reason, learning, blind;
You who through frailty stepped aside,
And you who never fell – *through pride*;
You who in different sects have shammed,
And come to see each other damned;
(So some folks told you, but they knew
No more of Jove's designs than you)
The world's mad business now is o'er,
20   And I resent these pranks no more.
I to such blockheads set my wit!
I damn such fools! – Go, go, you're bit.'

On Poetry: a Rhapsody

All human race would fain be wits,
And millions miss, for one that hits.
Young's universal passion, pride,
Was never known to spread so wide.
Say, Britain, could you ever boast
Three poets in an age at most?
Our chilling climate hardly bears
A sprig of bays in fifty years:

While every fool his claim alleges,
10　As if it grew in common hedges.
What reason can there be assigned
For this perverseness in the mind?
Brutes find out where their talents lie:
A bear will not attempt to fly:
A foundered horse will oft debate
Before he tries a five-barred gate:
A dog by instinct turns aside,
Who sees the ditch too deep and wide.
But man we find the only creature,
20　Who, led by folly, combats nature;
Who, when she loudly cries, 'Forbear',
With obstinacy fixes there;
And, where his genius least inclines,
Absurdly bends his whole designs.

　　Not empire to the rising sun,
By valour, conduct, fortune won;
Nor highest wisdom in debates
For framing laws to govern states;
Nor skill in sciences profound,
30　So large to grasp the circle round;
Such heavenly influence require,
As how to strike the Muses' lyre.

　　Not beggar's brat, on bulk begot;
Not bastard of a pedlar Scot;
Not boy brought up to cleaning shoes,
The spawn of Bridewell, or the stews;
Not infants dropped, the spurious pledges
Of gypsies littering under hedges,
Are so disqualified by fate
40　To rise in church, or law, or state,
As he, whom Phoebus in his ire
Hath *blasted* with poetic fire.

What hope of custom in the fair,
While not a soul demands your ware?
Where you have nothing to produce
For private life, or public use?
Court, city, country want you not;
You cannot bribe, betray, or plot.
For poets, law makes no provision:
50   The wealthy have you in derision.
Of state affairs you cannot smatter,
Are awkward when you try to flatter.
Your portion, taking Britain round,
Was just one annual hundred pound.
Now not so much as in remainder
Since Cibber brought in an attainder;
For ever fixed by right divine,
(A monarch's right) on Grub Street line.

Poor starveling bard, how small thy gains!
60   How unproportioned to thy pains!
And here a simile comes pat in:
Though chickens take a month to fatten,
The guests in less than half an hour
Will more than half a score devour.
So, after toiling twenty days,
To earn a stock of pence and praise,
Thy labours, grown the critic's prey,
Are swallowed o'er a dish of tea;
Gone, to be never heard of more,
70   Gone, where the chickens went before.

How shall a new attempter learn
Of different spirits to discern,
And how distinguish, which is which,
The poet's vein, or scribbling itch?
Then hear an old experienced sinner
Instructing thus a young beginner.

Consult yourself, and if you find
A powerful impulse urge your mind,
Impartial judge within your breast
80 What subject you can manage best;
Whether your genius most inclines
To satire, praise, or humorous lines;
To elegies in mournful tone,
Or prologue 'sent from hand unknown.'
Then rising with Aurora's light,
The Muse invoked, sit down to write;
Blot out, correct, insert, refine,
Enlarge, diminish, interline.
Be mindful, when invention fails,
90 To scratch your head, and bite your nails.

Your poem finished; next your care
Is needful, to transcribe it fair.
In modern wit all printed trash is
Set off with numerous breaks – and dashes –
To statesmen would you give a wipe,
You print it in *italic type*.
When letters are in vulgar shapes,
'Tis ten to one the wit escapes;
But when in CAPITALS expressed,
100 The dullest reader smokes a jest.
Or else perhaps he may invent
A better than the poet meant,
As learnéd commentators view
In Homer more than Homer knew.

Your poem in its modish dress,
Correctly fitted for the press,
Convey by penny post to Lintot,
But let no friend alive look into't.
If Lintot thinks 'twill quit the cost,
110 You need not fear your labour lost:
And, how agreeably surprised

Are you to see it advertised!
The hawker shows you one in print,
As fresh as farthings from the mint:
The product of your toil and sweating;
A bastard of your own begetting.

    Be sure at Will's the following day,
Lie snug, to hear what critics say.
And if you find the general vogue
120 Pronounces you a stupid rogue;
Damns all your thoughts as low and little,
Sit still, and swallow down your spittle.
Be silent as a politician,
For talking may beget suspicion:
Or praise the judgement of the town,
And help yourself to run it down.
Give up your fond paternal pride,
Nor argue on the weaker side;
For poems read without a name
130 We justly praise, or justly blame:
And critics have no partial views,
Except they know whom they abuse.
And since you ne'er provoked their spite,
Depend upon't their judgement's right:
But if you blab, you are undone;
Consider what a risk you run:
You lose your credit all at once;
The town will mark you for a dunce:
The vilest doggerel Grub Street sends,
140 Will pass for yours with foes and friends.
And you must bear the whole disgrace,
Till some fresh blockhead takes your place.

    Your secret kept, your poem sunk,
And sent in quires to line a trunk;
If still you be disposed to rhyme,
Go try your hand a second time:

Again you fail; yet safe's the word;
Take courage and attempt a third.
But first with care employ your thoughts,
150   Where critics marked your former faults:
The trivial turns, the borrowed wit,
The similes that nothing fit;
The cant which every fool repeats,
Town-jests, and coffee-house conceits;
Descriptions tedious, flat and dry,
And introduced the Lord knows why;
Or where you find your fury set
Against the harmless alphabet;
On A's and B's your malice vent,
160   While readers wonder whom you meant:
A public, or a private robber;
A statesman, or a South Sea jobber.
A prelate who no God believes;
A parliament, or den of thieves.
A house of peers, or gaming crew;
A griping monarch, or a Jew.
A pickpurse, at the bar, or bench;
A duchess, or a suburb wench.
Or oft when epithets you link,
170   In gaping lines to fill a chink;
Like stepping stones to save a stride,
In streets where kennels are too wide:
Or like a heel-piece to support
A cripple with one foot too short:
Or like a bridge that joins a marish
To moorlands of a different parish.
So have I seen ill-coupled hounds,
Drag different ways in miry grounds.
So geographers in Afric maps
180   With savage pictures fill their gaps;
And o'er unhabitable downs
Place elephants for want of towns.

But though you miss your third essay,
You need not throw your pen away.
Lay now aside all thoughts of fame,
To spring more profitable game.
From party merit seek support;
The vilest verse thrives best at court.
And may you ever have the luck
190 To rhyme almost as well as Duck;
And, though you never learned to scan verse,
Come out with some lampoon on D'Anvers.
A pamphlet in Sir Bob's defence
Will never fail to bring in pence;
Nor be concerned about the sale,
He pays his workmen on the nail.

Display the blessings of the nation,
And praise the whole administration,
Extol the bench of bishops round,
200 Who at them rail bid God confound:
To bishop-haters answer thus
(The only logic used by us),
What though they don't believe in Christ,
Deny them Protestants – thou liest.

A prince, the moment he is crowned,
Inherits every virtue round,
As emblems of the sovereign power,
Like *other* baubles of the Tower;
Is generous, valiant, just and wise,
210 And so continue till he dies.
His humble senate this professes,
In all their speeches, votes, addresses.
But, once you fix him in a tomb,
His virtues fade, his vices bloom;
And each perfection wrong imputed
Is fully at his death confuted.
His panegyrics then are ceased,

He's grown a tyrant, dunce and beast.
The loads of poems in his praise,
220 Ascending, make one funeral blaze.
As soon as you can hear his knell,
This god on earth turns devil in hell.
And lo, his ministers of state,
Transformed to imps, his levees wait:
Where, in the scenes of endless woe,
They ply their former arts below:
And as they sail in Charon's boat,
Contrive to bribe the judge's vote.
To Cerberus they give a sop,
230 His triple-barking mouth to stop:
Or in the ivory gate of dreams,
Project Excise and South Sea schemes:
Or hire their party pamphleteers,
To set Elysium by the ears.

Then poet, if you mean to thrive,
Employ your muse on kings alive;
With prudence gathering up a cluster
Of all the virtues you can muster:
Which formed into a garland sweet,
240 Lay humbly at your monarch's feet;
Who, as the odours reach his throne,
Will smile, and think 'em all his own:
For law and gospel both determine
All virtues lodge in royal ermine.
(I mean the oracles of both
Who shall depose it upon oath.)
Your garland in the following reign,
Change but the names, will do again.

But if you think this trade too base,
250 (Which seldom is the dunce's case)
Put on the critic's brow, and sit
At Will's, the puny judge of wit.

A nod, a shrug, a scornful smile,
With caution used, may serve awhile.
Proceed no further in your part,
Before you learn the terms of art:
(For you can never be too far gone,
In all our modern critics' jargon.)
Then talk with more authentic face,
260   Of 'unities, in time and place.'
Get scraps of Horace from your friends,
And have them at your fingers' ends.
Learn Aristotle's rules by rote,
And at all hazards boldly quote:
Judicious Rymer oft review:
Wise Dennis, and profound Bossu.
Read all the prefaces of Dryden,
For these our critics much confide in,
(Though merely writ at first for filling
270   To raise the volume's price, a shilling.)

A forward critic often dupes us
With sham quotations *Peri Hupsous*:
And if we have not read Longinus,
Will magisterially outshine us.
Then, lest with Greek he overrun ye,
Procure the book for love or money,
Translated from Boileau's translation,
And quote quotation on quotation.

At Will's you hear a poem read,
280   Where Battus from the table head,
Reclining on his elbow-chair,
Gives judgement with decisive air.
To him the tribe of circling wits,
As to an oracle submits.
He gives directions to the town,
To cry it up, or run it down.
(Like courtiers, when they send a note,

Instructing members how to vote.)
He sets a stamp of bad and good,
290 Though not a word be understood.
Your lesson learnt, you'll be secure
To get the name of connoisseur.
And when your merits once are known,
Procure disciples of your own.

For poets (you can never want 'em,
Spread through Augusta Trinobantum)
Computing by their pecks of coals,
Amount to just nine thousand souls.
These o'er their proper districts govern,
300 Of wit and humour, judges sovereign.
In every street a city bard
Rules, like an alderman his ward.
His indisputed rights extend
Through all the lane, from end to end.
The neighbours round admire his shrewdness,
For songs of loyalty and lewdness.
Outdone by none in rhyming well,
Although he never learnt to spell.

Two bordering wits contend for glory;
310 And one is Whig, and one is Tory.
And this, for epics claims the bays,
And that, for elegiac lays.
Some famed for numbers soft and smooth,
By lovers spoke in Punch's booth.
And some as justly fame extols
For lofty lines in Smithfield drolls.
Bavius in Wapping gains renown,
And Maevius reigns o'er Kentish Town:
Tigellius placed in Phoebus' car,
320 From Ludgate shines to Temple Bar.
Harmonious Cibber entertains
The court with annual birthday strains;

Whence Gay was banished in disgrace,
Where Pope will never show his face;
Where Young must torture his invention,
To flatter knaves, or lose his pension.

But these are not a thousandth part
Of jobbers in the poet's art,
Attending each his proper station,
330   And all in due subordination;
Through every alley to be found,
In garrets high, or underground:
And when they join their pericranies,
Out skips a book of miscellanies.

Hobbes clearly proves that every creature
Lives in a state of war by nature.
The greater for the smaller watch,
But meddle seldom with their match.
A whale of moderate size will draw
340   A shoal of herrings down his maw;
A fox with geese his belly crams;
A wolf destroys a thousand lambs.
But search among the rhyming race,
The *brave* are worried by the *base*.
If on Parnassus' top you sit,
You rarely bite, are always bit:
Each poet of inferior size
On you shall rail and criticize;
And strive to tear you limb from limb,
350   While others do as much for him.
The vermin only tease and pinch
Their foes superior by an inch.
So, naturalists observe, a flea
Hath smaller fleas that on him prey,
And these have smaller yet to bite 'em,
And so proceed *ad infinitum*:
Thus every poet in his kind,

Is bit by him that comes behind;
Who, though too little to be seen,
360 Can tease, and gall, and give the spleen;
Call dunces, fools, and sons of whores,
Lay Grub Street at each other's doors:
Extol the Greek and Roman masters,
And curse our modern poetasters.
Complain, as many an ancient bard did,
How genius is no more rewarded;
How wrong a taste prevails among us;
How much our ancestors outsung us;
Can personate an awkward scorn
370 For those who are not poets born:
And all their brother dunces lash,
Who crowd the press with hourly trash.

O, Grub Street! how I do bemoan thee,
Whose graceless children scorn to own thee!
Their filial piety forgot,
Deny their country like a Scot:
Though by their idiom and grimace
They soon betray their native place:
Yet *thou* hast greater cause to be
380 Ashamed of them, than they of thee;
Degenerate from their ancient brood,
Since first the court allowed them food.

Remains a difficulty still,
To purchase fame by writing ill:
From Flecknoe down to Howard's time,
How few have reached the low sublime!
For when our high-born Howard died,
Blackmore alone his place supplied:
And lest a chasm should intervene,
390 When death had finished Blackmore's reign,
The leaden crown devolved to thee,
Great poet of the *Hollow Tree*.

But, oh, how unsecure thy throne!
Ten thousand bards thy rights disown:
They plot to turn, in factious zeal,
Duncenia to a common-weal;
And with rebellious arms pretend
An equal privilege to *descend*.

    In bulk there are not more degrees,
400 From elephants to mites in cheese,
Than what a curious eye may trace
In creatures of the rhyming race.
From bad to worse, and worse they fall,
But who can reach to worst of all?
For though in nature depth and height
Are equally held infinite,
In poetry the height we know;
'Tis only infinite below.
For instance: when you rashly think,
410 No rhymer can like Welsted sink:
His merits balanced you shall find,
The laureate leaves him far behind.
Concanen, more aspiring bard,
Climbs downwards, deeper, by a yard:
Smart Jemmy Moor with vigour drops,
The rest pursue as thick as hops:
With heads to points the gulf they enter,
Linked perpendicular to the centre:
And as their heels elated rise,
420 Their heads attempt the nether skies.

    O, what indignity and shame
To prostitute the Muse's name,
By flattering kings whom heaven designed
The plagues and scourges of mankind.
Bred up in ignorance and sloth,
And every vice that nurses both.

Perhaps you say Augustus shines,
Immortal made in Virgil's lines,
And Horace brought the tuneful choir
430   To sing his virtues on the lyre,
Without reproach of flattery; true,
Because their praises were his due.
For in those ages kings we find,
Were animals of humankind,
But now, go search all Europe round,
Among the savage monsters crowned,
With vice polluting every throne
(I mean all kings except our own),
In vain you make the strictest view
440   To find a king in all the crew
With whom a footman out of place
Would not conceive a high disgrace,
A burning shame, a crying sin,
To take his morning's cup of gin.
Thus all are destined to obey
Some beast of burden or of prey.
'Tis sung Prometheus, forming man,
Through all the brutal species ran,
Each proper quality to find
450   Adapted to a human mind;
A mingled mass of good and bad,
The worst and best that could be had;
Then, from a clay of mixture base,
He shaped a king to rule the race,
Endowed with gifts from every brute,
Which best the regal nature suit.
Thus think on kings, the name denotes
Hogs, asses, wolves, baboons and goats,
To represent in figure just
460   Sloth, folly, rapine, mischief, lust.
O! were they all but Nebuchadnezzars,
What herds of kings would turn to grazers.

Fair Britain, in thy monarch blessed,
Whose virtues bear the strictest test;
Whom never faction can bespatter,
Nor minister nor poet flatter.
What justice in rewarding merit!
What magnanimity of spirit!
How well his public thrift is shown!
470 All coffers full except his own.
What lineaments divine we trace
Through all his figure, mien, and face;
Though peace with olive bind his hands,
Confessed the conquering hero stands.
Hydaspes, Indus, and the Ganges
Dread from his hand impending changes.
From him the Tartar, and Chinese,
Short by the knees entreat for peace.
The consort of his throne and bed,
480 A perfect goddess born and bred:
Appointed sovereign judge to sit
On learning, eloquence and wit.
Our eldest hope, divine Iülus,
(Late, very late, O, may he rule us.)
What early manhood has he shown,
Before his downy beard was grown!
Then think, what wonders will be done
By going on as he begun;
An heir for Britain to secure
490 As long as sun and moon endure.

The remnant of the royal blood,
Comes pouring on me like a flood.
Bright goddesses, in number five;
Duke William, sweetest prince alive.

Now sing the minister of state,
Who shines alone, without a mate.
Observe with what majestic port
This Atlas stands to prop the court:

Intent the public debts to pay,
500 Like prudent Fabius, by delay.
Thou great vicegerent of the King,
Thy praises every Muse shall sing:
In all affairs thou sole director,
Of wit and learning chief protector;
Though small the time thou hast to spare,
The church is thy peculiar care.
Of pious prelates what a stock
You choose to rule the sable flock!
You raise the honour of the peerage,
510 Proud to attend you at the steerage.
You dignify the noble race,
Content yourself with humbler place,
Now learning, valour, virtue, sense,
To titles give the sole pretence:
St George beheld thee with delight
Vouchsafe to be an azure knight,
When on thy breast and sides Herculean
He fixed the star and string cerulean.

Say, poet, in what other nation,
520 Shone ever such a constellation.
Attend ye Popes, and Youngs, and Gays,
And tune your harps, and strow your bays.
Your panegyrics here provide,
You cannot err on flattery's side.
Above the stars exalt your style,
You still are low ten thousand mile.
On Lewis all his bards bestowed
Of incense many a thousand load;
But Europe mortified his pride,
530 And swore the fawning rascals lied:
Yet what the world refused to Lewis,
Applied to George exactly true is:
Exactly true! Invidious poet!
'Tis fifty thousand times below it.

Translate me now some lines, if you can,
From Virgil, Martial, Ovid, Lucan;
They could all power in heaven divide,
And do no wrong to either side:
They teach you how to split a hair,
540   Give George and Jove an equal share.
Yet, why should we be laced so straight;
I'll give my monarch butter-weight.
And reason good; for many a year
Jove never intermeddled here:
Nor, though his priests be duly paid,
Did ever we desire his aid:
We now can better do without him,
Since Woolston gave us arms to rout him.

* * * * * * *Caetera desiderantur* * * * * * *

Verses Spoken Extempore by Dean Swift on his Curate's Complaint of Hard Duty

I marched three miles through scorching sand,
With zeal in heart, and notes in hand:
I rode four more to great St Mary,
Using four legs when two were weary.
To three fair virgins I did tie men
In the close band of pleasing hymen.
I dipped two babes in holy water,
And purified their mothers after.
Within an hour, and eke a half,
10   I preached three congregations deaf;
Which, thundering out with lungs long-winded,
I chopped so fast, that few there minded.
My emblem, the laborious sun,
Saw all these mighty labours done,
Before one race of his was run:
All this performed by Robert Hewit,
What mortal else could e'er go through it!

On his own Deafness

Vertiginosus, inops, surdus, male gratus amicis;
Non campana sonans, tonitru non ab Jove missum,
Quod mage mirandum, saltem si credere fas est,
Non clamosa meas mulier jam percutit aures.

Deaf, giddy, helpless, left alone,
To all my friends a burthen grown,
No more I hear my church's bell,
Than if it rang out for my knell:
At thunder now no more I start,
Than at the rumbling of a cart:
Nay, what's incredible, alack!
I hardly hear a woman's clack.

A Character, Panegyric, and Description of the Legion Club

As I stroll the city, oft I
Spy a building large and lofty,
Not a bow-shot from the College,
Half the globe from sense and knowledge.
By the prudent architect
Placed against the church direct;
Making good my grandam's jest,
Near the church – you know the rest.

    Tell us what this pile contains?
10   Many a head that holds no brains.
These demoniacs let me dub
With the name of 'Legion Club.'
Such assemblies, you might swear,
Meet when butchers bait a bear;
Such a noise, and such haranguing,

When a brother thief is hanging.
Such a rout and such a rabble
Run to hear jack-pudding gabble;
Such a crowd their ordure throws
20   On a far less villain's nose.

     Could I from the building's top
Hear the rattling thunder drop,
While the Devil upon the roof,
If the Devil be thunder-proof,
Should with poker fiery red
Crack the stones, and melt the lead;
Drive them down on every skull,
While the den of thieves is full;
Quite destroy that harpies' nest,
30   How might then our isle be blessed?
For divines allow that God
Sometimes makes the Devil his rod:
And the gospel will inform us,
He can punish sins enormous.

     Yet should Swift endow the schools
For his lunatics and fools,
With a rood or two of land,
I allow the pile may stand.
You perhaps will ask me, why so?
40   But it is with this proviso,
Since the House is like to last,
Let a royal grant be passed,
That the club have right to dwell
Each within his proper cell;
With a passage left to creep in,
And a hole above for peeping.

     Let them, when they once get in,
Sell the nation for a pin;
While they sit a-picking straws,

50   Let them rave of making laws;
     While they never hold their tongue,
     Let them dabble in their dung;
     Let them form a grand committee,
     How to plague and starve the city;
     Let them stare, and storm, and frown,
     When they see a clergy-gown.
     Let them, 'ere they crack a louse,
     Call for the orders of the House;
     Let them with their gosling quills,
60   Scribble senseless heads of bills;
     We may, while they strain their throats,
     Wipe our arses with their votes.

     Let Sir Tom, that rampant ass,
     Stuff his guts with flax and grass;
     But, before the priest he fleeces,
     Tear the bible all to pieces.
     At the parsons, Tom, halloo boy,
     Worthy offspring of a shoe-boy,
     Footman, traitor, vile seducer,
70   Perjured rebel, bribed accuser;
     Lay thy paltry privilege aside,
     Sprung from papists and a regicide;
     Fall a-working like a mole,
     Raise the dirt about your hole.

     Come, assist me, Muse obedient,
     Let us try some new expedient;
     Shift the scene for half an hour,
     Time and place are in thy power.
     Thither, gentle Muse, conduct me,
80   I shall ask, and thou instruct me.

     See, the muse unbars the gate;
     Hark, the monkeys, how they prate!

All ye gods, who rule the soul;
Styx, through Hell whose waters roll!
Let me be allowed to tell
What I heard in yonder Hell.

Near the door an entrance gapes,
Crowded round with antic shapes;
Poverty, and Grief, and Care,
90   Causeless Joy, and true Despair;
Discord periwigged with snakes,
See the dreadful strides she takes.

By this odious crew beset,
I began to rage and fret,
And resolved to break their pates,
Ere we entered at the gates;
Had not Clio, in the nick,
Whispered me, 'Let down your stick';
'What,' said I, 'is this the madhouse?'
100   'These,' she answered, 'are but shadows,
Phantoms, bodiless and vain,
Empty visions of the brain.'

In the porch Briareus stands,
Shows a bribe in all his hands:
Briareus the secretary,
But we mortals call him Carey.
When the rogues their country fleece,
They may hope for pence apiece.

Clio, who had been so wise
110   To put on a fool's disguise,
To bespeak some approbation,
And be thought a near relation;
When she saw three hundred brutes,
All involved in wild disputes;
Roaring till their lungs were spent,

'Privilege of parliament',
Now a new misfortune feels,
Dreading to be laid by the heels.
Never durst a muse before
120 Enter that infernal door;
Clio stifled with the smell,
Into spleen and vapours fell;
By the Stygian steams that flew,
From the dire infectious crew.
Not the stench of Lake Avernus,
Could have more offended her nose:
Had she flown but o'er the top,
She would feel her pinions drop,
And by exhalations dire,
130 Though a goddess, must expire.
In a fright she crept away,
Bravely I resolved to stay.

When I saw the keeper frown,
Tipping him with half a crown;
'Now,' said I, 'we are alone,
Name your heroes, one by one.'

'Who is that hell-featured bawler,
Is it Satan? No, 'tis Waller.
In what figure can a bard dress
140 Jack, the grandson of Sir Hardress?
Honest keeper, drive him further,
In his looks are hell and murther;
See the scowling visage drop,
Just as when he murdered Throp.

Keeper, show me where to fix
On the puppy pair of Dicks;
By their lantern jaws and leathern,
You might swear they both are brethren:
Dick Fitz-Baker, Dick the player,
150 Old acquaintance, are you there?

Dear companions hug and kiss,
Toast old Glorious in your piss.
Tie them, keeper, in a tether,
Let them stare and stink together;
Both are apt to be unruly,
Lash them daily, lash them duly,
Though 'tis hopeless to reclaim them,
Scorpion rods perhaps may tame them.

     Keeper, yon old dotard smoke,
160   Sweetly snoring in his cloak.
Who is he? 'Tis humdrum Wynne,
Half encompassed by his kin:
There observe the tribe of Bingham,
For he never fails to bring 'em;
While he sleeps the whole debate,
They submissive round him wait;
Yet would gladly see the hunks
In his grave, and search his trunks:
See they gently twitch his coat,
170   Just to yawn, and give his vote;
Always firm in his vocation,
For the court against the nation.

Those are Allens, Jack and Bob,
First in every wicked job,
Son and brother to a queer,
Brainsick brute, they call a peer.
We must give them better quarter,
For their ancestor trod mortar;
And at Howth, to boast his fame,
180   On a chimney cut his name.

There sit Clements, Dilkes, and Harrison,
How they swagger from their garrison.
Such a triplet could you tell
Where to find on this side Hell?

Harrison, and Dilkes, and Clements,
Souse them in their own excrements.
Every mischief's in their hearts,
If they fail 'tis want of parts.

Bless us, Morgan! Art thou there, man?
190　Bless mine eyes! Art thou the chairman?
Chairman to yon damned committee?
Yet I look on thee with pity.
Dreadful sight! What, learned Morgan,
Metamorphosed to a gorgon!
For thy horrid looks, I own,
Half convert me to a stone.
Hast thou been so long at school,
Now to turn a factious tool!
Alma Mater was thy mother,
200　Every young divine thy brother.
Thou a disobedient varlet,
Treat thy mother like a harlot?
Thou, ungrateful to thy teachers,
Who are all grown reverend preachers!
Morgan! Would it not surprise one?
Turn thy nourishment to poison!
When you walk among your books,
They reproach you with their looks;
Bind them fast, or from the shelves
210　They'll come down to right themselves:
Homer, Plutarch, Virgil, Flaccus,
All in arms prepare to back us:
Soon repent, or put to slaughter
Every Greek and Roman author.
While you in your faction's phrase
Send the clergy all to graze;
And to make your project pass,
Leave them not a blade of grass.

How I want thee, humorous Hogart!
220 Thou, I hear, a pleasant rogue art;
Were but you and I acquainted,
Every monster should be painted;
You should try your graving tools
On this odious group of fools;
Draw the beasts as I describe 'em,
Form their features, while I gibe them;
Draw them like, for I assure you,
You will need no caricatura;
Draw them so that we may trace
230 All the soul in every face.
Keeper, I must now retire,
You have done what I desire:
But I feel my spirits spent,
With the noise, the sight, the scent.'

'Pray be patient, you shall find
Half the best are still behind:
You have hardly seen a score,
I can show two hundred more.'
'Keeper, I have seen enough,'
240 Taking then a pinch of snuff;
I concluded, looking round 'em,
May their God, the Devil confound 'em.

An Epigram on Scolding

Great folks are of a finer mould;
Lord! how politely they can scold;
While a coarse English tongue will itch,
For whore and rogue; and dog and bitch.

Verses Made for the Women Who Cry Apples, etc.

APPLES

Come buy my fine wares,
Plums, apples, and pears,
A hundred a penny,
In conscience too many,
Come, will you have any;
My children are seven,
I wish them in heaven,
My husband's a sot,
With his pipe and his pot,
10   Not a farthing will gain 'em,
And I must maintain 'em.

ASPARAGUS

Ripe 'sparagrass,
Fit for lad or lass,
To make their water pass:
    O, 'tis a pretty picking
    With a tender chicken.

ONIONS

Come, follow me by the smell,
Here's delicate onions to sell,
I promise to use you well.
20   They make the blood warmer,
You'll feed like a farmer:
For this is every cook's opinion,
No savoury dish without an onion;
But lest your kissing should be spoiled,
Your onions must be thoroughly boiled;
        Or else you may spare

Your mistress a share,
The secret will never be known;
She cannot discover
30   The breath of her lover,
But think it as sweet as her own.

OYSTERS

Charming oysters I cry,
My masters come buy,
So plump and so fresh,
So sweet is their flesh,
No Colchester oyster,
Is sweeter and moister,
Your stomach they settle,
And rouse up your mettle,
40   They'll make you a dad
Of a lass or a lad;
And Madam your wife
They'll please to the life;
Be she barren, be she old,
Be she slut, or be she scold,
Eat my oysters, and lie near her,
She'll be fruitful, never fear her.

HERRINGS

Be not sparing,   ⎫
Leave off swearing,   ⎬
50   Buy my herring   ⎭
Fresh from Malahide,
Better ne'er was tried.
Come eat 'em with pure fresh butter and mustard,
Their bellies are soft, and as white as a custard.
Come, sixpence a dozen to get me some bread,
Or, like my own herrings, I soon shall be dead.

ORANGES

Come, buy my fine oranges, sauce for your veal,
And charming when squeezed in a pot of brown ale.
Well roasted, with sugar and wine in a cup,
60   They'll make a sweet bishop when gentlefolks sup.

Swift's Epitaph in St Patrick's Cathedral

WRITTEN BY HIMSELF IN LATIN

Hic depositum est Corpus
JONATHAN SWIFT S.T.D.
Hujus Ecclesiae Cathedralis
Decani,
Ubi saeva indignatio
Ulterius
Cor lacerare nequit.
Abi Viator
Et imitare, si poteris,
Strenuum pro virili
Libertatis Vindicatorem
Obiit 19° Die Mensis Octobris
A.D. 1745 Anno Aetatis 78.

W. B. Yeats's Version of Swift's Epitaph

Swift has sailed into his rest;
Savage indignation there
Cannot lacerate his breast.
Imitate him if you dare,
World-besotted traveller; he
Served human liberty.

NOTES

p. 23, 'The Humble Petition of Frances Harris'   Probably written in
1701. From 1699 to April 1701 Swift was chaplain to the Earl of
Berkeley, Lord Justice of Ireland, and lived with the family in Dublin
Castle where the poem is set. Frances Harris was a waiting woman to
Lady Berkeley   *Lady Betty's chamber:* Lady Elizabeth Berkeley
(1680–1769), the Earl's second daughter, who married Sir John
Germaine in 1706. She was one of Swift's most loyal friends   *Mrs
Dukes:* a footman's wife   *Whittle:* the Earl's valet   *Dame
Wadgar:* the old deaf housekeeper   *Lord Collway's folks:* a refer-
ence to the Earl of Galway, who, with the Earl of Berkeley, was being
succeeded as Lord Justice by the Primate and the Earl of Drogheda.
(The Lords Justice carried out the office of King's representative
in Dublin.) He was a Lord Justice for a second period from
1715–16   *Lord Dromedary:* the Earl of Drogheda (*c.*1650–1714),
who, with the Primate, was to succeed as a caretaker Lord Justice in
1701   *Cary:* the clerk of the kitchen   *the steward:* Ferris, whom
Swift called 'that beast' and 'a scoundrel dog'; see *Journal to Stella*, 21
December 1710   *Lady Shrewsbury:* probably the widow (d.1702) of
the fourteenth Earl   *three skips of a louse:* a saying frequently
repeated by Mrs Harris (F, 1735)   *service is no inheritance ...
money can't go without hands:* proverbial expressions, the last based on
'nothing is stolen without hands'   *Bedlam:* for Bedlamite, an
inmate of Bethlehem Hospital, London – hence, a mad person
cunning-man: a fortune teller, a conjuror, one who professed to be able
to discover stolen goods   *the chaplain:* Swift   *cast a nativity:*
draw a horoscope   *Mrs Nab:* name used for an abigail, a female
servant   *a learned divine:* Dr John Bolton, preferred to the Deanery
of Derry which Swift thought he ought to have had himself   *Harry:*

'a cant word of my Lord and Lady to Mrs Harris' (*F*, 1735)   *shall ever pray:* a formula for ending a petition

p. 26, 'Baucis and Philemon'   This poem was probably written in 1706. Swift revised it, on Joseph Addison's advice, in 1708. Swift was 'often wont to mention: that in a poem of not two hundred lines ['Baucis and Philemon'] Mr. Addison made him blot out fourscore, add fourscore, and alter fourscore' (Delany, *Observations* (1754), p. 19). It is based on Ovid, *Metamorphoses* VIII, 626-724, an account of a visit made by Jupiter and Apollo, in disguise, to the earth   *village ... Kent:* 'a village hard by Rixham' in Swift's draft of the poem, in the Pierpont Morgan Library, New York. Swift may have had Wrotham in mind   *Goody:* a contracted form of Goodwife, the equivalent of Mistress or Mrs   *jack:* this turned the spit which was used for roasting meat   *Joan of France ... English Moll, Fair Rosamund ... Robin Hood ... 'Little Children in the Wood':* various folk ballads, printed as chapbooks with crude woodcuts. Joan of France was Joan of Arc. English Moll was Mary Ambree, a female soldier, reputed to have fought at the siege of Ghent in 1584. Rosamund Clifford, daughter of Lord Clifford, was Henry II's mistress. *The Children in the Wood* was probably a domestic tragedy of 1599   *Right Divine:* the Divine Right of Kings   *coifs:* close-fitting skull caps   *pinners:* coifs with straps hanging down on each side, worn by women of rank   *colbertine:* open-work lace, French in origin, named after the French minister Jean Baptiste Colbert (1619-85)   *grogram:* a silk fabric, sometimes blended with wool or mohair   *forehead sprout:* a cuckold was supposed to sprout horns   *Goodman:* a yeoman, here equivalent to Goody, e.g. Mr

p. 31, 'An Elegy on the Supposed Death of Partridge, the Almanac Maker'   Written in 1708. John Partridge (1644-1715) was a shoemaker turned almanac writer, whose death Swift foretold in a hoax, *Predictions for the Year 1708*, later publishing *The Accomplishment of the First of Mr Bickerstaff's Predictions*, which gave details of Partridge's death. Partridge issued denials of his death but it was widely believed   *Bickerstaff:* a name adopted by Richard Steele (see note on him, p. 238) when he started the *Tatler* in 1709. The name probably

came from Lancashire; the family moved to Antrim in the Cromwel-
lian period, and a later dramatist, Isaac Bickerstaff (1733–1808), was
born in Dublin　　*Aries:* a sign of the Zodiac, the ram　　*cobbling:*
'Partridge was a cobbler' (*F,* 1735)　　*optics:* eyes, but with a hint of
the other meaning, a telescope or optic glass　　*list:* a strip of cloth
Boötes: the constellation of the Waggoner (which Partridge had
actually called 'Boots'), a transliteration of the Greek word　　*hornèd
moon:* an allusion to crescent-shaped clasps on the shoes of Patricians
hung by geometry: hung stiffly　　*barometry:* barometric observa-
tion, here probably weather-forecasting　　*boding:* sinister, fore-
boding　　*leather:* a reference to bats' wings　　*Mercury ... Venus:*
mercury was used in the treatment of venereal disease　　*Lucian:*
Greek writer (*c.*AD 117–80), born in Syria, an advocate whose satire,
notably in his *True Histories,* showed up the gulf between current
behaviour and the old beliefs and philosophies. He parodied the
current fashion for romances and fantastic adventures. The reference
here is to *Lucian, Opera* XI, 17　　*Philip:* Philip of Macedon
(281–226 BC), the father of Alexander the Great　　*the Bull:* the
constellation of Taurus　　*Argo:* the boat in which Jason sailed on his
expedition to obtain the Golden Fleece　　*Ariadne:* daughter of
Minos, King of Crete, she helped Theseus to escape from the labyrinth.
He subsequently deserted her and Bacchus later gave her a crown of
seven stars, made into a constellation after her death　　*ends:* a length
of thread pointed with a bristle　　*Sagittarius:* the constellation of
the archer Sagittarius　　*Vulcan ... his wife:* he was married to
Venus and cuckolded by Mars　　*Virgo:* the constellation of the
Virgin　　*strain a point:* this has sexual implications　　*She'll strain
... signs will be thirteen:* a footnote in the broadside supplies *Tibi
brachia contrahit Ingens Scorpius, etc.* (*F,* 1735), a quotation from
Virgil, *Georgics* I, 34–5: 'The blazing Scorpion already contracts his
arms of his own accord, and leaves you more than an equal proportion
of the sky'. This passage is addressed to Caesar (Augustus), who may
make himself into a new constellation in the vacant space 'between
Erigone and the Scorpion's pursuing claws'　　*But do not shed ... an
old friend:* these lines were omitted in *Miscellanies in Prose and Verse*
(1711) and subsequent editions　　*But do not shed:* the broadside
supplies as a footnote '*Sed nec in Arctoo sedem tibi legeris orbe*', etc.,

from Lucan, *De Bello Civili* I, 53   *Nor look asquint...:* the
broadside supplies as footnote a continuation (l. 55) of the passage
from Lucan '*Neve tuam videas oblique sidere Romam*'. The three lines,
addressed to Caesar (in a flattering passage telling him nature will let
him determine what deity he wishes to be and where he will establish
his throne when he seeks the stars at last), can be translated as 'Do not
choose your seat either in the Northern region or where the hot sky of
the opposing South sinks down: from these places your light would
look aslant at your city of Rome.'

p. 35, 'A Description of the Morning'   First published in Steele's
Tatler, 30 April 1709. It is a town eclogue, an ironic urban pastoral
to trace The kennel-edge: 'to find old nails' (F, 1735)   *Brickdust
Moll:* she was probably selling powdered brick for scouring   *to steal
for fees:* gaolers let out their prisoners to earn money, to pay the gaolers
for privileges and subsistence

p. 35, 'A Description of a City Shower'   First published in Steele's
Tatler, 17 October 1710. Swift thought it twice as good as 'A
Description of the Morning' (p. 35)   *the sink:* the sewer   *aches:*
then pronounced 'aitches'   *quean:* hussy   *Flirts:* flicks
'Twas doubtful ... dust: F, 1735, misquoting, draws attention to the
parallel with Sir Samuel Garth's *The Dispensary*, canto V, 176, ' 'Twas
doubtful which was sea, and which was sky'   *Sole coat ... stain:*
Miscellanies (1711) reads 'His only coat, where dust impressed with
rain / Roughen the nap and leave a mingled stain'   *daggled:*
splattered   *Templar:* a law student   *Triumphant Tories:* a large
Tory majority was returned at the general election in early October
1710. Robert Harley (1661–1724; see note on him, p. 213) formed a
Tory administration as Chancellor of the Exchequer and then as Lord
Treasurer. He was made Earl of Oxford after he recovered from being
stabbed by a French spy in 1711   *bully:* possibly a reference to
boisterous gangs of young men (of whom the slightly later so-called
Mohocks were typical)   *Laocoon:* a reference to Virgil, *Aeneid* II,
40–56   *From Smithfield, or St Pulchre's:* drainage from Smithfield
market met, at Holborn Viaduct, the drainage from the area of St
Sepulchre's Church, running down Snow Hill; the joint flow (contain-

ing offal from the market and butchers' shops) then ran into the Fleet
Ditch, then open and navigable at Holborn Bridge on the Thames

p. 37, 'Corinna'   Written in 1712 (*F*, 1735), and probably about Mrs
Mary de la Rivière Manley (1663-1724), daughter of Sir Roger
Manley and married to her cousin John Manley (apparently bigam-
ously). She became the mistress of the Warden of the Fleet Prison, John
Tilly, and of John Barber, a printer who became Lord Mayor of London.
She wrote *The Secret Memoirs from Atlantis* (1709), an erotic *roman-
à-clef* and political allegory. In 1710 her *Memoirs of Europe* were
published, and in 1711 she succeeded Swift as editor of the *Examiner*.
She wrote several plays and the largely autobiographical *Adventures of
Rivella* (1714)   *Marries for love ... runs in debt:* her love affairs
were well known; she may have been imprisoned for debt   *Curll's:*
Edmund Curll (1683-1747), a London bookseller notorious for piracy,
disliked by both Swift and Pope. He published obscene books as well as
standard works. Arbuthnot said his biographies added a new terror to
death   *Her commonplace book ... Utopia:* these four lines were
omitted in *F*, 1735, but included in *Miscellanies. The Last Volume*
(1727, for 1728)   *Atlantis ... Memoirs of the New Utopia:* Mrs
Manley's anti-Whig *New Atlantis* was published in 1709, her *Memoirs
of Europe* in 1710. It has been suggested that the *Memoirs of the New
Utopia* may refer to *Memoirs of a Certain Island Adjacent to the
Kingdom of Utopia* (1724-5) by Mrs Eliza Haywood (*c.*1693-1756),
but the date of publication seems to rule this out

p. 38, 'Cadenus and Vanessa'   Probably written at Windsor in the
autumn of 1713, and first published in 1726 (though it had not been
intended for publication). Cadenus is an anagram of Decanus (Latin for
Dean) and Swift had been installed as Dean of St Patrick's Cathedral,
Dublin, in 1713. Vanessa was Esther or Hester Vanhomrigh (1687/
8-1723). Swift made up the name from the Van of Vanhomrigh and
Essy, a diminutive of Esther. He also called her Mishessy. After the
death of her father, an Irish merchant of Dutch origin, appointed
Commissary-General, she moved to London in 1707 with her mother
and other members of the family. Swift became a visitor to their home
and taught Vanessa rather as he had earlier taught Stella (Esther

Johnson). His relationship with Vanessa, however, did not follow the pattern of his friendship with Stella. Vanessa had a passionate nature; he rebuked her for indiscretion, but, despite his advice, she followed him to Ireland in 1714. She lived at Celbridge Abbey, County Kildare, situated on the Liffey some miles from Dublin. After various stormy scenes, she died in 1723. Some have suggested that references to coffee in their correspondence suggest a sexual relationship, but this is mere surmise. What caused their final break is not known, though there is a suggestion that it was a letter from Vanessa to Stella (possibly enquiring if she and the Dean were married) which Swift silently threw on the table in her house in Celbridge before leaving. The ultimately unhappy relationship remains a mystery   *Pleading ... queen:* in a court of love presided over by Venus, goddess of love, of whom there was a cult in Cyprus   *His altar ... smokes:* worshippers were no longer sacrificing to him   *His mother's aid:* Venus was Cupid's mother   *equipage:* possibly a coach and horses with servants in which to parade in the park in London (in the Ring at Hyde Park or in the Mall in St James's Park)   *toilets:* dressing tables; here probably making their toilets, or getting up and then going to bed   *'Nor further those deponents . . .':* legal terminology   *the sea, my place of birth:* in classical mythology Venus sprang from the foam of the sea   *daggled:* splattered   *so nice:* so closely balanced   *their king's permission:* Apollo's   *the Graces:* the three sister goddesses who represented beauty and charm   *Fleta's, Bractons, Cokes:* legal authorities: *Fleta*, a Latin treatise (*c.*1290), edited by John Selden in 1647 and so called because the anonymous author was in the Fleet Prison in London; Henry de Bracton (d.1268) wrote *De Legibus et Consuetudinibus Angliae*; Sir Edward Coke (1552–1634) wrote *Four Institutes* and *Law Reports*, which became basic texts for students of law   *Ovid:* Publius Ovidius Naso (43 BC–AD 17), the Roman poet whose *Amores* or *Ars Amatoria* are probably intended here   *Virgil ... Dido's case:* Virgil told the story of Dido and Aeneas in *Aeneid* I–IV; she was the Queen of Carthage who fell in love with Aeneas when he was shipwrecked on the Carthaginian coast. By order of the gods, he forsook her and she killed herself   *Tibullus's reports:* Albius Tibullus (*c.*50 BC–19 BC), a Roman elegiac poet who wrote about his love for Delia, and others   *Cowley ... Waller:* Abraham Cowley

(1618–87) and Edmund Waller (1606–87) had been influential love poets   *bills, and answers:* written submissions of grievances (bills) and defences (answers)   *Demur, imparlance, and essoign:* requests for delays in legal proceedings. Demurrer admits an opponent's statements but denies that legal relief is entitled, and asks for this point to be decided; imparlance asks for an extension of time in answering a case, allowing for a theoretical settlement; and essoign, or essoin, offers an excuse for not appearing in court at the appointed time   *Clio:* the muse of history   *Lucina:* Juno, Queen of Heaven, in her capacity as goddess of childbirth   *amaranthine:* never fading   *Titan:* the sun   *Pallas:* Pallas Athene (Minerva in Latin mythology), goddess of wisdom   *my own:* Cupid; who carried a bow   *Olympus:* Mount Olympus in Greece, the home of the gods and goddesses *five thousand pound:* Vanessa inherited a quarter of her father's estate of £20,000, but all the estate came to her as her mother, brothers and sister died before her   *the martial maid:* Pallas Athene, who was also a goddess of war   *by Homer told . . . scold:* possibly a reference to the episode in *Iliad* XXI, where Hera abuses Artemis and boxes her ears   *Atalanta's star:* Atalanta was a virgin who did not want to marry, and killed her suitors   *a new Italian:* an opera singer *purlieus of St James:* the fashionable area in London's West End, near St James's Palace   *dishabille:* fashionable negligent undress *That present times . . .:* Harold Williams, *Swift's Poems* II, 697, suggests that Swift had in mind a letter, written on 23 June 1713, by Vanessa in which she praised the ancients 'who used to sacrifice everything for the good of the commonwealth; but now our greatest men will, at any time, give up their country out of pique, and that for nothing' (*Correspondence* II, 47)   *Montaigne:* Michel Eyquem de Montaigne (1533–92), French essayist and sceptical philosopher *Mrs Susan:* a name often used for a maid   *the Ring:* in Hyde Park, where fashionable people drove in their carriages   *breaks:* breaks up   *Tunbridge:* Tunbridge Wells, in south-west Kent, a fashionable spa and social centre, particularly popular in the seventeenth and eighteenth centuries   *rallied:* made fun of   *old Queen Bess:* Elizabeth I of England   *red:* rouge   *hoop:* a whalebone stiffener for a petticoat   *Flanders lace:* it was popular and often smuggled into England   *colbertine:* open lacework, French in origin, named after the French Minister, Jean Baptiste Colbert (1619–88)   *a mask:* masks were frequently worn to protect the wearer's complexion *patch her face:* to stick a beauty spot, usually a patch of black silk, on the face or on exposed flesh to emphasize contrasts between the black patch and the complexion or to hide blemishes   *ombre:* a card game for three players   *Plutarch's Morals:* Mestrius Plutarchus (*c.*AD 46 –*c.*120), a Greek historian, biographer and philosopher. The *Morals* are short treatises on various subjects; he is also known for his *Parallel Lives*, forty-six portraits of great characters of the ages preceding his own   *his poetic works:* possibly a reference to the *Miscellanies in Prose and Verse* of 1711, or else Vanessa may have asked to read his poems   *not in years a score:* probably a typically vague comment (this would set the poem back to 1707 or 1708 if regarded as accurate, since Vanessa was born in 1687/8)   *a gown of forty-four:* Swift was this age between November 1711 and 1712   *She wished her tutor were her lover . . . a secret glance:* these eight lines are omitted in *F*, 1735; they were included in the London edition published by James Roberts in 1726 but were later suppressed   *'a bite':* a hoax, joke, deception   *. . . imbibed:* the following two lines, 'From him transfused into her breast / With pleasure not to be expressed' are omitted in *F*, 1735 but were included in the 1726 version published by James Roberts   *Construing:* translating and explaining   *equipages:* in their full array   *project:* a projector was, implicitly, irresponsible. Venus had been in this case   *Coram Regina prox' die Martis:* 'Before the Queen on Tuesday next' (that is, in the Court of the Queen's Bench)   *humbly showing:* the introductory formula in a petition. Cf. the 'Humbly showeth' of 'The Humble Petition of Frances Harris', p. 23   *'Oyez!':* a call by a court officer (or the public crier) to command attention and silence; it was usually repeated thrice

p. 64, 'The Author upon Himself'   Written during Swift's stay (from 3 June to 16 August 1714) with his friend the Rev. John Geree (d. 1761), the rector of Letcombe Bassett in Berkshire, who came from Farnham, near Moor Park, and was close to Sir William Temple's family. Swift left London on 31 May 1714, despairing of reconciling Oxford (see note on *Harley* below) and Bolingbroke (see note on *St John* below), and stayed in the country until mid-August, Queen Anne having died on 1 August   *hag:* Elizabeth Percy, Duchess of Somerset (1667–1722); the daughter of the Earl of Northumberland. She married the Earl of Ogle at the age of twelve; widowed a year later, she married Thomas Thynne in 1681. He was murdered in 1682, possibly by her lover, the Count of Königsmark. In the same year she then married a Whig politician, the Duke of Somerset. Later she became a favourite of Queen Anne and was appointed Mistress of the Robes. Swift thought that she blocked his preferment; she had been enraged by his poem 'The Windsor Prophecy' (1711), which refers to her as 'Carrots' and refers also to the story that she had suggested the murder of her husband Thomas Thynne   *A crazy prelate:* Dr John Sharp (1645–1714), who became Archbishop of York in 1691. He advised Queen Anne on preferments, and Swift thought that his own career in the Church was hindered by Sharp because of *A Tale of a Tub*, the author of which was unfit, according to Sharp, for a bishopric   *a royal prude:* Anne, Queen of England (1665–1714), daughter of James II, who married George, Prince of Denmark, in 1683 and succeeded to the throne in 1702. She disliked Swift, particularly because of *A Tale of a Tub* and 'The Windsor Prophecy'   *Child's or Truby's:* 'a coffee-house and tavern near St Paul's, much frequented by the clergy' (*F*, 1735)   *Harley:* Robert Harley (1661–1724), Secretary of State 1704–8, formed a Tory administration in 1710 after a successful general election. He became the first Earl of Oxford in 1711; dismissed in 1714, he was impeached and released after two years' imprisonment in the Tower of London. He was a friend of Swift and Pope and began the Harleian collection of books and manuscripts, now housed in the British Library. It consists of over 7000 volumes of manuscripts, 350,000 pamphlets and 50,000 books. Augmented by Harley's son, it was bought in 1753 by Parliament after his death   *Windsor:* the Queen lived in Windsor Castle   *St John:* 'the Secretary of State, now Lord Bolingbroke, the most universal genius in Europe' (*F*, 1735). Henry St John (1678–1751), created first Viscount Bolingbroke, shared the leadership of the Tory party with Harley. He negotiated the Treaty of Utrecht in 1713. He was plotting a Jacobite restoration when Queen Anne died, was dismissed and fled to the Continent, returning to England in 1723, hoping to be readmitted to political life. Disappointed, he spent from 1735 to 1742 in France. His works included *A*

Letter on the Spirit of Patriotism (1749) and *The Idea of a Patriot King* (1740)   *Finch:* 'Late Earl of Nottingham who made a speech in the House of Lords against the author' (*F*, 1735). Daniel Finch (1647-1730) succeeded to the earldom in 1682 and became sixth Earl of Winchelsea in 1725; he held public office from 1681 to 1693, and was Secretary of State from 1702 to 1704. He led the High Church party. Lord President of the Council in 1714, he was dismissed in 1716, having advocated more lenient treatment of the Jacobite Lords after the 1715 Rising. Known as 'Dismal', he made dull speeches, in one of which he alluded to 'a certain Dean ... hardly suspected of being a Christian' *Walpole and Aislabie:* 'Those two made speeches in the House of Commons against the Author, although the latter professed much friendship for him' (*F*, 1735). Sir Robert Walpole (1676-1745) was created Earl of Orford in 1742 when he resigned office. A Whig, he was Secretary-at-War 1708-10 and became Treasurer of the Navy in 1710; in 1712 he was expelled from the House and sent to the Tower of London for alleged corruption. After the accession of George I he became Chancellor of the Exchequer and First Lord of the Treasury in 1715, a post from which he resigned in 1717 but resumed in 1720. He was Britain's first Prime Minister (1721-42); he secured a Whig majority in the House of Commons by bribery. Swift and he were diametrically opposed to each other; he was a shrewd, unscrupulous manipulator and manager. John Aislabie was Tory MP for Ripon, Yorkshire, but in 1713-14 was in league with the Whigs   *Perkin:* Perkin Warbeck (1474-99), a Flemish impostor, a pretender to the throne, who was executed in the Tower of London on a charge of attempting to escape from imprisonment. (He had previously surrendered on promise of a pardon)   *York ... Lambeth ... treatise:* a reference to Swift's *A Tale of a Tub*, in which he claimed he attacked corruption in religion, not religion itself. Lambeth is the residence of the Archbishop of Canterbury. See note on *A crazy prelate* above *sues for pardon:* 'It is known that his Grace sent a message to the Author, to desire his pardon, and that he was very sorry for what he had said and done' (*F*, 1735)   *Madam Königsmark ... her murdered spouse:* see note above on the *hag*, the Duchess of Somerset   *the vengeful Scot:* 'the proclamation was against the Author of a pamphlet, called *The Public Spirit of the Whigs* [1714] against which the Scotch

Lords complained' (*F*, 1735). After a complaint in the House of Lords, the printer and publisher were arrested and a reward of £300 offered for identification of the author of this 'seditious libel', an attack on Richard Steele (see note on him, p. 238), though it was well known that Swift had written it. Proceedings were dropped on a technicality *Delaware:* 'Lord Delaware [John West, sixth Baron De La Warr or Delaware (1663–1723), a courtier], then Treasurer of the Household, always caressing the Author at Court. But during the trial of the printers before the House of Lords, and while the proclamation still hung over the Author, his Lordship would not seem to know him, till the danger was past' (*F*, 1735)   *The Scottish nation . . . their friend:* 'The Scotch Lords treated and visited the Author more after the proclamation than before, except the Duke of Argyle, who would never be reconciled' (*F*, 1735). John Campbell, second Duke of Argyle (1680–1743), a soldier as well as politician, was active in the suppression of the 1715 Rising; he became a Field Marshal. Swift had originally liked him

p. 66, 'In Sickness'   Swift arrived in Dublin on 24 August 1714, deeply depressed by political events; this poem was written in October 1714 and reflects his melancholy at leaving his friends in England, his disappointment about his own prospects now that the political party with which he had been associated had lost power – he was being attacked in various lampoons   *kind Arbuthnot:* John Arbuthnot (1667–1735) became a close friend of Swift after they met in 1710. A member of the Scriblerus Club, he was Queen Anne's physician, and wrote *The History of John Bull* (1712), a Tory satire, a collection of pamphlets issued anonymously which argued for the ending of the war with France. John Bull, 'an honest, plain-dealing fellow', a 'boon companion', represents England; Lewis Baboon, Louis XIV of France; Lord Strutt, Philip of Spain; and Nicholas Frog, the Dutch. Swift means here that Arbuthnot does not sufficiently look after his own interests and career   *burden: F*, 1735 gives the older form 'burthen'

p. 67, 'Horace, Lib. 2, Sat. 6'   Probably written at Letcombe Bassett in early August 1714; it was first printed in 1727   *terrace walk . . . a wood:* Swift had been presented to the living of Laracor, County

Meath (and allied parishes) in 1700, and put much work into improving the grounds. In 1714 he found that his trees had been carried off by a spiteful neighbour   *rood:* a quarter of an acre   *this side Trent:* south of the river Trent; that is, nearer to London   *the Channel:* St George's Channel, that part of the Irish Sea between Ireland and Wales   *Lewis:* Erasmus Lewis (1670–1754), a Welshman and diplomat who was Under-Secretary of State in 1710. A friend of Swift and other members of the Scriblerus Club, he was a client of Harley (see note on him, p. 213) and arranged Swift's first meeting with him in October 1710   *The toil, the danger:* given favourable winds to or from Holyhead, it took about eight days to accomplish the journey between London and Dublin   *five hundred pound:* what it cost Swift to install himself in the Deanery of St Patrick's Cathedral, Dublin   *levee day:* when the Minister received petitioners and other visitors   *ribbons blue and green:* the insignia of the Order of the Garter (revived by Harley) and the Order of the Star   *my Lord Bolingbroke ... warrant:* see note on *St John,* p. 213. The Secretaries of State signed official documents   *Harley:* see note on him, p. 213. Swift first met Harley on 4 October 1710   *country signs:* Harold Williams, *Swift's Poems,* I, 201, gives two lines which Stella added in her transcript of the poem (now in Woburn Abbey): 'And mark at Brentford how they spell / Hear is good Eal and Bear to cell'   *Pope:* Alexander Pope (1688–1744), introduced to London literary life by the playwright William Wycherley (1641–1715), was a friend of Joseph Addison (see note on *Addison ... distressed,* p. 238) but drifted away from his circle and became a member of the Scriblerus Club. His translations of Homer were financially rewarding and were most influential. His range included his early pastorals, *The Rape of the Lock* (a mock-epic), *Windsor Forest, An Epistle to Dr Arbuthnot, The Dunciad, An Essay on Man,* miscellaneous satires and the two satirical dialogues of *One Thousand Seven Hundred and Thirty Eight*   *Parnell:* The Rev Thomas Parnell (1679–1718), an Irish poet and member of the Scriblerus Club, who became Archdeacon of Clogher in Ireland. His poems were published posthumously in 1722   *Gay:* John Gay (1685–1732), poet and dramatist, a member of the Scriblerus Club. He wrote *Trivia* (1716), *Fables* (1727) and *The Beggar's Opera* (1728)   *Staines:* then a market town in Middlesex, on the London side of

Windsor, from which it is about six miles distant; it is about fifteen miles from Hyde Park Corner in London   *Windsor:* one of the Queen's residences, Windsor Castle, in Berkshire   *Charing Cross:* in London, where royal proclamations were read   *the Emperor treat:* the Emperor of Austria, Charles III of Spain, who succeeded his brother Joseph I (1678–1711) as Emperor of Austria. He was not involved in the negotiations for peace in 1713

p. 71, 'The Author's Manner of Living'   Probably written between 1715 and 1718 in Swift's early occupation of the Deanery, to judge by two of his letters, to Pope of 28 June 1715 and to Charles Ford of 20 December 1718. The poem was first published in *F*, 1746, VIII, 320   *scraps . . . board-wages:* servants' wages paid for them to spend on food, rather than living on scraps left over from Swift's meals

p. 71, 'Mary the Cook-Maid's Letter to Dr Sheridan'   Probably written about October 1718, first published in *Miscellanies. The Third Volume* (1732)   *Dr Sheridan:* Thomas Sheridan (1687–1738), clergyman and schoolmaster. He had a school in Capel Street, Dublin, and a country house at Quilca, County Cavan, where Swift was a visitor. In 1735 Sheridan moved to another school at Cavan. He was unhappily married and usually in dire financial straits. He was a good scholar and translated Persius and Juvenal. One of his sons, Thomas (1719–88), was an actor and author, the father of Richard Brinsley Sheridan, the dramatist and theatre-owner, orator and MP (1751–1816)   *Knave in your teeth:* an expression of defiance   *hoddy-doddy:* a person with a dumpy figure   *called you goose:* probably a reference to Swift's poem 'Sheridan, a Goose'   *'sweetheart':* Swift called his cook thus; she was, according to Delany (*Observations* (1754), pp. 186–7), 'large and robust, with a face disfigured by smallpox and wrinkled by age'   *concerned:* drunk   *come-rogues:* comrades   *eat grass on his grave:* based on a proverbial expression, 'to eat of the goose that will graze on your grave', meaning to outlive someone. This is a reference to the last line of Sheridan's poem 'A Highlander Once Fought', included in *The Whimsical Medley* (1808). The comparison of Sheridan to a goose is part of a series of squibs and rejoinders between Swift and Sheridan   *to tell truth . . . Devil:* a proverbial saying   *Saunders:* Swift's highly regarded servant, Alexander McGee, whom he called Saunders, 'the butler' (*F*, 1735), who died in 1722 in his twenty-ninth year. Swift placed a tablet in his memory in St Patrick's Cathedral   *dishclout:* a remark made to men or boys who interfered in kitchen matters   *written hand:* cursive script with the letters linked

p. 73, 'Stella's Birthday, 1718'   This poem, written in 1718[/19], is the first of the poems Swift wrote annually to Stella on her birthdays (13 March). Stella was the name Swift gave to Hester (her baptismal name, but she called herself Esther) Johnson (1681–1728), whom he first met in 1689 at Moor Park, Sir William Temple's home in Surrey. 'Swift's most valuable friend', she was the daughter of Edward Johnson and his wife Bridget, who was housekeeper at Moor Park. In 1701 Stella moved to Dublin with her companion Rebecca Dingley, Swift thinking that her money would go further in Ireland. Stella's health deteriorated after 1722. When she died on 28 January 1728, Swift in his misery could not bring himself to attend her funeral in St Patrick's Cathedral and began his *Memoir* of her life in the Deanery as her interment was taking place. Some scholars have suggested that she was a natural child of Sir William Temple; some have suggested that she was secretly married to Swift. The poem was first published in *Miscellanies. The Last Volume* (1727, for 1728)   *thirty-four:* she was in fact thirty-eight in March 1719. Swift was usually inaccurate when he mentioned her age   *at sixteen:* she was eight in 1689, but he may allude to his second stay at Moor Park, which began in 1696. Her health improved greatly when she was sixteen and she became, in Swift's words, 'beautiful, graceful, and agreeable'

p. 74, 'A Quiet Life and a Good Name'   Probably written in 1719, this poem may relate to Sheridan's (see note on *Dr Sheridan*, p. 217) marriage, though Swift often wrote upon the subject of ill-assorted couples   *'seek peace and ensue it':* from the Bible, I Peter III:11. Pat Rogers has drawn attention to Thomas Hobbes, *Leviathan* (1651) I, 14 (*Jonathan Swift. The Complete Poems* (1983), p. 687)   *the very nick:* of time   *Od's-buds:* God's blood   *Jamaica ... truck the carrion for tobacco:* Jamaica was associated with the slave trade; truck is to trade; the carrion is a wretched person; and the slaves worked in the tobacco plantations in Jamaica   *a riding:* a skimmity ride, mocking the couple (Thomas Hardy deals with one in chapter 29 of *The Mayor of Casterbridge* (1886))

p. 76, 'Phyllis; or, The Progress of Love'   Probably written in 1719 or 1720, this poem was first published in *Miscellanies. The Last Volume* (1727, for 1728)   *wished:* desired, a vulgarism. Swift underlined 'wish'd' in his copy of the *Miscellanies* and glossed it as a tradesman's phrase   *Crop:* a crop-haired horse   *toilet:* dressing table   *'Marriages ... heaven':* proverbial phrase   *unwholesome:* a reference to venereal disease   *Staines ... the Old Blue Boar:* see note on *Staines*, p. 216. The name of the inn is probably invented

p. 79, 'The Progress of Beauty'   Probably written in 1719, the date heading the poem in Stella's transcript (now at Woburn Abbey), though Faulkner gives 1720; the poem was first published in *Miscellanies. The Last Volume* (1727, for 1728)   *Diana:* goddess of the moon   *Celia:* a name for a nymph in love poetry   *The soot ... and sweat:* these lines were not included in *Miscellanies* nor in *F*, 1735, but are in Stella's transcript   *complexions:* her make-up   *The paint ... her joints:* these lines were not included in *F*, 1735, but are in Stella's transcript   *Venus:* goddess of beauty and love   *White lead:* used in cosmetics; women who used it sometimes suffered the fatal effects of lead poisoning   *Lusitanian dish:* Portuguese ware was popular at the time   *china-ware:* chamber pots   *In the Pall Mall ... fair:* these lines were not included in *Miscellanies* nor in *F*, 1735, but are in Stella's transcript   *Pall Mall:* a fashionable London street, running between the Haymarket and St James's Palace   *the glasses:* the windows of your sedan chair   *Partridge:* John Partridge the astrologer (see note on him, p. 206)   *Cancer:* the sign of the Crab, but Swift here seems to imply cancer of the breast (the 'Milky Way')   *Gadbury* John Gadbury (1627–1704), an astrologer, a predecessor of Partridge, who was accused of conspiracy in 1690 but proved his innocence. He wrote *De Cometis* (1665)   *swain Endymion is not sound:* Endymion, the youth loved by Diana, is not free of venereal disease, is unhealthy   *Mercury's her foe:* Mercury is the planet nearest the sun; mercury, or quicksilver, was used in the treatment of venereal disease, with poisonous side-effects   *Flamsteed:* the Rev. John Flamsteed (1646–1719), the first Astronomer Royal (1675). He made a catalogue of the stars   *Luna's fate:* the moon's   *restore a nose:* one eaten away by syphilis   *Two balls . . . left:* these lines were not included in *Miscellanies*, nor in *F*, 1735, but are in Stella's transcript

p. 83, 'To Stella, who Collected and Transcribed His Poems'   This poem, first published in *Miscellanies. The Last Volume* (1727, for 1728), was dated 1720 in *F*, 1735, but 1723 seems a more likely date *Inigo Jones:* Jones (1573–1652), the great English classical architect, introduced the Palladian style into England; he designed the Queen's House at Greenwich and the Banqueting Hall at Whitehall. He also designed the masques of Ben Jonson and introduced the proscenium arch and moveable scenery into the theatre   *stout:* then a cant word for strong beer (*F*, 1735)   *Chloe, Sylvia, Phyllis, Iris:* conventional names for ladies in love poems   *tippling underground:* in some drinking den in a cellar   *beating flax . . . bloody tracks:* hard labour, a punishment inflicted on those imprisoned in the Bridewell (a house of correction for disorderly women); punishment by the lash *Curll's collection:* see note on *Curll*, p. 209   *Maevius:* a poetaster mentioned in Virgil's *Eclogues* III, 90   *crambo:* rhyme, from the game of crambo in which one player challenges another to find a rhyme *lost her nose:* from the effects of syphilis   *Etna's fire:* Mount Etna is a volcano in Sicily   *Phoebus' rays:* Phoebus Apollo was the god of the sun   *Ajax:* a Greek leader at the siege of Troy, who, when the arms and armour of Achilles were awarded to Odysseus, was so enraged that, Athene having struck him with madness, he killed a flock of sheep, thinking they were Greeks. Ashamed of his action, he committed suicide

p. 88, 'An Elegy on the Much Lamented Death of Mr Demar, the Famous Rich Usurer, who Died the Sixth of July, 1720'   This poem, written in 1720, was first published in two Dublin broadsides; it was reputedly written when Swift and some friends heard the news of Demar's death in Thomas Sheridan's (see note on *Dr Sheridan*, p. 217) house in Capel Street, Dublin   *Mr Demar:* Joseph Demar or Damer

(1630–1720), a commander of horse in the Parliamentary forces in the Civil War, who went to France after the Restoration and then set up as a money-lender in Dublin   *steward:* here Demar is in his capacity as a broker, land agent and lender of money   *Pluto ... shades:* Pluto was ruler of Hades, the Underworld; there tended to be confusion between Pluto and Ploutos, the god of wealth   *pelf:* money, wealth *under hand and seal:* the final formula in a legally binding document (above the signature)   *obligation:* liability to pay a sum of money *a groat:* an English silver coin, worth four pennies, taken out of circulation in the seventeenth century   *interest:* this has several meanings – interest paid on a loan, a legal title, and self-interest *London Tavern:* a Dublin tavern in Fishamble Street (near St Patrick's Cathedral) where Demar transacted his business   *touched the pence:* got money by underhand means   *others touched the pot:* when they were drunk   *shot:* the bill   *Old as he was:* he died at the age of ninety   *moidores:* a Portuguese gold coin used in England at the time   *current:* alive, active   *cried down:* publicly decried *change:* his death (change may also suggest a pun on exchange, a place where brokerage was conducted)   *bills:* of exchange (also bills of mortality, the record of deaths)   *His heirs ... chest:* the broadsides, as well as some early editions, printed these lines as:

> *His heirs for winding-sheet bestowed*
> *His moneybags together sewed.*
> *And that he might securely rest,*
> *Have put his carcass in a chest*

p. 89, 'Verses from Cadenus to Vanessa in Letters'   The title and subtitles have been supplied by the present editor. These three sets of lines were included in two letters, the first two in a letter of 13/20 July 1720 and the third in one of 12 August 1720. They were first published in Sir Walter Scott's edition of Swift's *Correspondence* (1814) XIX, 426–7, 435   *[The verses he promised]: Nymph:* Vanessa. See headnote to 'Cadenus and Vanessa', p. 209   *[An Epigram]:* These lines Swift described as 'an Epigram that concerns you not', in his letter of 13/20 July 1720 to Vanessa   *[Cad is weary of Town]:* Included in a letter of 12 August 1720 to Vanessa   *Cad:* Cadenus, Dean Swift;

see headnote to 'Cadenus and Vanessa', p. 209   *drink my coffee:* some critics have argued that the phrase has a secret sexual meaning

p. 91, 'An Excellent New Song on a Seditious Pamphlet'   These lines were written in the year 1720 and relate to the row caused by Swift's *Proposal for the Universal Use of Irish Manufacture* (1720). The printer, Edward Waters, was found not guilty when charged with sedition, but the Lord Chief Justice sent the jury back nine times; a special verdict was finally reached. The uncancelled version of the preamble read as follows: 'The author having writ a treatise, advising the people of Ireland to wear their own manufactures; that infamous wretch Whitshed prosecuted Waters the printer with so much violence and injustice, that he kept the jury nine hours, and sent them away eleven times, till out of mere weariness they were forced to give a special verdict.' The Chief Justice was William Whitshed (1656–1727). A Whig, he was Solicitor-General for Ireland, 1709, Chief Justice of the King's Bench in Ireland, 1714, and Chief Justice of the Common Pleas, 1726   *Packington's Pound:* a popular sixteenth-century ballad or dance tune (used by Gay in *The Beggar's Opera*)   *tabbies:* watered silk taffeta   *Robert Ballentine:* not known   *journeyman Waters:* see headnote above   *In England the dead:* legislation from 1667 (which was not repealed until 1815) required that corpses should be buried in woollen shrouds; it was a measure to protect the wool trade   *Teague:* slang term for an Irishman (akin to 'Paddy')   *living dog . . . dead lion:* from the Bible, Ecclesiastes IX:4, later a proverbial saying   *horns pull in:* like snails, that is, curtail activity; there is also the suggestion of cuckoldry   *the Dean's book:* Swift's pamphlet, *A Proposal for the Universal Use of Irish Manufacture*   *Corum Nobus:* a vulgar version of the Latin *Coram nobis,* 'before us' (meaning before the Court of the King's Bench)   *swingingly:* immensely, but there is probably a punning suggestion of swinging, hanging   *come off clean:* escape, but with a suggestion of clean linen

p. 92, 'The Run upon the Bankers'   Written in 1720, it was described as 'printed some years ago, and it should seem by the late failure of two Bankers to be somewhat prophetic, it was therefore thought fit to be reprinted' (*F,* 1735). In a letter of 30 August 1734,

Swift commented to the Earl of Oxford that 'two of our chief Bankers have broke for near two hundred thousand pounds', and that others were 'leaving off their business'. The poem may have been prompted by the general events of the period, notably the South Sea Bubble, about which Swift wrote 'The Bubble' in 1720 which ends:

> *The nation too late will find*
> *Computing all their cost and trouble*
> *Directors' promises but wind,*
> *South Sea at best a mighty Bubble*

The earliest printed version was printed as a broadside by Samuel Terry of Cork   *Corrupts and stagnates:* this refers to the view that the blood conveyed corrupt 'humours' through the system; there is a pun on circulation of the blood and of money   *Quakers:* they refused to pay tithes to the established Church   *levee:* a gathering of clients or suitors, here applied to a group of duns, bailiffs or debt collectors   *on the nail:* (slang) at once   *birds . . . jays:* a reference to Aesop's fable about the jay who strutted about wearing peacock's feathers until the other birds stripped him of this finery   *the wisest monarch:* Solomon; see the Bible, Proverbs XXVI:5: 'For riches certainly make themselves wings; they fly away as an eagle towards heaven'   *silver plumes:* the goose quills used by a scrivener in drawing up documents   *The wish of Nero:* according to Suetonius, in *Lives of the Caesars* VI, 10, the Emperor Nero wished he could not write when he had to sign death warrants   *images of wax:* the use of wax images to damage enemies through magic; also the images on seals, pressed into wax to authenticate official or legal documents   *conjuror . . . the bloody bond:* sealed or signed in blood; conjuror suggests an element of magic   *the writing on the wall:* see the Bible, Daniel V:5-30, for the account of the moving hand seen at the feast given by Belshazzar, King of Babylon, writing *'Mene, mene, tekel upharsin'*, which presaged the King's death and the end of his kingdom   *call:* the summons by God on Judgement Day, but also a demand for payment of an instalment   *Weighed . . . found light:* see the Bible, Daniel V:27: 'Thou art weighed in the balance and art found wanting'

p. 95, 'The Description of an Irish Feast'   This poem was described as translated in 1720 (*F*, 1735). Swift asked for a literal translation of Hugh MacGauran's ninety-six line Irish poem 'Plearaca na Ruarcach', which was set to music by Turlough Carolan (1670–1738), the blind poet and composer. Tradition has it that Swift admired Carolan and entertained him at the Deanery in Dublin   *O'Rourk's:* Brian O'Rourke was an Irish chieftain who rebelled against the English in 1580   *Usquebagh:* whiskey (from Irish *uisge beatha, usquebaugh*, the water of life, *uisge* meaning whiskey or water)   *madder:* a wooden vessel, generally of a square shape   *kercher:* handkerchief   *the searcher:* possibly an excise official searching for illegal liquor   *ramping:* romping   *Margery Grinagin:* name of an Irish woman   *Bring straw:* Swift omitted the four preceding lines:

> *Here's to you, dear Mother*
> *I thank you, dear Pat;*
> *Toss this down your throat.*
> *I'm the better of that.*

a Yean: another Irish name for a woman (*F*, 1735); 'a' is vocative   *skenes:* daggers or short swords (*F*, 1735), from the Irish *scian*, a knife or dagger   *Lusk:* a village with a round tower and ancient church about fourteen miles north of Dublin   *castle of Slane:* overlooking the Boyne valley in County Meath, about thirty miles north-west of Dublin   *Carrickdrumrusk:* Carrick-on-Shannon, County Leitrim (Irish, *Cara Droma Ruisg*)   *The Earl of Kildare:* possibly the 'Great Earl' of Kildare, the eighth; or else Gerald Fitzgerald, the eleventh Earl (d.1585)   *Moynalta:* not identified   *their mother:* their nurse or foster-mother   *wame:* belly   *arse:* Swift omitted the racy last twenty-four lines of the Irish poem. They are supplied in Scott's edition, XIV, 140

p. 97, 'Stella's Birthday, 1720'   Probably written in March 1721   *Angel Inn:* a common inn sign   *tapster:* barman   *thirty-six:* Stella was actually forty   *supplies:* provides a substitute for   *to so small: Miscellanies. The Last Volume* (1727, for 1728; also 1731, 1733 and 1736) give 'but to small'   *Nailed to her window . . . invite:* these two lines are omitted in *F*, 1735, but were included in Stella's transcription, now at Woburn Abbey   *beauty's queen:* Venus

p. 99, 'A Satirical Elegy on the Death of a Late Famous General'
This poem was first published in the *Gentleman's Magazine* XXXIV,
244, May 1764   *His Grace:* John Churchill, first Duke of Marl-
borough (1650–1722), the victor of Blenheim, was rewarded hand-
somely. Dismissed from public employment in 1711, he was restored to
his honours on the accession of George I. The text is from *F*, 1765; it
was also published in Deane Swift's edition of *The Works of Dr
Jonathan Swift* (1765). Deane Swift (1707–83) was the son of Swift's
first cousin, also Deane Swift, the son of Godwin Swift (see
Introduction). Swift developed 'a great esteem' for him. Deane Swift
wrote *An Essay on the Life, Writings and Character of Dr Jonathan
Swift* (1755) and was a useful editor of his work   *last loud trump:*
from the Bible, I Corinthians XV:52   *so old:* he was seventy-two
when he died on 16 June 1722   *his funeral ... hearse:* the funeral
took place with great pomp on 9 August 1722, the hearse being drawn
by eight horses *widow's sighs ... orphan's tears:* he was responsible for
many becoming widows and orphans

p. 100, 'The Progress of Marriage'   This poem, written in January
1721/2, was first published in *F*, 1765 and in Deane Swift's edition of
The Works of Dr Jonathan Swift (1765), on which the present text is
based   *A rich divine:* Benjamin Pratt (*c.*1669–1721), a contempor-
ary of Swift at Trinity College, Dublin, and a friend during Harley's (see
note on him, p. 213) administration. He became a Fellow of Trinity
College, Dublin, was appointed Provost in 1710, but replaced by
Richard Baldwin in 1717; he then became Dean of Down   *related
to an Earl:* Lady Phillipa Hamilton, daughter of the sixth
Earl of Abercorn   *the Cyprian queen:* Venus   *bid in form:*
formally invited   *Juno:* Queen of Heaven, protectress of women
Mistress Iris: the messenger of the gods and goddess of the rainbow
Hebe: the goddess of youth; she could restore youth and beauty to the
old   *The swain is rich:* Baldwin (see note on *A rich divine* above)
had considerable means and enjoyed social life; he incurred criticism for
spending too much time in London away from his duties in Dublin as
Provost of his College   *stomach:* appetite   *Her chairmen:* the

men who carried her sedan chair   *the family:* the household
His lady has twelve times miscarried: F, 1765 reads 'Poor Lady Jane has
thrice miscarried'   *the Bath:* Bath, a spa in south-west Eng-
land   *Venus:* she was born of the sea   *Achelous' spring:*
Achelous was a river god. Hercules broke his horn and in compensation
he received the cornucopia of Amalthea, the horn of plenty (Amalthea
was a goat and had suckled Zeus)   *hornèd flood:* the river god
sometimes had a bull's head, and the bull's horn was associated with
fertility   *genial virtue:* procreative energy   *his horn:* a cuckold's
horn   *boiling fountain:* the warm water of the springs at
Bath   *slip:* lose   *season:* at Bath, but there is an implication of its
being the best time to conceive a child   *raffling-rooms:* where a dice
game was played   *toys:* diversions   *the Cross Bath ... others:*
this had a reputation for curing infertility   *ensign:* the lowest rank
of commissioned army officer   *jointure:* her inheritance, a provi-
sion made by a husband for his wife by settling property on her at the
time of marriage for her to use after his death

p. 105, 'Stella at Woodpark'   The poem was probably written at
Woodpark in October 1723. Stella seems to have been staying at
Charles Ford's (see note on *Don Carlos* below) home, Woodpark (about
eleven miles from Dublin on the road to Trim, County Meath), about
the time of Vanessa's death (2 June 1723), while Swift went to the
south of Ireland in June; the exact date of his return is not known, but
it is certain that he was back in Dublin by 20 September. The present
text follows that of *F*, 1735, but that version was a combination of two
poems, of 22 and 76 lines (the first entitled 'Stella's Distress on the 3rd
fatal day of October 1723'; the second headed by the quotation from
Horace which *F*, 1735 gives as an epigraph). The problem is dealt with
by D. Nichol Smith, *The Letters of Jonathan Swift to Charles Ford*
(1935), pp. 197-202, and Harold Williams, *Swift's Poems* II, 744 and
748-9. Swift did not alter his copy of *F*, 1735   *Epigraph:* Horace,
Epistles I, XVIII, 31-2: Eutrepalus used to give costly clothes to
someone if he wished to harm him   *Don Carlos:* Swift's nickname
for Charles Ford (1682-1714), a close friend of Swift and Stella, who
had inherited the estate of Woodpark, County Meath. He was
appointed Gazeteer in 1712   *half a year:* probably imprecise, but as

Stella returned to Dublin on 3 October, she may have gone to Woodpark in April. Swift was there twice between the end of March and early May 1723, and Stella and Mrs Dingley may have gone there when he was staying with Ford. Swift's letter of 20 September (*Correspondence* II, 466), however, suggests the ladies stayed four months   *nice:* choosy, pernickety   *fumette:* the smell of game when high   *purling streams:* a classical phrase in pastorals *Liffey:* the river which runs through Dublin   *sossing:* lounging *stomach:* appetite   *piddle:* pass water   *Pontac:* a sweet wine from Pontac, near Pau in the south of France   *Archdeacon Wall:* Rev. Thomas Walls (?1672–1750), whose wife was Stella's friend. Archdeacon of Athenry, he was also master of St Patrick's Cathedral School, but later became Vicar of Castleknock near Dublin. The Walls lived in Queen Street, Dublin   *Ormond Quay:* 'where both the ladies lodged' (*F*, 1735), on the north bank of the Liffey in Dublin, about half a mile from St Patrick's Cathedral. (Stella and Mrs Dingley also lived in Capel Street, to the east of Ormond Quay)   *entry:* entrance hall   *Lady Day:* 25 March   *grisette:* a seamstress, a working girl *houses: F*, 1735 reads 'lodgings'   *Delf:* Delftware, less expensive than chinaware   *the spark:* usually a young man-about-town; it may be an ironic allusion to Ford   *stomach:* here, disposition or attitude

p. 108, 'Pethox the Great'   Described as written in the year 1723 (*F*, 1735), this poem was first published in *Miscellanies. The Last Volume* (1727, for 1728). The poem's title is an anagram of the pox or syphilis *herald:* the word is used, as in the College of Heraldry, to mean an expert in genealogy   *Vulcan:* the god of fire. Because Venus, his wife, committed adultery with Mars, god of war, he was the patron of cuckolds   *Scamander:* the river near Troy, originally called Xan-thus, which took its new name from Scamander, a Cretan leader who brought his people to Phrygia and helped in the building of Troy. He leapt into the river in a battle and it boiled. See Homer, *Iliad* XXX, 136–382   *all before:* scars on the whole body, including the genital region   *neighbouring Gaul:* syphilis was associated with France *Parthenope:* the ancient name of Naples, another place associated with syphilis; the name Parthenope was derived from that of one of the sirens, whose body was cast up there   *Vesputio:* Amerigo Vespucci

(1451–1512), supposed by some to have discovered America in 1497 before Columbus   *painted skin:* a reference to American Indians, known as redskins   *Epicurus:* Greek philosopher (*c.*340–270 BC) who laid the basis for the view that the Universe's formation was owed to the chance collision of atoms   *production:* generation   *rubies:* scars and sores   *bird of Pallas:* the owl, Bubo; but bubo also means a swelling in the groin   *Byzantians:* Turks   *a wooden tower:* a sweating tub used in the treatment of venereal disease   *Regulus:* Marcus Attilius Regulus as consul reduced Brundisium (267 BC); he was in command of Roman forces in Africa, was defeated and captured by the Carthaginians in 255 BC, in the first Punic War. Having been sent on parole to Rome with Carthaginian envoys, he dissuaded the Roman Senate from agreeing to their proposals and returned to Carthage where he was tortured to death   *billet-doux:* a love letter *Proteus:* in Greek mythology a sea god who could change his shape at will   *Hermes:* the Greek equivalent of the Roman god Mercury (glossed as Mercury in *F*, 1735), who was the son of Jove by Maia, one of the Pleiades. Mercury was used in the treatment of syphilis

p. 111, 'Stella's Birthday, 1725'   Written in March 1724–5, this poem was first published in *Miscellanies. The Last Volume* (1727, for 1728)   *off the hooks:* in bad spirits   *Sheridan:* see note on *Dr Sheridan*, p. 217   *Delany:* see note on him, p. 237   *The god of wit, and beauty's queen:* Apollo and Venus   *fifty-six ... forty-three:* fifty-seven and forty-four if the poem was written in March 1725, but if, though it is unlikely, the ages are correct, the poem could have been written in 1723–4   *dimmish grown ... deaf:* Swift's sight and hearing had deteriorated; he was very deaf in 1724 and in 1725; he was worried about his sight in 1725

p. 113, 'Verses Left in a Window of Dublin Castle'   Probably written in January 1725; first published in 1779. The lines may have been prompted by Swift's first visit to Dublin Castle during the Lord Lieutenancy (1724–30) of John Carteret (1690–1763), the second Baron, and second Earl of Granville (1744). Despite ordering the prosecution of the author, printer and publisher of the *Drapier's Letters*, he recommended the abandonment of Wood's proposed coinage which had occasioned them. He and Swift became warm friends. The reply supposed to have been written by him was probably by Sir William Fownes (Swift, *Correspondence* III, 230): 'My very good Dean, there's few come here / But have something to ask or something to fear'

p. 113, 'To Quilca'   Probably written in summer 1725 (*F*, 1735) when Swift stayed, from spring to late September, with Thomas Sheridan (see note on *Dr Sheridan*, p. 217) at Quilca, in County Cavan 'about forty miles from Dublin'   *A rotten cabin, dropping rain:* during Swift's visit the weather was particularly wet and cold   *smoke; Stools ... broke:* the chimney was in a bad state, the furniture equally so   *poor Sheelah:* a lady's maid, or else a nurse   *Want ... Theft:* for Swift's comments on the visit, see *Prose Works*, ed. H. Davis, V, pp. 219–22, and a letter he wrote to Charles Ford on 16 August 1725, *Correspondence*, ed. Harold Williams (1963–5), p. 89

p. 114, 'Stella's Birthday, 1727'   Headed 13 March 1726/7, it was first published in *Miscellanies. The Last Volume* (1727, for 1728). It was the last of Swift's birthday poems for Stella, who died on 28 January 1728   *Janus:* the two-faced Roman god to whom the month January was dedicated: he could look back on the old year and forward to the new

p. 116, 'Clever Tom Clinch Going to be Hanged'   Described in *F*, 1735 as written in the year 1726, it was first printed in that edition   *Holborn:* the procession from Newgate to Tyburn (where executions took place) led via Holborn   *the George:* a tavern on the south side of Holborn. The procession usually stopped for drinks on the way to Tyburn   *last speech:* street-hawkers sold speeches by the condemned to those attending executions   *whittle:* 'a cant word for confessing at the gallows' (*F*, 1735)   *Wild:* Jonathan Wild (1683–1725), a criminal, a 'thief-taker' who organised thefts in London until he was executed at Tyburn. He was the inspiration for Peachum in John Gay's *The Beggar's Opera*; both Daniel Defoe and Henry Fielding wrote lives of him

p. 117, 'Advice to the Grub Street Verse-Writers'   Described as written 'in the year 1726' when it first appeared in *F*, 1735   *paste:* a wrapping for pastries   *Curll:* see note on him, p. 209

p. 118, 'The Furniture of a Woman's Mind'   'Written in the year 1727' (*F*, 1735, in which it first appeared), it was also included in *Miscellanies. Volume the Fifth* (1735)   *scarlet coat:* a soldier *cut and dry:* prepared in advance   *swown:* swoon   *clubs:* informal meetings of friends   *patch:* see note on *patch her face*, p. 209 *Molly:* a maid   *Admires:* wonders at   *women:* the original 'woman' was corrected thus in Swift's copy of *F*, 1735   *robustious:* a vulgarism, a cross between robust and boisterous   *Mrs Harding:* Mrs Sarah Harding, widow of John Harding, a Dublin printer who printed the *Drapier's Letters* and who was imprisoned and prosecuted, and died in prison on 19 April 1725. Mrs Harding was imprisoned along with her husband, and later published The *Intelligencer* (1728–9), a weekly paper jointly written by Swift and Thomas Sheridan (see note on *Dr Sheridan*, p. 217). It lasted for nineteen numbers, a twentieth appearing in the spring of 1729. Swift's satires 'Mad Mullinix and Timothy' (p. 122) and 'Tim and the Fables' appeared in it

p. 120, 'Holyhead. September 25, 1727'   This poem was written at Holyhead in September 1727. It was not published. ('The Power of Time', also written then, appeared in *F*, 1735.) The contents of the MS volume, a journal in which it is written, were not published until 1882 *at Holyhead:* Swift, fearing Stella might well have died before his return, left London on 18 September, was in Chester four days later, but through tiredness and various mischances did not reach Holyhead until 24 September. He missed the packet boat, and because of adverse winds and weather could not sail for Ireland until 29 September, though half an hour after first putting out the ferry had to turn back *Convict:* convicted   *A packet:* the ferry which carried passengers and mail on a regular service   *a friend:* Stella   *the land I hate:* Swift landed at Carlingford, County Louth, and then had nearly seventy miles to travel to Dublin. Another poem in the journal, 'Ireland', begins

Remove me from this land of slaves
Where all are fools, and all are knaves,
Where every knave and fool is bought,
Yet kindly sells himself for nought.

this bleaky shore: Anglesey

p. 121, 'An Elegy on Dicky and Dolly'   The elegy was probably written in 1728; it was first published in 1732 by James Hoey of Skinner Row, Dublin, and subsequently by *F*, 1765 and in Deane Swift's edition of *The Works of Dr Jonathan Swift* (1765). On 8 April 1728 Dorothea Stopford, daughter of James Stopford of Tara Hill, then Countess of Meath, married as her second husband Lieutenant-General Richard Gorges (her previous husband, Edward Brabazon, fourth Earl of Meath, had died on 27 February 1707/8; she was his second wife). The newly married couple died within four days of each other. She was to have been buried in Dublin, but the General died on 12 April at his family seat, Kilbrew, County Meath, and both were buried at Kilbrew on 14 April 1728. Swift commented in the *Journal to Stella*, 25 February 1711/12: 'Countess Doll of Meath is such an owl that wherever I visit people are asking me whether I know such an Irish lady; and her figure and her foppery'   *jointure:* see note, p. 226   *Meath:* the sixth Earl of Meath, Chetworth Brabazon (1686–1763)   *The son:* presumably by the General's first marriage   *Cuff:* John Cuff of Desart, who married Gorges's daughter   *Alicant:* from Alicante, in Spain

p. 122, 'Mad Mullinix and Timothy'   This poem was written and published in 1728, in the eighth number of the *Intelligencer*, a weekly journal published by Mrs Sarah Harding in Dublin (see note on her, p. 147). It was included in *Miscellanies. The Third Volume* (1732) and *F*, 1735. Mullinex (or Molyneux) was a deranged Dublin beggar who proclaimed Tory views; Timothy was the Hon. Richard Tighe (?1678–1736), a Whig politician mentioned in the *Journal to Stella* (he was then living in London). He was MP for Belturbet in the Irish parliament and a member of the Irish Privy Council. In 1725 he reported to Lord Carteret, the Lord Lieutenant, on a sermon preached by Dr Thomas Sheridan (see note on *Dr Sheridan*, p. 217): both Swift and Sheridan resented this and made Tighe an object of savage satire. His family had supplied Cromwell's troops with bread; hence the reference to an oven in 'Tom Mullinex and Dick' (p. 130), while in 'A Character, Panegyric, and Description of the Legion Club' he is called Dick Fitz-Baker   *hardly twenty:* a decided underestimation of their numbers   *an earl . . . public debts:* John Pratt, Deputy Vice-Treasurer of Ireland, got into financial difficulties (he owed Swift a large sum of money, most of which Swift recovered), and in the Irish House of Lords the Earl of Barrymore had supported an inquiry into the public accounts in 1727   *statesman bishop:* probably the Primate, Hugh Boulter (1672–1742), Archbishop of Armagh from 1724   *Avignon:* in the south of France, then a Papal State; the Pretender was there in 1727   *Avignon . . . These brangling jars:* between these lines the *Intelligencer* version printed the following lines, omitted in *F*, 1735:

> M.   *In every arse you run your snout,*
> *To find this damned Pretender out,*
> *While all the silly wretch can do*
> *Is but to frisk about like you.*
> *But Tim, convinced by your persuasion,*
> *I yield there might be an invasion,*
> *And you who never fart in vain*
> *Can fart his navy back again.*

> T.   *Zounds, sir.*   M.   *But to be short and serious*
> *For long disputes will only weary us*

Martin Marall: Dryden's play *Sir Martin Mar-all, or the Feign'd Innocence* (1668). See Act V, 2   *Thersites:* see Homer, *Iliad* II, 212–71; he was known for his vicious ill-temper   *Keck:* retch   *Glorious:* a reference to William of Orange   *his statue:* in College Green, Dublin   *from below:* a fart   *the true mother:* whether the Pretender born on 10 June 1688 at St James's Palace, London, was the son of Mary of Modena, second wife of James II, was in doubt, some believing that he was smuggled into St James's Palace in a warming-pan   *the witch of Endor:* see the Bible, I Samuel XXVIII:7–25   *Faustus:* a reference to Christopher Marlowe's *The Tragic History of*

Dr Faustus (1604)   *Queen of Sheba's lap:* see the Bible, I Kings
X:1–13   *The Duke of Lorraine:* the Old Pretender, James Francis
Edward Stuart (1688–1766), son of James II and Mary of Modena
Sabra's sake: the daughter of Ptolemy whom St George rescued from
the dragon   *frank my letters:* MPs could send letters free by writing
their names on the covers   *Jacks:* Jacobites   *May-game:* object
of ridicule   *the sable guard:* vagrants   *the cinder-picking fair:*
girls who rake the ashes to get cinders for re-use   *Horace says ...
Ephippia:* in Horace, *Epistles* I, XIV, 43, the ox wishes for the horse's
trappings   *Dr Lee:* Lee was a 'deceased clergyman whose footman
he was' (*F*, 1735). The original version in the *Intelligencer* read, 'How
much improv'd by Dr —', which Harold Williams, *Swift's Poems* III,
779, glossed as 'Dr D.' or Doctor Delany   *Your block:* your head
(like a wig-block, on which a wig was placed)   *toupee and snake:*
different styles of wig   *bonnyclabber:* clotted sour milk

p. 130, 'Tom Mullinex and Dick'   Probably written in 1728, this
poem was first published in *Miscellanies. The Tenth Volume* (1745).
For Mullinex and Dick, see headnote to 'Mad Mullinix and Timothy', p.
231   *an oven:* Cromwell's troops were supplied with bread by
Dick's (Richard Tighe's) family   *borees:* country dances   *the
blackguard boys:* vagrants, street arabs   *Stentor:* the Greek herald in
the Trojan War, renowned for the strength of his voice

p. 131, 'Dick, a Maggot'   Probably written in 1728, this poem was
first published in *Miscellanies. The Tenth Volume* (1745). It deals with
Richard Tighe (see headnote to 'Mad Mullinix and Timothy', p. 231
Drawcansir: a bully in *The Rehearsal* (1671) by George Villiers,
second Duke of Buckingham (1627–87)   *wainscot* dark in colour
Tartar: fierce, savage

p. 132, 'An Answer to the Ballyspellin Ballad'   Probably written by
Swift in September 1728, and published by Faulkner in Dublin in that
year, this was a reply to a ballad Thomas Sheridan (see note on *Dr
Sheridan*, p. 217) had written on the spa (known for its chalybeate
waters) of Ballyspellan in County Kilkenny into which he put all the
rhymes he could find to 'Ballyspellin'. Swift, however, with a friend

(possibly Sir Arthur Acheson (see note on *Market Hill* below), with whom he was staying when he wrote the 'Answer'), found fifteen more. Sheridan had followed the example of John Gay's 'Molly Mog' (1726), a crambo ballad in the writing of which Swift and Pope may have shared. When it first appeared, in *Mist's Weekly Journal*, it was described as 'writ by two or three men of wit' when they were 'lying at a certain inn at Buckingham, where the daughter of the house was remarkably pretty', and whose name was Molly Mog   *drabs:* girls in Sheridan's ballad   *Llewellyn:* possibly the Welsh poet Llewellyn ab Gryffydd (d.1282), included by Sheridan for the rhyme   *Doctor Pelling:* also included for the rhyme; possibly Dr Edward Pelling (d.1718), an Anglican clergyman   *teagues:* Irishmen, here intended to indicate social inferiors   *sowens:* food 'made of oatmeal and sometimes of the shellings of oats' (*F*, 1762)   *Market Hill:* the family estate, near Armagh, of Sir Arthur (1688–1749) and Lady Acheson (d.1737). Sir Arthur, the fifth Baronet, was an Irish MP from 1727 and Sheriff of County Armagh. Market Hill is now known as Gosford Castle; Sir Arthur's eldest son Archibald (b.1718) became the first Viscount Gosford   *Sheelah:* the lady's maid or nurse at Quilca, Sheridan's house in County Cavan (see note, p. 217)   *mawkins:* sluts, drabs   *Holland:* fine lace   *For Holland:* 'Of Holland' is read by Joseph Horrell, *Collected Poems of Jonathan Swift* (1958) I, 331   *grisettes:* working girls   *the Bell Inn:* in Market Hill   *Enniskillen:* in County Fermanagh, to the west of Market Hill   *blowze:* a blowsy girl   *stiver ... skilling:* coins of little value   *leaks* urinates

p. 135, 'Verses Occasioned by the Sudden Drying Up of St Patrick's Well near Trinity College, Dublin'   This poem's date of composition is not certain but is probably 1729, the year the well went dry; it was first published by Faulkner in 1762. Swift's notes, included in that edition, are cited here   *holy zeal ... fame ... once favourite:* Swift's note alludes to Festus Avienus (*fl*.370), whose poem 'De Oris Maritimis' used this expression concerning Ireland   *Italy:* Swift comments that because St Patrick was educated in and received his mission in Italy, it can be called his native land   *Renowned:* Swift cites Julius Solinus, Polydore Virgil and Giraldus Cambrensis

Colchus . . . Jason: Swift remarks that Orpheus (or whoever wrote the poem on the Argonautica) and Adrianus Junius say that Jason sailed to Ireland   *Thee . . . Pallas . . . unknown:* Pallas Athene, goddess of the arts. Swift here cites Tacitus, *Agricola,* as saying that the harbours of Ireland were better known to the trading part of the world than those of Britain   *Caledonians:* Swift comments that Fardon, Hector Boethius, Buchanan 'and all the Scotch historians' agree that Fergus of Ireland was the first King of Scotland, and his descendants reigned after him   *thy base invaders:* Swift's note tells how Dermot Mac-Morrough, King of Leinster, invited Strongbow, the Earl of Pembroke, to help him to regain his kingdom, promising him his daughter and dominions. Strongbow obtained all of Leinster, and the Irish rulers submitted to Henry II when he came to Ireland   *human knowledge and divine:* here Swift cites the Venerable Bede for the effect of St Patrick's conversion of the Irish begun by Palladius and others, the creation of seminaries of learning and of literature in addition to religion   *the venomed serpent:* St Patrick reputedly expelled snakes from Ireland   *the magpies:* Swift's note remarks on magpies arriving in Ireland a short time before the year 1700   *the croaking race:* frogs, too, he comments, were not known in Ireland until 1700   *fur and lawn:* the judges and bishops – a reference to judges who (like peers) wore ermine and to bishops who wore lawn sleeves   *the new-devouring vermin:* Norway rats came to Ireland after 1700, according to Swift's note   *nursery of arts:* Trinity College, Dublin, founded by Queen Elizabeth in 1591   *Hippocrene:* the fountain of the Muses on Mount Helicon, Boetia, the source of poetic inspiration in Greek legend   *foreign:* English   *for:* instead of   *tide:* a reference to the tide waiters, customs officials, who examined incoming ships   *brass:* a reference to Wood's planned coinage for use in Ireland, the subject of Swift's *Drapier's Letters* (see note, p. 236) *that mongrel breed:* absentee landlords

p. 138, 'Drapier's Hill'   Probably written in the summer of 1729, this poem was first published in August 1729, in *Fog's Weekly Journal*; it is included in *F*, 1735 and *Miscellanies. Volume the Fifth* (1735) *purchased land:* Swift was '£100 the poorer' after he abandoned the idea (apparently by October 1729) of building a house at Drumlack on land owned by Sir Arthur Acheson, north of Market Hill. 'The Dean's reasons for not building at Drapier's Hill', included in Deane Swift's edition, *The Works of Dr Jonathan Swift* (1765) and *F*, 1765, indicates some coolness between Swift and the Achesons, as well as his realization of the impracticability of the plan   *Sir Arthur:* Sir Arthur Acheson (see note on *Market Hill*, p. 234). He married Anne, the daughter of Philip Savage, in 1715. Swift often stayed with the Achesons at Market Hill and wrote several teasingly affectionate poems about Lady Acheson   *Drapier's Hill ... the Drapier ... Letters:* Swift adopted the name M. B. Drapier when he attacked the proposal that William Wood, a Wolverhampton entrepreneur, should be licensed to issue a new coinage (of halfpence and farthings) for Ireland. Swift wrote the *Drapier Letters*, seven prose pieces, between 1724 and 1725. A month after the issue of the patent, the Irish Revenue Commissioners complained twice, to the Lord Lieutenant, then to the Treasury. Walpole finally conceded defeat, and the patent, intended to provide funds for Gräfin Melusine von der Schulenberg (Duchess of Munster from 1719), George I's mistress, was withdrawn   *signs... medals ... prints ... handkerchiefs:* 'Medals were cast; many signs hung up; and handkerchiefs made with devices in honour of the Author, under the name of M. B. Drapier' (*F*, 1735)   *Cooper's Hill:* a topographical poem, published in 1642, by Sir John Denham (1615–69), who was born in Dublin. Cooper's Hill is four miles from Limerick

p. 138, 'A Pastoral Dialogue'   Though *F*, 1735 dates this as written in 1728, it may have been written in September 1729; it first appeared in *Miscellanies. The Third Volume* (1732)   *hight:* (archaic) called *Gosford knight:* Sir Arthur Acheson (see note on *Market Hill*, p. 234). The Achesons took the title of Gosford (after Sir Arthur's great-grandfather 'Sir Archibald of Gosford in Scotland') when they succeeded to the peerage. They rebuilt Market Hill as Gosford Castle *in counterview:* opposite   *spud:* a knife or tool for weeding *thistle for Sir Arthur's sake:* alluding to the Acheson family's Scottish ancestry, the thistle being the emblem of Scotland. *F*, 1735 glosses Acheson as 'a great lover of Scotland'   *tobacco plug:* a twist or a cut from a block of tobacco, used for chewing   *Dennis:* the Achesons' butler   *Tady ... long-bullets:* Tady may be for Thady, an Irish name; long-bullets or long-bowls was a skittle game akin to ninepins *gossip:* godmother   *brogues:* shoes   *sowens:* an oaten dish (see note, p. 234)

p. 140, 'On Burning a Dull Poem'   Written 'in the year 1729', and first published in *F*, 1735 and *Miscellanies. Volume the Fifth* (1735)   *An ass's hoof ... poisonous juice:* the Styx, an Arcadian spring, was so cold that its waters were poisonous; only vessels made from horses' or asses' hoofs could contain them, they were so corrosive. There may be a reflection here of Ben Jonson's use of the phrase 'the dull ass's hoof' in 'An Ode to Himself' and in the Epilogue to *The Poetaster* (1602)

p. 141, 'A Libel on the Reverend Dr Delany and His Excellency John, Lord Carteret'   Swift wrote this as a second reply to Delany's poem 'Epistle to Lord Carteret' (1729; dated 1730); his first reply was 'An Epistle upon an Epistle', probably published late in 1729. 'A Libel ...' was first published early in February 1730   *Dr Delany:* Patrick Delany (1685/6–1767). Educated at and a Fellow of Trinity College, Dublin, he became Chancellor of Christ Church Cathedral, Dublin, in 1728, Chancellor of St Patrick's Cathedral, Dublin, in 1730 and Dean of Down in 1744. He was a friend of Thomas Sheridan (see note on *Dr Sheridan*, p. 217) and of Swift (from about 1718), who regarded him as 'the most eminent preacher we have.' He was one of Swift's executors, and regarding Orrery's *Remarks* (1752) as calumnious, answered them with *Observations upon Lord Orrery's Remarks upon the Life and Writings of Dr Jonathan Swift* (1754), the only account of Swift written by a close friend, and one who knew him in his full vigour. He wrote pamphlets, sermons and scholarly works, defending polygamy, the crimes of King David and the dietary laws of the Old Testament   *Lord Carteret:* see headnote to 'Verses Left in a Window of Dublin Castle', p. 228   *boasting:* referring to Delany's 'Epistle'   *cup and can:* proverbial for familiar companions   *Congreve ... Montagu:* William Congreve (1670–1729), Swift's schoolfellow at Kilkenny College, fellow undergraduate at Trinity College, Dublin, and lasting friend. He gave up his successful career as a dramatist in 1700. He held several sinecures, Charles Montagu, the first Earl of Halifax, being a

good patron to him as well as to Joseph Addison and Matthew Prior
crazy: sickly, delicate   *chair:* pay for a sedan chair   *Paean's fire:*
a hymn to Apollo   *Steele:* Richard Steele (1672–1729), an Irish-
born author who wrote comedies, began the *Tatler* in 1709, and wrote
for the *Spectator*. He wrote various political pamphlets and was
manager of the Drury Lane Theatre, retiring to Wales through ill-
health and dying there in 1729   *owned . . . writ:* Swift is alluding to
Tickell's view that Steele had taken credit for writings by Addison,
something Steele denied   *Thus Gay:* see note, p. 216. Swift is
alluding to 'The Hare and Many Friends', in Gay's *Fables* (1727); Gay
became associated with the hare who 'complied with everything'
servile usher's place: Gay did not accept the offer of the post of
'gentleman-usher' to George II's daughter Princess Louisa (then two
years old) in 1727   *Addison . . . distressed:* Joseph Addison
(1672–1719), whose travels in Europe had been publicly financed, later
became an MP, secretary to the Lord Lieutenant of Ireland (1708–10),
and was Secretary of State (1717–18). He first met Swift in 1710 and,
though their politics differed, they remained friends   *Pope . . . of a*
queen: Alexander Pope (see note on him, p. 216) met Swift in 1713; a
fellow Scriblerian, he was Swift's main host in 1726 and 1727. They
collaborated in joint *Miscellanies*, an I Pope played a considerable part
in the publication of Swift's later poems. Here Swift alludes to a story
that Pope left home to avoid a visit from Queen Caroline   *Homer*
dead: Pope's translations of Homer's *Iliad* (1715–20) and *Odyssey*
(1725–6) made him financially independent   *Pindus' head:* Mount
Pindus, the Muses' seat in Thessaly   *smoke:* discover, see through
Bolingbroke . . . Pulteney: for Bolingbroke, see note on St John, p. 213.
William Pulteney (1684–1764), a statesman and friend of various
writers, was Secretary-at-War 1714, and very briefly First Lord of the
Treasury in 1746   *The Viceroy . . . retire:* Lord Carteret retired in
April 1730   *Walpole:* see note on him, p. 214   *Before a play:* in
a prologue (dedicated to some patron)   *Philips:* Ambrose Philips
(1674–1749), known as 'Namby Pamby', a poet praised for his
pastorals, who held several government posts, being secretary to
Archbishop Boulter in 1724, an Irish MP in 1727 and Judge of the
Prerogative Court in 1732   *the tripod of Apollo:* of Pythia, the
priestess of Apollo, at Delphi; the oracle there was dedicated to Apollo

Belzebub's Black Hall: for Beelzebub, Prince of Wales; see the Bible, Matthew XII:24. Black Hall suggests Whitehall

p. 147, 'An Excellent New Ballad; or, The True English Dean to be Hanged for a Rape'   Written 'in the year 1730' and first published as an anonymous broadside in Dublin in that year   *Steele:* see note on him, p. 238   *Dean of Ferns:* Dr Thomas Sawbridge was prosecuted on 2 June and acquitted on 15 June 1730. He had been appointed Dean of Ferns in County Wexford in 1728. Swift remarked in a letter that 'the plea he intended was his being drunk when he forced the young woman [Susanna Runcard]; but he bought her off'. The broadside version reads 'For who wou'd have *F—ns* without a *Commendum?*'   *jure ecclesiae:* (Latin) 'by the Church's law'   *commendam:* a bonus, an extra. The Latin phrase *in commendam* was used of the tenure of a benefice, held with the revenues   *Smedley:* Rev. Jonathan Smedley (b.1670/1); 'that rascal Smedley', in Swift's words, became Dean of Killala in 1718, and Dean of Clogher in 1724. In politics a Whig, he wrote a newspaper supported by government funds (*c.*1722) and attacked Swift and Pope in 1728, for which he appeared in Pope's *The Dunciad.* He went to Madras in 1729, but thereafter nothing is known of him   *rochet:* linen surplice worn by a bishop   *Atherton's shape:* John Atherton (1598–1640), Bishop of Waterford and Lismore, who was charged with and hanged for unnatural vice   *Chartres:* Francis Chartres (1675–1732), a rascally Scottish landlord, usurer and gambler. A Whig, he had tried unsuccessfully to bribe his way into Parliament in 1727. He was convicted of rape in 1730 but was released from prison, through, it was suggested, Walpole's intervention   *hempen cape:* hangman's noose made of rope

p. 150, 'The Lady's Dressing Room'   Written 'in the year 1730' (*F,* 1735), this poem first appeared in 1732   *Betty:* presumably Celia's maid   *alum flower:* alum powder   *Tripsy:* a pet dog   *puppy water:* made from the guts of a puppy or a pig   *coifs and pinners:* see note, p. 206   *thick and thin:* a proverbial expression, without paying attention to any hindrance   *Pandora's box . . . Epimethus:* Pandora's husband, Epimethus, though advised against doing so, opened the box Jove gave Pandora: every evil that plagues the world flew out, though hope did stay in the box　'Those secrets of the hoary deep': cf. Milton, Paradise Lost II, 890–1　plumped: dropped into liquid　Repeating . . . shits: not included in the version in F, 1732 and F, 1735, but restored in F, 1737　the Queen . . . ooze?: Venus rose from the sea　Statira: the daughter of Darius, married to Alexander the Great; she is one of the two heroines of Nathaniel Lee's (?1653–92) tragedy The Rival Queens (1670). She was stabbed to death by Alexander's first wife, Roxana, whom he had banished　pocky quean: a prostitute or disreputable woman marred by smallpox scars

p. 155, 'A Beautiful Young Nymph Going to Bed'　'Written for the honour of the fair sex, in 1731' (F, 1735), the poem (with 'Strephon and Chloe' and 'Cassinus and Peter') first appeared in a London quarto pamphlet in December 1734, a month before F, 1735, Mrs Barber (see headnote to 'Corinna', p. 208) having brought these poems (with three others) to Matthew Pilkington in London in 1733 to negotiate their publication　Drury Lane: then a haunt of prostitutes　Covent Garden: also a raffish area in London　three-legged: one leg was broken　plumpers: pads or discs used to fill out hollows in the cheeks (possibly caused by venereal disease)　shankers: chancres, ulcers caused by venereal disease　front: forehead　Bridewell: see note on beating flax . . . bloody tracks, p. 220　the compter: a prison resembling Bridewell, controlled by the sheriffs　Jamaica: where some convicts were transported　Alone . . . by no planter: this theme may have been prompted by Aphra Benn (1640–89), whose novel Oroonoko (c.1678) dealt with the treatment of a royal slave in the West Indies; a dramatized version by Southerne was staged in 1695. F, 1735 supplies a note with a Virgilian quotation from Aeneid IV, 467–8: 'et longam incomitata videtur / Ire viam'. Harold Williams, Swift's Poems II, 583, suggests a recollection of Gay's opera Polly (1729)　Fleet Ditch: see note on From Smithfield, or St Pulchre's, p. 208　rubs: distressing encounters　clubs: here groups of dissenters or societies for the reform of manners　issue-peas: globular bodies placed in an incision to drain putrid matter from the body　Shock: name for a lap-dog

p. 157, 'The Character of Sir Robert Walpole'   This poem may have been written in autumn 1731; it was first published in 1733   *Robert Walpole:* see note on him, p. 214   *his peace:* possibly the Peace of Seville of 1729   *spaniel of Spain:* Walpole's policy towards Spain did not seem strong enough to the opposition

p. 157, 'The Place of the Damned'   'written in the year 1731' and first published in a broadside in that year   *I will tell:* Swift's correction of *F*, 1735's 'I'll tell'   *flammed:* deceived by a false account

p. 158, 'Helter Skelter; or, The Hue and Cry after the attorneys, Going to Ride the Circuit'   First published in a broadside of late 1731, the attribution of this poem to Swift has been queried by some scholars, though it has been included in the canon since 1775   *attorneys:* lawyers; originally this had the meaning 'solicitor'   *tilters:* swords   *Cambric:* fine linen (from Cambrai in France)   *holland:* linen   *letters:* monograms   *lim:* limbo, meaning the pawnshop   *Thorough:* through   *vacation's over:* the assize courts, attended by itinerant judges and lawyers, were held outside Dublin during the vacation period of the Dublin courts

p. 160, 'Verses on the Death of Dr Swift, D.S.P.D.'   This poem was being written in December 1731 and was probably completed late in that month, notes being added to it subsequently. There are several versions, the best text being that of *F*, 1739, which gives the full-length version (484 lines) of the poem. 'The Life and Genuine Character of Dr Swift' had been published in 1733 and consisted of 202 lines. The 'Verses on the Death of Dr Swift' was a London edition of 1739, edited and cut by William King and Alexander Pope from Swift's 484 lines to 381 lines. The initials in the title stand for Dean of St Patrick's, Dublin   *maxim in Rochefoucauld:* from duc François de la Rochefoucauld (1613–80), *Reflexions ou Sentences et Maximes Morales* (1665)   *'In all distresses . . . us':* lines influenced by George Granville, *The History of Adolphus* (1691), p. 48; see Christopher Ricks, 'Notes on Swift and Granville', *Review of English Studies* XI, 1960, pp. 412–13   *Pope . . . Gay . . . Arbuthnot:* see notes, pp. 216 and 215   *old vertigo:* the

giddiness, labyrinthine vertigo, and ringing or buzzing in the ears
produced by Ménière's disease, from which Swift had suffered
intermittently since 1690. It was named after Prosper Ménière
(1799–1862), a French physician; its aetiology was not ascertained until
1861   *Charles the Second:* Charles II lived from 1630 to 1685
stomach: appetite   *tropes:* figures of speech   *Approves:* proves,
confirms   *passing-bell:* bell rung to announce a death or funeral
all...public uses: not completely, as there were some personal bequests
Drapier: Swift's note (*F*, 1739) stated that though he imagined the
scribblers of the prevailing political party would libel him after his death,
others would remember him with gratitude for the service that he had
done to Ireland 'under the name of M. B. Drapier, by utterly defeating
the destructive project of Wood's halfpence, in five letters to the people
of Ireland, at that time read universally, and convincing every reader'
Lady Suffolk: Henrietta Howard, Countess of Suffolk (?1687–1767),
Bedchamber Woman to Princess Caroline and mistress of the Prince of
Wales, later George II. She married Charles Howard (later ninth Earl
of Suffolk) in 1706; he died in 1733 and she married George Berkeley
two years later. She lived at Marble Hill, Twickenham, where she
entertained the Scriblerians. She was a good friend to Swift   *the
medals:* medals promised by the Princess (later Queen Anne) to Swift
in return for his gift of Irish poplin (see Swift's *Correspondence* III,
392)   *Chartres:* see note, p. 239   *Sir Robert's levee:* Walpole's
(see note on him, p. 214). *F*, 1735 describes Walpole's inviting Swift to
dinner in 1726, and Swift, finding him 'no great friend' to Ireland,
'would see him no more'   *without his shoes:* a slang phrase for
being hanged   *Will:* William Pulteney (see note on *Bolingbroke...
Pulteney*, p. 238). *F*, 1739 describes Pulteney as opposing Walpole's
measures   *Bolingbroke: F*, 1739 describes Walpole as treating him
'most injuriously'. Bolingbroke (see note on *St John*, p. 213), on his
return to England, was not allowed to sit in the House of Lords
Curll: 'the most infamous bookseller of any age or country', accused of
publishing three volumes by Swift (*F*, 1739) 'who never writ three page
of them' (see note on him, p. 209)   *Tibbalds, Moore, and Cibber:*
[Lewis] Tibbald: fictive name of Lewis Theobald (1688–1744), 'King
Dunce' in Pope's *The Dunciad*, a dramatist, poet, critic and editor of
Shakespeare (1734). James Moore Smythe (1702–34), an author

'whose father was gaoler at Monaghan'. Colley Cibber (1671–1757), playwright, a manager of Drury Lane Theatre from 1712. He was appointed Poet Laureate in 1730. He was made King Dunce in the 1743 edition of Pope's *The Dunciad*. He is best known for his *Apology* (1740), an autobiography   *my letters:* Curll published lives, letters, and last wills and testaments of the nobility and Ministers of State as well as of criminals hanged at Tyburn   *Arbuthnot a day:* a pun, 'Arbuth' not a day (see note on *kind Arbuthnot*, p. 215   *the vole:* in quadrille, to win all the tricks   *Lintot:* Bernard Lintot (1675–1736), a bookseller with whom Pope quarrelled after Lintot had published several of his works, including the highly successful translations of Homer   *Duck Lane:* where secondhand books were sold *pastry-cook's:* to be used as wrappings for pies or linings for cooking utensils   *spick and span:* neat and new   *birthday poem:* a poem in honour of the King's birthday which Cibber, as Poet Laureate, was expected to produce annually   *Stephen Duck:* known as the thresher poet, he was a Wiltshire farm labourer (1705–56) whose complimentary verses gained him Queen Caroline's favour; he was given various offices, became Vicar of Byfleet, and drowned himself when in a depressed state   *the Craftsman:* described (*F*, 1739) as 'an excellent paper', in which Pulteney and Bolingbroke combined to discredit Walpole; it first appeared in December 1726   *Henley:* Rev. John Henley (1692–1756), a preacher who wrote pro-Walpole material in *The Hyp Doctor*. The note in *F*, 1739 described him as 'generally reputed crazy'   *Woolston's tracts:* Rev. Thomas Woolston (1670–1733), who was deprived of a Fellowship at Sidney Sussex College, Cambridge, in 1721, and tried for blasphemy in 1729 *God's in Gloucester:* possibly a proverbial expression; it is less likely to refer to the appointment of a new bishop there in 1733   *the Rose:* a tavern on Drury Lane, popular with playgoers   *stars and garters:* Walpole received the Order of the Garter in 1726   *And to her Majesty . . . come from him:* these lines are not printed in *F*, 1739; they were quoted (with a variant in the first line) by Mrs Pilkington, *Memoirs* (1748) I, 91, and occur in annotated copies (which belonged to John Forster and Professor Edward Dowden)   *David's lesson:* Psalm CXLVI:3   *six hundred pound:* the note in *F*, 1739 alludes to the £300 reward proclaimed, at the instance of the House of Lords in

England, in 1713 for the identification of the author of the *Public Spirit of the Whigs*, and to the £300 proclamation in Ireland for the identification of the author of *The Drapier's Fourth Letter reconcile his friends: F*, 1739 refers to the falling into 'variance' of the ministry: Harcourt, the Chancellor, and Bolingbroke, the Secretary, were discontented with Oxford, the Treasurer, for his mildness towards the Whigs   *left the court:* Swift retired to the country ten weeks before the fall of the ministry   *Ormonde's valour:* James Butler, Duke of Ormonde (1665–1745), a Jacobite who joined the Prince of Orange and fought at the Battle of the Boyne (1690). He was Lord Lieutenant of Ireland 1703–5, 1710–11 and 1713. In 1712 he succeeded Marlborough as Captain-General, was dismissed in 1714, and attainted in 1715. He fled to France, played a prominent part in organizing the Rising and continued to be influential in Jacobite affairs. Swift greatly admired and liked him; it was through the Duke that he became Dean of St Patrick's Cathedral   *that precious life:* Queen Anne died on 1 August 1714   *wrath and vengeance: F*, 1739 refers to the rage and revenge of the Whigs on their return to power. They 'impeached and banished the chief leaders of the Church Party, stripped all their adherents of what employments they had'. . . . They gave the greatest preferments in the Church in England and Ireland 'to the most ignorant men, fanatics were publicly caressed, Ireland utterly ruined and enslaved, only great Ministers heaping up millions. . . .' *solemn league and covenant:* the agreement of 1643 which provided for the establishment of Presbyterianism and the suppression of Roman Catholicism   *the Tower:* where the Earl of Oxford was confined *the land of slaves and fens:* Ireland, where Swift feared for his safety while libels were written against him; there were rumours of a proclamation offering £5 for his arrest. He was 'insulted in the street, and at nights was forced to be attended by his servants armed' (*F*, 1739) *familiar friends . . . heels:* an echo of the Bible, Psalm XII, 9   *cheat:* Wood and his proposed coinage for Ireland   *monster on the bench:* William Whitshed (see headnote to 'An Excellent New Song on a Seditious Pamphlet', p. 222)   *Scroggs . . . or old Tresilian:* William Scroggs (?1623–83), Lord Chief Justice from 1678 to 1681; he was impeached in 1680 and removed from office. Sir Robert Tresilian, Chief Justice at the time of the Peasant's Revolt, was hanged in 1388 for

treason   *Nor feared he ... regarded:* from the Bible, Luke XVIII:2
topics: points of law   *middling kind:* in Ireland he 'only conversed
with private gentlemen of the clergy or laity, and but a small number
of either' (*F*, 1739)   *no right or power:* a reference to the
Declaratory Act of 1720   *Biennial squires:* the Irish Parliament met
every second year, the administration being 'in the hands of the Lord
Lieutenant, or, in his absence, three Lords Justices'   *Go snacks:*
share the pickings or sports   *rapparees: F*, 1739 describes them as
highwaymen, 'Irish soldiers who in small parties' used to plunder the
Protestants   *keep the peace:* act as magistrates   *job:* this sug-
gests jobbery, something dishonest   *the tax:* landowners influenced
the routes of the toll roads or turnpikes to suit their properties   *a
house for fools and mad:* St Patrick's Hospital, Dublin, opened in 1757
and still functioning

p. 175, 'Verses on I Know Not What'   These may have been
written in 1732, the present title appearing on the reverse of a paper
on which Swift wrote the poem, which was first published in 1765 in
The Works of Dr Jonathan Swift, ed. Deane Swift (1765), and in *F*,
1765

p. 175, '[A Paper Book is Sent by Boyle]'   This was written after
Swift's sixty-fifth birthday (30 November 1732) and first published in
the *Gentleman's Magazine* in June 1733 and subsequently in *F*, 1735
(Vol. IV)   *Boyle:* John Boyle (1707–62), fifth Earl of Orrery (whose
Remarks (1752) are the first biographical study of Swift), sent Swift as
a birthday present a book 'very richly bound and clasped with gold' with
a poem on the first page, the rest being blank   *Delany:* see note on
Dr Delany, p. 237. His present was a silver standish or writing stand,
also accompanied by verses. Boyle's and Delany's verses were first
published in the *Gentleman's Magazine* in January 1733

p. 176, 'On the Day of Judgement'   Possibly written in 1731 and
first published in the *St James's Chronicle, or, British Evening Post*,
9–12 April 1774, the version followed in this edition

p. 176, 'On Poetry: a Rhapsody'   Probably written in 1732; first published in December 1733   *Young's ... passion:* Young's satires, *The Universal Passion: the Love of Fame* (1725–8), later published as *Love of Fame* (1728), by the Rev. Edward Young (1683–1765), the poet known for his 'Night Thoughts' (1742–4) and 'Conjectures on Original Composition' (1759)   *foundered:* lame   *beggar's brat:* a boy used by a beggar to induce pity   *Bridewell:* see note on *beating flax ... bloody tracks,* p. 220   *Phoebus:* Phoebus Apollo, Greek god of poetry   *hundred pound:* the Poet Laureate's annual stipend. *F,* 1735 points out in a footnote that it was paid to 'one Cibber, a player' (see note on him, p. 243)   *attainder ... Grub Street line:* a legal process stopping a criminal's heir inheriting titles or property. Cibber's (see note on *Tibbalds, Moore, and Cibber,* p. 242) lack of worth has meant the succession to his post is for ever the right of Grub Street hacks, either through the stupidity of Cibber or of the King   *spirits to discern:* see the Bible, I Corinthians XII:10   *'sent from hand unknown':* conventional phrase used in connection with prologues or epilogues to plays   *Aurora's light:* the dawn   *wipe:* a reproof or a jibe *smokes:* recognizes   *Lintot:* see note on him, p. 243   *Will's:* a coffee-house on the north side of Russell Street, Covent Garden, a favourite meeting place of poets   *swallow down:* control your anger   *quires:* unbound sheets   *A's and B's:* initials disguising the identity of persons satirized   *statesman ... jobber:* a suggestion that Walpole (see note on him, p. 214) was linked with South Sea stock-jobbers who made money dealing in South Sea Company stock (which led to the bursting of the South Sea Bubble in 1720–1)   *A house of peers ... or a Jew:* these two lines were not included in *F,* 1735 because it did not seem safe to print them at the time. See G. P. Mayhew, *Rage or Raillery* (1967) for these and other lines omitted from *F,* 1735   *kennels:* open drains, usually in the centre of a street   *marish:* marsh   *And may you ... D'Anvers:* these lines were omitted in *F,* 1735   *Duck:* Stephen Duck (see note on him, p. 243)   *D'Anvers:* 'Caleb D'Anvers', a name used by Bolingbroke and Pulteney when writing the *Craftsman* (see note, p. 243)   *Sir Bob:* Walpole   *on the nail:* see note, p. 214   *Display ... thou liest:* these eight lines were omitted in *F,* 1735   *baubles of the Tower:* the Crown Jewels, still kept there   *His panegyrics ... beast:* omitted in *F,* 1735   *Charon's boat:* Charon ferried the dead to Hades across the river Styx; the dead offered a cake as a 'sop' to Cerberus, the three-headed dog belonging to Pluto that guarded his dominions   *gate of dreams: F*, 1735 quotes in a footnote Virgil, *Aeneid* VI, 873-4: *'sunt geminae Somni portae - Altera candenti perfecta nitens elephanto'* ('there are two gates of sleep, one shining with the gleam of ivory, the other of transparent horn')   *Excise:* a reference to Walpole's Excise Bill, which he had to withdraw   *puny judge:* a pun on puisne (or junior) judge and puny   *'unities ... Aristotle's rules:* the unities meant that the action of a play should occur within twenty-four hours and take place in one locality   *Rymer:* Thomas Rymer (1641-1713), a critic known for his *Short View of Tragedy* (1691); he was Historiographer Royal, and when he died Swift hoped for the post, was recommended for it by Bolingbroke but was not appointed   *Dennis:* John Dennis (1657-1734), critic, dramatist and poet   *Bossu:* René le Bossu (1631-80), a French critic   *Peri Hupsous: On the Sublime*, reputedly by Dionysius Cassius Longinus (c.AD 213-73), but probably written in the first century   *Boileau's translation:* translated in 1712 by Leonard Welsted (1688-1747), a poet who became Commissioner of Lotteries in 1731. Welsted said he worked from the Greek, but Swift suggests his translation was based on that of 1674 by Nicolas Boileau (1636-1711), an influential French writer whose *L'Art Poetique* was published in 1674   *Battus:* possibly Dryden (or possibly Addison) may be intended; it is, however, probably a general portrait   *Augusta Trinobantum:* the ancient name of London, from the tribe of the Trinobantes   *bays:* a wreath of bay leaves   *Smithfield drolls:* shows at Bartholomew Fair held at the end of August   *Bavius ... Maevius:* poetasters (see note on *Maevius*, p. 220)   *Tigellius:* Hermogenes Tigellius, a mimic and writer patronized by Julius Caesar and Augustus   *Ludgate ... Temple Bar:* at the east and west ends of Fleet Street, the area of the book trade   *Cibber ... birthday strains:* see note on *birthday poem*, p. 243   *Gay banished:* Gay's (see note on him, p. 216) opera *Polly* (1728) was prohibited   *pension:* Edward Young (see note on *Young's ... passion*, p. 246) had flattered Walpole by addressing his poem 'The Instalment' to him (it celebrated Walpole's receiving the Order of the Garter). Young was given a pension of £200 in consequence   *pericranies:* brains (from pericranium)   *Hobbes:*

a reference to ideas in *Leviathan* (1651), Part I, chapter 13, by Thomas Hobbes (1588–1679)   *Flecknoe:* Richard Flecknoe (?1600–78), a priest and minor poet, mocked by Dryden and Pope   *Howard:* Edward Howard (1624–?1700), a poet and playwright; his brother, Sir Robert, also wrote poems and plays of indifferent quality   *Blackmore:* Sir Richard Blackmore (1654–1729), epic poet and physician to both William III and Queen Anne; a dull Whig political author   *Great poet ... Tree:* William Luckyn, first Viscount Grimston (?1683–1756), a Whig MP and long-winded speaker, a minor poet and playwright, author of a play, *The Lawyers' Fortune, or Love in a Hollow Tree* (1705), which was received with ridicule   *Duncenia:* an invented name for the Kingdom of Dunces   *descend:* continuous descent in a line of dunces is indicated, also the art of sinking in verse   *Leonard Welsted:* see note on *Boileau's translation*, p. 247. F, 1735 footnotes 'rashly' in the previous line with a reference to the *Treatise on the Profound* (see note on *Peri Hupsous*, p. 247) and to Pope's *Dunciad*   *Concanen:* Matthew Concanen (1701–49), an Irish writer, who became, surprisingly, according to Pope, Attorney-General in Jamaica in 1732   *Jemmy Moore:* see note on *Tibbalds, Moore, and Cibber*, p. 242. James Moore Smythe (1702–34), author of a play, *The Rival Modes* (1727), ridiculed in *The Dunciad*   *Perhaps you say . . . grazers:* these lines were omitted in F, 1735   *Prometheus:* in Greek legend a demi-god, son of the Titan Iapetus who made man out of clay; he stole fire from Olympus and taught man the use of it   *Nebuchadnezzars:* see the Bible, Daniel IV:31–3, where Nebuchadnezzar, King of Babylon, was, for his impiety, made to eat grass   *thy monarch:* George II   *How well ... own:* omitted in F, 1735   *Hydaspes ... Ganges:* the footnote in F, 1735 quotes Virgil, *Aeneid* VI, 795–9: '*Super et Garamanthus et Indos Proferet imperium. . . .*' ('[Augustus] will extend his empire beyond the Garamantes and the Indians. . . .')   *Short by the knees:* kneeling, from Horace, *Epistles* I, XII, 28   *The consort:* Queen Caroline   *Iülus:* also called Ascanius, the son of Aeneas; a reference to the Prince of Wales, Frederick Louis (1707–51), father of George III   *goddesses:* the five daughters of George II and Queen Caroline   *Duke William:* William Augustus, Duke of Cumberland (1721–65), second son of George II. Known as 'Butcher Cumberland', he commanded the

English army at Culloden (1746)   *minister of state ... mate ...*
Atlas: Sir Robert Walpole's wife Catherine was unfaithful; he had an
illegitimate daughter by his mistress; and he had a portly body
Fabius: Quintus Fabius Maximus (d.203 BC), the Roman consul and
dictator (217 BC), called Cunctator (the Delayer) in the second Punic
War because of his caution, which wore down Hannibal's forces. The
footnote in *F*, 1735 quotes *'Unus homo ... rem'* from Virgil, *Aeneid*
VI, 846 ('You, the single man who restores the state by delaying')
the sable flock: clergymen   *St George ... string cerulean:* St George
was patron of the Order of the Garter (awarded to Walpole in 1726),
which had a blue ribbon   *Lewis:* Louis XIV of France   *his pride:*
France was defeated in the War of the Spanish Succession   *Martial:*
Marcus Valerius Martialis (?40–?104 AD), Latin poet and epigramma-
tist, born in Spain, a friend of Seneca and Lucan   *Lucan:* Marcus
Annaeus Lucanus (AD 39–65), Latin poet, born in Spain. As leader of
the Pisonian conspiracy was ordered to commit suicide. He was the
author of the *Pharsalia*   *an equal share:* F, 1735 supplies a footnote:
'Divisium Imperium cum Jovi Caesar habet' ('Caesar has divided
sovereignty with Jove'), attributed to Virgil   *butter-weight:*
eighteen ounces (not the usual sixteen) to the pound, hence a generous
measure   *Woolston:* see note on *Woolston's tracts*, p. 243
Caetera desiderantur: (Latin) 'the rest is missing'

p. 192, 'Verses Spoken Extempore by Dean Swift on his Curate's
Complaint of Hard Duty'   It is not certain when these lines were
written; they were first published in the *Gentleman's Magazine* in
December 1734. The curate was Robert Hewit, probably from a parish
adjoining the Dean's in Dublin   *great St Mary:* probably St Mary's
Parish, Dublin   *hymen:* marriage   *purified:* a reference to the
churching of women after they have given birth

p. 193, 'On his own Deafness'   Probably written in September 1734
(several versions exist) and first published in English in the *Dublin
Evening Post*, 26 October 1734, in Latin and English in the *Dublin
Journal*, 29 October 1734. The poem's draft (different from later
published versions) is in the Henry Huntington Library, San Marino,

California. Faulkner's edition of 1746, containing both Latin and English versions, supplies the present text

p. 193, 'A Character, Panegyric, and Description of the Legion Club' Swift completed what he described as a 'very masterly' poem in April 1736; it was first published under the title 'S—t Contra Omnes' in that year. It was prompted by his desire to support the clergy when a report of a committee of the Irish House of Commons backed the views of various freeholders who had protested against pasturage tithes. The title indicating the Irish Parliament is taken from the Bible, Luke VIII:30, 'And Jesus asked him, What is thy name? And he said, Legion: because many devils were entered into him'   *a building ... the College:* the Parliament House, on the north side of College Green opposite Trinity College, is now the Bank of Ireland. Its foundation stone was laid in 1728 and it was completed in 1739   *the prudent architect:* Sir Edward Lovett Pearce (d.1733)   *the church:* St Andrew's, also known as the Round Church   *Near the church:* a proverbial saying which ended 'and far from God'   *jack-pudding:* a jester   *less villain's nose:* the criminals publicly hanged were less villainous than the Members of Parliament   *den of thieves:* see the Bible, Matthew XXXI:13   *harpies' nest:* in classical mythology the harpies were fabulous monsters (with a woman's face and a bird's wings and claws) supposed to act as ministers of divine vengeance *his lunatics and fools:* see 'Verses on the Death of Dr Swift', ll. 479–80 *gosling:* suggesting immaturity   *Sir Tom ... papists ... regicide:* Sir Thomas Prendergast (d.1760), who succeeded as second baronet, 1709; an MP and Postmaster-General for Ireland, 1733; he became a Protestant. His father had been rewarded with a baronetcy for giving evidence about a plot in which he had been involved to assassinate William III in 1696   *ye gods:* this and the succeeding imagery is based on Virgil, *Aeneid* VI, in which Aeneas visits the Underworld *Styx:* see note on *Charon's boat*, p. 246   *Clio:* the muse of history; in Virgil's *Aeneid* the Sybil who conducts Aeneas   *Briareus:* in classical mythology a giant with a hundred hands and fifty heads *Carey:* Walter Carey (1685–1757), an MP who was secretary to the Lord Lieutenant of Ireland, and held other places; he was a supporter of Walpole   *three hundred brutes:* the 300 Irish Members; each of

the 150 constituencies had two seats   *laid by the heels:* arrested
Lake Avernus: in classical mythology supposedly the entrance to the
lower regions; it is in Campania   *Waller... Hardress:* John Waller,
an Irish MP, grandson of Sir Hardress Waller, who had been a judge at
the trial of Charles I   *Throp:* Roger Throp (d.1736), rector of
Kilcorman, County Limerick, who had been engaged in a legal battle
with Waller, his patron, who had apparently treated him very badly
pair of Dicks ... Dick Fitz-Baker ... Dick the player: Richard Tighe and
Richard Bettesworth. For Tighe, see headnote to 'Mad Mullinix and
Timothy' (p. 231); he is called Fitz-Baker here because his family
supplied bread to Cromwell's troops. See also 'Tom Mullinex and Dick',
p. 130. Richard Bettesworth (1688/9–1741), educated at Trinity
College, Dublin, was called to the Irish bar and became Serjeant-at-Law
in 1716. He was MP for Philipstown (1721) and Midleton (1727). Swift
lampooned him in other poems, 'The Yahoo's Overthrow' and 'On the
Words – Brother Protestants'. He was called 'the player' because of his
pompous diction at a period when a bill was before the Irish House of
Commons containing a clause to commute the tithes on flax. He vowed
revenge on Swift (the clergy having successfully petitioned against the
measure) and swore to cut Swift's ears off with a penknife   *old
Glorious:* William III   *smoke:* discover his identity   *Wynne:*
not identified; there were three MPs named Wynne   *tribe of
Bingham:* Sir John Bingham, Bt (*c.*1690–1749), and his brother Henry,
both MPs   *Allens ... peer:* John Allen, son of Lord Allen, and
Robert Allen, his brother. They were the sons of Joshua Allen, the
second Viscount (1685–1742), a friend and then an enemy of Swift; he
opposed the Corporation of Dublin awarding Swift the Freedom of the
City)   *Howth:* Howth Castle, north of Dublin, where John Allen
worked as an architect   *Clements, Dilkes, and Harrison:* Henry
Clements was MP for Cavan; Nathaniel Clements for Duleek; Michael
O'Brien Dilkes for Castlemartyn; and William Harrison for Bannow
Morgan ... committee: Dr Marcus Antonius (or Anthony) Morgan
(b.1702/3), who represented the Borough of Athy, County Kildare,
chaired the committee which reported on the complaint of the
freeholders against the pasturage tithes. The Commons passed a
resolution in support of the graziers   *Flaccus:* an allusion to Horace,
whose full name was Quintus Horatius Flaccus (65 BC–8 BC)

Hogart: William Hogarth (1697–1764), the artist and engraver, whose art obviously appealed to Swift

p. 200, 'An Epigram on Scolding'   The date of composition is not known; it was first published in 1746

p. 201, 'Verses Made for the Women Who Cry Apples, etc.'   The date of composition of these verses is not known, though they relate to Dublin; they were first published by Faulkner in 1746   *'sparagrass:* asparagus   *Colchester oyster:* these oysters from Essex were famous from Roman days   *make you a dad:* oysters are supposed to increase virility   *Malahide:* about eight miles north of Dublin, a coastal village famous for its oysters   *bishop:* a mulled wine drunk with oranges or lemons and sugar, possibly deriving from the Dutch *bisschop*

p. 203, 'Swift's Epitaph in St Patrick's Cathedral'   This Latin epitaph written by Swift drew upon Juvenal, Satire I, 79, for its idea of indignation, and possibly Swift's employment of the late Latin word *vindicator* may have been suggested by Dryden's use of the word in his essay *A Discourse Concerning the Original and Progress of Satire*, where he describes Juvenal as a vindicator of Roman liberty. It is placed in St Patrick's Cathedral, Dublin, where Swift was interred in 1745

p. 203, 'W. B. Yeats's version of Swift's Epitaph'   Yeats completed this version in September 1930; it was first published, untitled, in the *Dublin Magazine*, October–December 1931. Yeats altered the first line and added the adjective 'world-besotted'

INDEX OF TITLES

INDEX OF FIRST LINES

A NOTE ON THE TEXT

The texts in the present edition have been taken where possible from George Faulkner's Dublin edition of Swift's *Works*, Volume II, the *Poetical Works* of 1735 (there is a supplement with poems in Volume IV), which is referred to in the Notes as *F*, 1735. Swift was deeply concerned in the preparation of this edition; the proofs were read to him and received his careful attention – later Pope described the edition as being under Swift's 'own eye'. The text of this present edition is modernized and regularized as regards the use of capitals and italics, the spelling and punctuation. The sources of poems not included in Faulkner's 1735 edition are indicated in the Notes. As far as possible the texts are arranged in chronological order.